Foreword

Although problems of homelessness rightly attract our attention because those affected need immediate help, the condition of a significant proportion of the United Kingdom housing stock is also an important problem which is all too often overlooked. Living in sub-standard housing is not just a miserable experience for those affected – there is increasing evidence of a link between poor housing and poor health, especially for children and older or disabled people who spend more time than average in their homes. Poor conditions can also mean danger (from electrical wiring, steep stairs) or social stigma, especially for children, with all the related effects. Poor housing can also inhibit attempts to regenerate an area economically and socially. Sub-standard conditions thus deserve a high priority in our attempts to tackle housing and the broader social and economic problems.

The nature of house condition problems varies across the UK. In Scotland, the national house condition survey identified dampness as a key issue. Scotland's legacy of tenement housing also brings with it particular challenges when it comes to persuading a multiplicity of owners to get together to repair common elements such as roofs. In Northern Ireland, as in Scotland, some of the worst conditions are found in remote rural dwellings without access to modern services and amenities. Rural housing problems are found in Wales too but there is also the immense task of regenerating housing in the Valleys, much of it presenting a structural challenge and often in the ownership of older people on very low incomes. In England, the sheer scale of the task of renovating the pre-1919 terraced stock in the inner areas of the larger cities and towns and in former mining areas appears daunting. Concerns about some of the inter-war stock, and even some post-war dwellings, are also emerging throughout the UK.

The Joseph Rowntree Foundation concerns itself with a wide range of housing and social problems and in 1995 the Foundation identified poor housing conditions and housing renewal policies as one of its priorities for the next few years and appointed Professor Philip Leather as its adviser on these issues. In the same year the Foundation approved seven research projects looking at various aspects of this topic, followed by four additional projects in 1997. To provide a background to this work and to produce a consistent picture of problems and policies across the UK as a basis for debate on appropriate policy solutions, the Foundation also supported the preparation of this report, which is a comprehensive update of an earlier study, *Renovation file*, published in 1993 by the Anchor Trust. This new edition concerns itself with house conditions in all tenures. It draws together data from the four national house condition surveys and a wealth of other sources and aims to present a historical perspective on both the problems and the policies. It includes a great deal of local data which individual authorities, housing associations and other organisations will find useful in comparing their problems and policies with other areas. Given the growing importance of private investment in dealing with sub-standard housing, the report also devotes attention to the work which people fund for themselves and the contribution that this makes to tackling poor housing problems.

The state of UK housing is essential reading for all those with an interest in or concern about the condition of the nation's housing stock. Just three years from the end of this century, we still have a great deal of housing which belongs to the last century in terms of the conditions it provides to its occupants. I hope that the report will contribute to the urgent task of finding ways to increase investment to ensure that the housing stock of the 21st century is something we can be proud of.

Raymond Young
Director of Research and Innovation Services, Scottish Homes

The state of UK housing

A factfile on dwelling conditions

Philip Leather and Tanya Morrison

The POLICY

P~P

PRESS

First published in Great Britain in 1997 by
The Policy Press
University of Bristol
Rodney Lodge
Grange Road
Clifton
Bristol BS8 4EA
Telephone: (0117) 973 8797
Fax: (0117) 973 7308
E-mail: tpp@bris.ac.uk

In association with the Joseph Rowntree Foundation.

ISBN 1 86134 045 1

Philip Leather is Professor of Housing and **Tanya Morrison** is Research Officer at South Bank University, London.

The Joseph Rowntree Foundation has supported this project as part of its programme of research and innovative development projects, which it hopes will be of value to policy makers and practitioners. The facts presented and views expressed in this report, however, are those of the authors and not necessarily those of the Foundation.

The Policy Press is working to counter discrimination on grounds of gender, race, disability, age and sexuality.

Printed in Great Britain by Hobbs the Printers Ltd. Cover design by Qube, Bristol.

Acknowledgements

A large number of people and organisations have provided assistance with data used in the preparation of this report. Anne Kirkham, Terry McIntyre and Simon Nichol from the Department of the Environment (DoE) in England provided access to data on housing conditions, renewal areas and group repair. We are also grateful to Henry Small for providing data on renovation grant activity in England. Brendon Hilbourne, and Ed Swires-Hennessy at the Welsh Office, John McPeake, Lynne Reavie and Trevor McCartney at the Northern Ireland Housing Executive (NIHE), and Raymond Young and Jennifer Waterton at Scottish Homes were also extremely helpful in providing access to house condition survey data and information on progress with grants, demolitions and other indicators, including much unpublished material.

Much of the information on local levels of demolitions, grant provision, and investment in the public and housing association sectors comes from official sources, such as *Local Housing Statistics* and *Housing and Construction Statistics* published by HMSO and we gratefully acknowledge the value of these sources.

Many tables, figures and maps in this report make use of data from the 1991 English, 1991 Scottish, 1991 Northern Ireland and 1993 Welsh House Condition Surveys. The 1993 Welsh House Condition Survey (WHCS) data was supplied by the Welsh Office from special tabulations using the WHCS database. Data for England, Scotland and Northern Ireland was mainly produced by the authors from original survey data supplied by the DoE, Scottish Homes, and the NIHE. Much of the data has not been previously published, but in a small number of instances there are minor differences between the figures in this report and those in the published survey reports which arise from differences in the bases used in tables, adjustments to weightings, the treatment of missing values, or rounding. Responsibility for the figures in this report lies with the authors and not with the organisations which provided access to the survey data.

Contents

List of tables, figures and maps viii
Key to sources for figures and maps xii
Summary... 1

Chapter 1: Introduction.. 7

Chapter 2: Measuring poor housing conditions... 8

Chapter 3: Housing conditions in the United Kingdom

Unfit dwellings or dwellings below the tolerable standard 12
Missing amenities 14
Disrepair.. 14
Mean repair costs per dwelling 15
The pattern of unfitness in the private sector stock 16
Contrasts between urban and rural areas 16
Trends in house condition 19

Chapter 4: Housing conditions and the dwelling stock

Age of the stock 20
Dwelling type.. 20
Age and type of dwelling.. 22
The pattern of older private sector properties... 23
Dwellings in poor condition by age 23
Dwellings in poor condition by type 26
Tenure... 29
Tenure and age of dwelling 29
Tenure and dwelling type.. 31
Dwellings in poor condition by tenure 32
An overview of dwellings in poor condition.. 32
Heating, insulation and energy efficiency 36

Chapter 5: People living in poor conditions

Income... 39
Employment status... 39
Household characteristics... 42
Age group 46
Gender of household head 48
Length of residence.. 49
Ethnic origin... 50
An overview of households living in poor conditions.. 51

Chapter 6: Housing renewal policies 54

Chapter 7: Tackling poor housing conditions
  Clearance 57
  Grants to owners... 60
  Grants per 1,000 dwellings 63
  Area renewal 82
  Improving the local authority stock 88
  The role of housing associations 94
  Dealing with adaptations 96
  Home improvement agencies 100

Chapter 8: Public investment in housing renovation
  Renovation's share of public expenditure.................................... 106
  Renovation expenditure 107

Chapter 9: Private investment in housing renovation
  Private expenditure 111
  Building society lending... 122
  Building industry output 123

Chapter 10: European comparisons.. 126

References... 130
Appendix A: Detailed tables 132
Appendix B: Key data on housing conditions and renovation activity by local authority 178

List of tables, figures and maps

Tables

2.1   The standard of fitness for human habitation and the tolerable standard.................11

3.1   Housing conditions in the UK (1991/93) 13

3.2   Reasons for unfitness/BTS, UK (1991/93)...14

3.3   Authorities in England and Wales with the highest proportion of unfit private sector dwellings (1986)..17

4.1   Authorities in England and Wales with the highest proportion of pre-1919 private sector dwellings (1986) 23

4.2   Dwellings in poor condition by age, Britain (1991/93) 25

4.3   Dwellings in poor condition by type, Britain (1991/93)............................27

4.4   Dwellings in poor condition by tenure, Britain (1991/93) 32

5.1   Older households in unfit dwellings, England (1991) 46

5.2   Households in unfit dwellings by age and gender of head of household, England (1991)..48

6.1   Key stages in the development of housing renewal policy, Britain..........56

7.1   Authorities in England and Wales with the highest rate of demolitions and closures per 1,000 private sector dwellings (1978-93)..............................58

7.2   Minor works assistance by type, England (1990-94)................................66

7.3   Authorities in England and Wales with the highest rate of 1985 Act grant payments per 1,000 private sector dwellings (1978-94)...........................67

7.4   Authorities in England and Wales with the highest rate of renovation grant payments per 1,000 private sector dwellings (1990-94)...........................69

7.5   Authorities in England and Wales with the highest rate of DFG payments per 1,000 private sector dwellings (1990-94) 71

7.6   Authorities in England and Wales with the highest rate of MWA payments per 1,000 private sector dwellings (1990-94) 74

7.7   100% grants and average grant as % of costs of work, renovation grants and DFGs, England (1990-94)...75

7.8   Authorities in England and Wales with the highest rate average payments for mandatory renovation grants (1994/95)...76

7.9   Authorities in England and Wales with the highest rate average payments for mandatory DFGs (1994/95) 79

7.10 Grants by tenure of recipient, England and Wales (1990-94) 82

7.11 Renewal areas by standard region, England..85

7.12 Group repair schemes and dwellings in schemes, England (1991-95).......87

7.13 Housing action area declarations and completions, Scotland (1978-94)..................88

7.14 Authorities in England and Wales with the highest rate of renovation to their own stock per 1,000 council dwellings (1978-94)......................................92

7.15 Authorities in England and Wales with the highest rate of HA renovation per 1,000 private sector dwellings (1978-94) 95

7.16 An estimate of spending on equipment and adaptations, Britain (1994/95) 100

7.17 Output of government-funded home improvement agencies in England and Wales (1994/95).. 101

9.1 Expenditure on repairs, maintenance and decoration by region, UK (1994-95)... 113

9.2 Average weekly spending on repairs, maintenance and decoration by income, owner-occupiers, UK (1994-95) 113

9.3 Average weekly spending on repairs, maintenance and decoration by income as a percentage of income, owner-occupiers, UK (1994-95)............................ 114

9.4 Spending on repairs, maintenance and decoration and related matters, UK (1994-95)... 115

9.5 Value of work carried out by households by tenure, England (1991) 116

9.6 Value of work carried out by landlords and others, England (1991) 117

9.7 Type of work by tenure, England (1991).. 117

9.8 Value of work carried out by households by tenure, Scotland (1991) 122

Figures

3.1 Housing conditions in the UK (1991/93)... 12

3.2 Mean repair costs, UK (1991/93) 15

3.3 Unfit housing by urban/rural location, UK (1991/93)....................................... 17

4.1 Age of housing stock, UK (1993).. 21

4.2 Type of dwelling stock, UK (1993) 21

4.3 Components of housing stock by age and type, UK (1991/93) 22

4.4 Unfit/BTS dwellings by age, UK (1991/93)... 26

4.5 Dwellings in disrepair by age, UK (1991/93).. 27

4.6 Unfit/BTS dwellings by type, UK (1991/93)... 28

4.7 Unfit/BTS dwellings by age and type, UK (1991/93) 29

4.8 Tenure of dwellings, UK (1994).. 30

4.9 Age of dwelling by tenure, Britain (1993)... 30

4.10 Dwelling type by tenure, Britain (1993) 31

4.11 Unfit dwellings by tenure, UK (1991/93).. 33

4.12 Unfit dwellings by age and tenure, England (1991)... 34

4.13 Unfit dwellings by age and tenure, Wales (1993).. 34

4.14 BTS dwellings by age and tenure, Scotland (1991) 35

4.15 Unfit dwellings by age and tenure, Northern Ireland (1991)............................. 35

4.16 Central heating by tenure, England, Northern Ireland and Scotland (1991).......... 36

4.17 Incidence of loft insulation, UK (1982 and 1992) 37

4.18 Depth of loft insulation, UK (1982 and 1992) 37

4.19 SAP ratings by tenure, England (1991).. 38

5.1 Households living in poor conditions by income group, England (1991).............. 40

5.2 Households living in poor conditions by income group, Wales (1993).................. 40

5.3 Households living in poor conditions by income group, Scotland (1991).............. 41

5.4 Households living in poor conditions by income group, Northern Ireland (1991) . 41

5.5 Households living in poor conditions by employment status, England (1991)....... 42

5.6 Households living in poor conditions by employment status, Scotland (1991)....... 43

5.7 Households living in poor conditions by employment status, Northern Ireland (1991).. 43

5.8 Households living in poor conditions by type, England (1991) 44

5.9 Households living in poor conditions by type, Wales (1993).............................. 44

5.10 Households living in poor conditions by type, Scotland (1991).......................... 45

5.11 Households living in poor conditions by type, Northern Ireland (1991)................ 45

5.12 Households living in poor conditions by age group, England (1991) 46

5.13 Households living in poor conditions by age group, Wales (1993)...................... 47

5.14 Households living in poor conditions by age group, Scotland (1991)................... 47

5.15 Households living in poor conditions by age group, Northern Ireland (1991)..........48
5.16 Households living in poor conditions by length of residence, England (1991) 49
5.17 Households living in poor conditions by ethnic origin, England (1991) 50
5.18 Households living in poor conditions by ethnic origin, Scotland (1991)..................50
5.19 Households living in unfit dwellings by income and tenure, England (1991)..........51
5.20 Households living in unfit dwellings by income and tenure, Wales (1993)..............52
5.21 Households living in unfit dwellings by income and tenure, Scotland (1991)..........52
5.22 Households living in unfit dwellings by income and tenure, Northern Ireland (1991)...53
7.1 Dwellings demolished or closed, Britain (1969-93) 57
7.2 Grants by type, England (1969-94) 61
7.3 Grants by type, Wales (1969-94) 62
7.4 Grants by type, Scotland (1969-94)...62
7.5 Grants by type, Northern Ireland (1977-94)...63
7.6 Grants per 1,000 privately owned dwellings, UK (1969-94)....................................64
7.7 Grants by type under the old system, UK (1969-94) 65
7.8 Grants by type under the new system, England and Wales (1994) 66
7.9 Average value of grants, UK (1979-94) 75
7.10 Grant payments by number of pre-1919 dwellings, England and Wales (1978-94) 80
7.11 Grants in HAAs and GIAs, England (1975-89)..83
7.12 Size distribution of declared renewal areas, England and Wales............................86
7.13 Changing proportion of spending in renewal areas by source, England...................86
7.14 Improvements in Scottish HAAs by source (1979-95)...89
7.15 Renovations to LA stock, England (1969-94)..90
7.16 Renovations to LA stock, Wales, Scotland and Northern Ireland (1969-94) 91
7.17 Average value per dwelling of LA, HA and private sector renovations, England (1979-94) 91
7.18 Renovations to HA stock, England (1969-94) 94
7.19 Renovations to HA stock, Wales, Scotland and Northern Ireland (1969-94)...........95
7.20 Grants for people with disabilities, England (1979-94) 97
7.21 Grants for people with disabilities, Wales (1979-94) 99
7.22 Take up of HEES by tenure, England (1990-93)..103
7.23 Take up of HEES by dwelling type, England (1990-93)..103
7.24 Take up of HEES by dwelling age, England (1990-93)..104
8.1 Percentage shares of public expenditure on housing by programme, England (1979-93)...106
8.2 Percentage shares of public expenditure on housing by programme, Wales (1981-95) 107
8.3 Percentage shares of public expenditure on housing by programme, Northern Ireland (1985-95) 108
8.4 Public expenditure on housing renovation, England (1979-95)............................109
8.5 Public expenditure on housing renovation, Wales (1981-94)................................109
8.6 Public expenditure on housing renovation, Northern Ireland (1985-95) 110
9.1 Household expenditure on repair, maintenance and decoration, UK (1986-94)...111
9.2 Household expenditure on repair, maintenance and decoration, 1986-94 by tenure, UK (1993/94 prices)...112
9.3 Value of expenditure on building work by tenure, England (1991) 115
9.4 Average value of work carried out by household income, England (1991)............118
9.5 Average value of work carried out by age of household head, England (1991).....119
9.6 Average value of work carried out by household type, England (1991).................119
9.7 Average value of work carried out by length of residence, England (1991)..........120
9.8 Average value of work carried out by age of dwelling, England (1991) 121
9.9 Average value of work carried out by general repair cost, England (1991)...........121
9.10 Average value of work carried out by value of dwelling, England (1991)..............122
9.11 Building society lending by type of property, Britain (1973-92)............................123

9.12 Ratio of first-time buyers to existing owners by age of dwelling, Britain (1994/95) 124

9.13 Output on housing repair and maintenance, Britain (1985-94) 124

9.14 Output on housing repair and maintenance by size of firm, Britain (1990, 1992, 1994) 125

10.1 Proportion of owner-occupied dwellings in the European Community 126

10.2 Proportion of pre-1919 dwellings in the European Community 127

10.3 Decreases in dwelling stock per 1,000 dwellings in the European Community ... 127

10.4 Proportion of dwellings with a bath/shower in the European Community 128

10.5 Proportion of dwellings with central heating in the European Community 129

Maps

3.1 Unfitness per 1,000 privately owned dwellings, England and Wales (1986) 18

3.2 Below tolerable standard per 1,000 privately owned dwellings, Scotland (1995) ... 19

4.1 Percentage of pre-1919 privately owned dwellings, England and Wales (1986) 24

7.1 Dwellings demolished or closed per 1,000 privately owned dwellings, England and Wales (1978-91) 59

7.2 Grants under the old system per 1,000 privately owned dwellings, England and Wales (1978-91) 68

7.3 Grants per 1,000 households by area, Scotland (1990-93) 69

7.4 Renovation grants per 1,000 privately owned dwellings, England and Wales (1990-94) 70

7.5 Disabled facilities grants per 1,000 privately owned dwellings, England and Wales (1990-94) 72

7.6 Minor works assistance per 1,000 privately owned dwellings, England and Wales (1990-94) 73

7.7 Average value of mandatory renovation grants, England and Wales (1994/95) 77

7.8 Average value of mandatory DFGs, England and Wales (1994/95) 78

7.9 Average value of improvement grants by area, Scotland (1993) 80

7.10 Location of renewal areas, England and Wales 84

7.11 Renovations to LA stock per 1,000 publicly owned dwellings, England and Wales (1978-91) 93

7.12 Renovations to HA stock per 1,000 privately owned dwellings, England (1978-94) 98

7.13 Location of government-funded home improvement agencies, Britain (1995/96) 102

7.14 Location of LEACs 105

Key to sources for figures and maps

The note (**a-r**) that appears in the title of figures and maps refers to the following sources:

a   1991 EHCS, 1991 SHCS, 1991 NIHCS: analysis of data; 1993 WHCS: special tabulations

b   OPCS (1994)

c   DoE, SDD and Welsh Office (various years)

d   1991 EHCS: analysis of data

e   1993 WHCS: special tabulations

f   1991 SHCS: analysis of data

g   1991 NIHCS: analysis of data

h   Dunster et al (1994)

i   DoE, unpublished data

j   Robertson and Bailey (1996)

k   Wilcox (1995)

l   CSO (various years)

m   BSA/CML (various years)

n   European Commission (1993)

o   DoE, unpublished data; Welsh Office, unpublished data

p   Scottish Office (various years)

q   Care and Repair (1995)

r   Energy Savings Trust

Summary

Poor housing conditions in the United Kingdom

Although there have been frequent national surveys of housing conditions in England, Scotland, Wales and Northern Ireland, there is no overall source of information on poor housing conditions covering the whole of the United Kingdom, nor any single source of data on measures to deal with these problems. It is the aim of this study to fill that gap and to raise awareness of housing condition problems across the UK.

The measurement of poor housing conditions is a difficult and complex task but the variety of definitions used in national surveys, differences in the way surveyors are briefed, and variations in the way in which repair costs are estimated make comparisons between countries in the UK impossible. There is no obvious reason to justify the lack of comparability.

Unfit dwellings or dwellings below the tolerable standard

In 1991, some 1,638,000 occupied dwellings in the UK were either unfit for human habitation or below the Scottish tolerable standard (BTS) – this represented about 7% or one in 14 dwellings in the UK in 1991. This problem was most severe in Wales where 13.3% of dwellings were unfit to live in. The proportion of dwellings lacking one or more basic amenities follows a similar pattern, with Wales again having the most severe problems.

Disrepair

Problems of disrepair are more widespread than unfitness, with almost one in five dwellings in England having urgent repair costs of more than £1,000 in 1991. In Scotland, the proportion of dwellings with repair costs over £3,000 was about 10%. In Northern Ireland, a quarter of dwellings had comprehensive repair costs of more than £5,000. In Wales, the repair cost standard was not comparable with those used elsewhere but 20% of dwellings had general repair costs of more than £1,500 and 4% had costs in excess of £5,000.

The pattern of unfitness/below tolerable standard

Unfitness is by no means evenly distributed. Areas with high levels of unfitness included a large group of rural or industrial districts in the north of England, notably North East Lancashire, northern cities or urbanised districts such as Manchester, Liverpool and Calderdale, parts of rural Wales and the South Wales valleys, a group of cities or industrial areas in the Midlands, and in the south, Bristol, Bath and some London boroughs. The area south of the Wash to Bristol Channel line stands out clearly as an area with below average unfitness levels compared with Wales and the north of England.

In Scotland, the problem of poor conditions in rural areas is prominent, with the Western Isles, Argyll, Skye, Ross and Cromarty, Lochaber and Orkney having between 20% and 30% of their privately owned stock below standard. Glasgow also shows a very high level of BTS private sector dwellings (10%), but the equivalent figure for Edinburgh is much lower (4%). The proportion of dwellings which were unfit was similar in urban and rural areas in England and Wales, but in Scotland and Northern Ireland levels of rural unfitness/BTS were markedly higher.

Trends in house condition

Trends in house condition are difficult to assess because of differences in the interpretation of standards and changes in the definition of house condition indicators between surveys. The number of dwellings lacking one or more basic amenities has shown a clear and consistent decline over time, but trends in unfitness/BTS and disrepair are less clear, partly as a result of changes to standards. There was probably a reduction in unfitness and disrepair over the 1986-91 period as rising house prices encouraged owners to invest, but investment levels during the subsequent housing market recession remain to be seen.

Housing conditions and the dwelling stock

Poor housing conditions are closely related to the age of the dwelling stock. The post-1964 stock has the lowest level of unfitness/BTS in all cases, and the proportion of dwellings in each age band which are unfit increases steadily with age before rising sharply for the pre-1919 stock. However, there are significant levels of unfitness in the inter-war stock in Wales and Scotland.

In England, converted flats and terraced houses are the most likely types of dwellings to be unfit. In Wales, terraced houses also stand out as the most likely type of dwelling to be in poor condition. In Scotland, converted flats are the most likely

to be in poor condition, although tenements also have relatively high repair costs. In Northern Ireland, detached dwellings in rural areas are the most problematic.

Dwellings in poor condition by tenure

Vacant dwellings are the most likely to be in poor condition, but in the occupied stock the private rented sector has the highest proportion of dwellings in poor condition. In the remaining stock, conditions vary, but the greater size of the owner-occupied stock means that in numerical terms the majority of occupied unfit dwellings are found in this sector.

People living in poor conditions

People on low incomes are more likely to live in poor housing conditions. In England, for example, more than one in 10 households with an income of less than £4,000 per annum lived in unfit dwellings compared with only one in 35 of those with an income of £24,000 or more. At least three quarters of those living in unfit housing or housing in serious disrepair had incomes below £12,000 in 1991. There is, however, still a minority of more affluent households living in poor conditions, especially in England.

The types of household which experience poor conditions are very similar throughout the UK. Older people and younger people just starting their housing careers are the groups most likely to live in poor conditions, with middle-aged people generally better housed. Within older age groups the tendency to live in poor conditions is much greater after the age of 75. In England the proportion of households living in unfit housing rises from 6.6% for households headed by a person aged between 60 and 64 to 13.2% for households headed by a person aged 85 or more.

Younger men are more likely to live in unfit dwellings than younger women, but from the age of 30 onwards households headed by women are more likely to experience unfit living conditions, with 13.6% of households headed by women in the 40-59 age band falling into this category. Data on ethnic origin and poor housing conditions is only available for England and Scotland. In both countries households with a head from a minority ethnic community were generally more likely to live in poor conditions than those from the white community.

Tackling poor housing conditions

Clearance

The level of demolition has declined sharply from more than 80,000 dwellings per annum in the early 1970s to some 4,200 in 1992, an annual replacement rate of less than one in every 4,750 dwellings. The present level of clearance is widely regarded by professionals as too low, but with a high proportion of older houses in individual ownership it is both difficult and expensive to implement clearance programmes. Any sustained recovery in demolition levels would require the provision of additional capital resources.

Grants to owners

Provision of capital grants to assist home owners with the improvement, repair and adaptation of their homes reached a peak in the 1982-84 period, when almost 300,000 grants per annum were provided across the UK. In England, provision has subsequently fallen back to only about 60,000 per annum in the 1990s. In Wales the decline from the mid-1980s has been less pronounced. In Scotland provision has also fallen from the 60,000 grants provided in 1984 to about 20,000 per annum since 1990. In Northern Ireland there was a high level of grant provision throughout the 1980s but in the 1990s this has fallen to around 7,000

per annum. Currently the number of grants is thus only about one third of the early 1980s level.

Setting these levels of provision against the size of the housing stock reveals that until the late 1980s investment levels in Northern Ireland generally exceeded those elsewhere in the UK. After a slow start the number of grants in Scotland per 1,000 privately owned dwellings increased rapidly in the late 1970s and has generally remained above the level in England or Wales. Grant provision in Wales has exceeded that in England and in the late 1980s it became comparable with Scotland and Northern Ireland. In England, provision has remained consistently the lowest, at less than 10 grants per 1,000 private sector dwellings. As a result, Glasgow, Belfast and Cardiff have received far higher levels of investment than many comparable cities in England.

The authorities with the highest rates of grant provision overall are predominantly Welsh, including both urban and rural districts. In England the majority of authorities with high levels of provision are rural and few large urban authorities have given a large number of grants relative to the size of their stock. Data for Scotland at local authority (LA) level is not available for an extended period, but in recent years rural areas in north Scotland, such as the Western Isles, Skye and Lochalsh, Sutherland, Lochaber, Caithness provided the highest number of grants per 1,000 dwellings, followed by some of the larger cities such as Aberdeen, Edinburgh and Glasgow.

Dealing with adaptations

In 1994, total grant provision for equipment and adaptations in the UK through disabled facilities grants (DFGs), minor works assistance (MWA), and improvement grants amounted to £109m. Spending fell in real terms in the early 1990s, contrary to the common perception, but in 1994 rose again

3 ∎

to an all-time high. Other sources of spending on equipment and adaptations include social services (an estimated £75m in 1994/95), and capital and revenue spending by LAs and housing associations (HAs) on their own stock (£126m). There is no spatial pattern to the distribution of authorities active in the provision of DFGs.

The size of grants provided

There is a perception that grant levels have risen sharply since the introduction of the new system in 1990. In real terms, however, the increase has been less dramatic, at least in England. Average grant values rose from about £4,000 in 1979 (at 1993/94 prices) to almost £8,000 in the mid-1980s, and to about £10,000 in 1994 under the new system. In Wales, however, the average increased more rapidly after 1990 to £18,000 in 1994. In Scotland, where the old system remained in place, grants have also increased but more steadily, rising from about £3,500 in 1979 to £7,500 in 1990. Since then there has been a slight fall in real terms. In part, the increases in average grant levels under the new system are due to the higher effective grant percentages paid under the new system in England and Wales. On average, renovation grants covered 85% of the total costs of grant-aided work in 1993/94, with DFGs covering an average of 91%. Some 61% of renovation grants and 81% of DFGs covered 100% of the cost of works in 1993/94.

Grant recipients

There has been no ongoing monitoring of the characteristics of grant recipients. A study carried out for the Department of the Environment (DoE) in the system's early period of operation showed that during the first two years of operation, 48% of renovation grant approvals were awarded to people over 60, a much higher proportion than under the old system. In addition, 75% of DFG approvals were awarded to those aged 60 or more. As a result of the test of resources, grants were closely targeted on those with low incomes. In total, 60% of those who had grants approved were in receipt of some form of state benefit. In terms of tenure, private landlords have fared badly under the new system compared with the old system.

Area renewal

Local authorities can declare special areas where they will focus their housing renewal activities. In England and Wales, some 104 renewal areas had been declared by March 1995, containing about 145,000 dwellings. In England, renewal areas are predominantly located in the north (60%) and the Midlands (32%). The North West has 40% of the declared renewal areas. Overall public expenditure on renovation in renewal areas in England was about £123.4m in 1993/94. Some 59% of investment came from LA sources, 34% from HAs (including Housing Association Grant [HAG] and LAHAG), and 7% from private sources. New build by HAs and the private sector remains the largest component of renewal area investment, accounting for 38% of the total in 1993/94. Some 29% of spending took the form of grant aid, demolitions accounted for 13% of spending, followed by group repair (10%). If demolition costs are added to new build, over 50% of renewal area expenditure was on new development, indicating the extent to which activities in these areas go beyond housing renovation.

The mechanism for area-based renewal in Scotland has remained the Housing Action Area (HAA). By the end of 1994, about 1,700 HAAs had been declared. New declarations remained at close to 100 per annum until 1991, after which there was a steep decline in activity. Housing Action Areas in Scotland typically contain far fewer dwellings than those in England and Wales. Housing associations have been the dominant force for improvement, but their contribution was at its greatest in the early 1980s. Since 1992, grant take up by individual owner-occupiers, as in England and Wales, has come to dominate the profile of activity.

Area improvement has never been a dominant element of renewal programmes in the UK, except in a small number of local areas where these policies have been pursued more intensively. Grants in General Improvement Areas (GIAs), HAAs, or renewal areas rarely exceeded 15% of all grants given. The abolition of mandatory renovation grants in 1996 may increase the proportion of investment in renewal areas.

Improving the local authority stock

Substantial house condition problems are found in the LA sector. The majority of poor condition LA dwellings were constructed after 1945. In addition to the need for improvements to amenities and repairs in the traditionally built housing stock, there are substantial problems of repair in the non-traditional stock, especially in Scotland. Renovation levels reached a maximum in the late 1980s when many LAs made use of accumulated capital receipts to improve the condition of their stock. The number of LA dwellings renovated overtook the number of private sector dwellings renovated in 1978, and since 1990 LA renovation has run at almost three times the level of private sector renovation. The exception to this picture is Wales, where LA renovation has generally been much lower than the level of grant provision to the private sector. Activity levels have generally been highest in the south east and the south west of England and in parts of the Midlands. It is notable that the majority of metropolitan districts with large public sector stocks have not been able to achieve as much renovation relative to the size of their stock as smaller districts.

The role of housing associations

In England, there was a rapid increase in the level of renovations by HAs as a result of the introduction of HAG in 1975. The level of renovation activity fluctuated between 10,000 and 20,000 throughout the 1980s before falling to below 6,000 per annum for most of the 1990s. This decline has been partly attributed to the new arrangements for funding HAs introduced by the 1988 Housing Act. Lower levels of HAG and the requirement that associations should bear any cost over-runs in full have made rehabilitation much less attractive than new build schemes. A similar decline has occurred in the remainder of the UK.

In the past the majority of HA renovation work has been undertaken on dwellings purchased from private sector owners, so this activity has made an important contribution to the alleviation of poor housing conditions in the private sector. Housing association renovations have been heavily concentrated in urban areas with a high proportion of private sector housing in poor condition, including London and the larger metropolitan areas or cities.

Renovation's share of public expenditure

Renovation took an increasing share of public expenditure during the 1980s while new building declined. Expenditure on LA renovation has taken the main share of spending throughout the 1979-95 period, accounting for over half of all renovation expenditure in most years. Private sector renovation spending only approached spending on the LA stock in the early 1980s during the repair grants boom. Investment in renovation by housing associations has remained consistently below both other programmes. Only reductions in unit costs since 1990 have sustained the volume of LA renovation output.

Private investment in housing renovation

In addition to public expenditure on renovation, individual households invest a substantial amount of their own resources, amounting to over £30bn in England in 1991. Relatively little is known about this investment. In real terms there was a fall in spending by households in repair and maintenance between 1986 and 1988, followed by an increase in spending between 1989 and 1991, when the average across all households exceeded £400. In subsequent years the total fell back to only £336 in 1994.

As might be expected, home owners spend more than those in other tenures on repair, maintenance and decoration. Expenditure in 1994 was greatest among the 30-49 and 50-64 age groups and least among those under 30 and over 75. Among home owners, spending was highest in Northern Ireland, Scotland, Wales, the North and Greater London, and lowest in East Anglia, the Midlands, the South East and the South West. This may be related to the age profile of the dwelling stock. Expenditure increased with income both for households as a whole and for home owners, but the proportion of total income devoted to these items decreased as income rose.

The future

The abolition of mandatory renovation grants in England and Wales through the 1996 Housing Grants, Construction and Regeneration Act will relieve pressures on LA budgets but may lead to a reduction in public spending if hard-pressed LAs cut back on grant provision. In the absence of new measures to encourage private spending and to make it more effective, there is a strong prospect that housing conditions for low income home owners and those in the private rented sector may deteriorate in the medium and long term.

Chapter 1

Introduction

This report aims to provide a comprehensive overview of poor housing conditions in the United Kingdom and to examine progress in dealing with these problems. Although there have been frequent national surveys of housing conditions in England, Scotland, Wales and Northern Ireland, there is no overall source of information on poor housing conditions covering the whole of the UK, nor any single source of data on measures to deal with these problems. This report is intended, as far as data sources permit, to fill that gap. Wherever possible, the report presents a UK-wide picture, although in a few cases data for one part of the UK (usually Northern Ireland) is not available.

The state of UK housing is a follow-up to *Renovation file*, a report published by Anchor Housing Trust in 1993, and has been comprehensively revised to incorporate the results of the 1991 round of national house condition surveys (1993 in Wales) and to update the sections on progress in dealing with poor conditions by the addition of the most recent data available. Additional material on area

renewal, group repair, and energy conservation has been incorporated, and the range of local data available for Scotland has been extended. As with *Renovation file*, this report makes heavy use of graphs and charts, but in response to requests there is an extensive selection of detailed tables providing supporting and background information. The report also includes a selection of indicators relating to individual local authorities (LAs).

Extensive reference is made in tables, maps and figures below to the four national house condition surveys. Information has been obtained from the published reports of the surveys (see References), from special tabulations produced by the Welsh Office from the 1993 Welsh House Condition Survey (WHCS), and from direct analysis of the 1991 English, Scottish and Northern Ireland house condition surveys (EHCS, SHCS, and NIHCS respectively). The relevant source is indicated in each instance (see p xii).

Local data is based on districts in existence at 31 March 1996.

Chapter 2

Measuring poor housing conditions

The measurement of poor housing conditions is a difficult and complex task and comparisons between countries within the UK are made more problematic by differences in the definitions used. Some definitional variations stem from differences in national legislation on housing standards within the UK, but others stem from variations in the methodologies of the national house condition surveys.

In this report, three main aspects of poor housing conditions are distinguished:

■ *Unfit for human habitation* or *below tolerable standard (BTS):* fitness for human habitation is an important statutory concept which applies in England, Wales and Northern Ireland; in Scotland, the minimum standard is the tolerable standard. The fitness standard plays an important role in determining whether a LA is obliged to take action to deal with poor conditions. In England and Wales between 1990 and 1996 it also determined whether property owners were entitled to mandatory grant aid to deal with poor housing conditions (1992 onwards in Northern Ireland). It is likely to continue to be an important determinant of grant priorities in the future. The definition of unfitness remained unchanged from 1957 to 1990, when a new definition was set out in the 1989 Local Government and Housing Act and subsequent circulars and codes of guidance (the equivalent Order in Northern Ireland came into effect in 1992). The information in this report on unfitness relates to the new standard. The determination of whether an individual property is unfit or not is a matter for

skilled judgement rather than precise measurement and one of the key problems in comparing housing conditions is to obtain consistency in the interpretation of this standard by different surveyors. The tolerable standard, which in its current format is set out in the 1987 Housing (Scotland) Act, fulfils a similar role in Scotland. Table 2.1 (p 11) sets out the components of the two standards for comparison. The changes to the fitness standard introduced in the rest of the UK in 1990 and 1992 brought the two standards more closely into line but some differences remain – most significantly, the tolerable standard excludes reference to serious disrepair and does not specifically require exclusive use of a suitably located wash hand basin and a bath or shower. There are also differences in relation to dampness (the tolerable standard makes no link between dampness and the health of the occupants). As a result, the tolerable standard is now less stringent than the fitness standard applied throughout the remainder of the UK.

■ *Lacking or sharing amenities:* the absence of certain basic amenities, such as a WC, a sink, a wash hand basin, a bath or shower, and supplies of hot and cold water have been important measures of poor conditions which have also had statutory importance as the basis for determining entitlement to grant aid in some cases. The presence or absence of amenities is more easily determined than unfitness but even here there are differences in definition between surveys. Some refer to the availability of an *indoor* WC or a *readily accessible* WC, while others find an outdoor WC acceptable. Some surveys also refer to the *exclusive use* of amenities by a single household while others appear to accept the sharing of amenities by more than one household. As a result of these differences, comparisons of amenity levels between surveys must be made with caution. Provision of amenities has become less important as an indicator of poor housing conditions in recent years as the number of dwellings which lack amenities has declined significantly.

■ *Disrepair:* there is no statutory definition of disrepair and a variety of definitions have been used in surveys. A common approach is to measure the costs of bringing a dwelling up to a particular standard, often that which would be required to qualify for a mortgage from a building society, or to meet the standard of work required after provision of grant aid. There are many problems in defining these standards with precision, and in measuring the costs of repair. Identifying the nature and the scale of house condition problems is the first stage. This involves what are often difficult judgements about the scale of repair, especially where the relevant building elements are inaccessible. Some surveys also attempt to identify problems which will emerge in the future, for example, within the next 10 years, as well as existing deficiencies. After this, it is necessary to arrive at a decision about what needs doing to remedy a problem, including the crucial choice between repair and replacement. Finally, the derivation of repair costs from this information is also complex. The first problem is the source of detailed data on the prices of specific jobs. Costs based on public sector renovation contracts have been extensively used in the past but have the disadvantage that they are often below the costs that would be charged for small-scale jobs in the private sector. The repair costs of specific elements may also fail to take into account overhead costs or the costs of dealing with consequential repairs. On the other hand,

when costs are derived from a large number of separate elements it may also be that economies of scale would be achieved in practice. From this it can be seen that estimates of repair costs, while valuable in summing up the significance of disparate elements of disrepair, are perhaps best seen as relative rather than absolute. As a result of differences in the definitions used in the national house condition surveys it has proved impossible to find a consistent definition of disrepair for use throughout the UK, but the following are the most commonly used in this report:

a) *Urgent repairs:* in England and Northern Ireland, urgent repairs are works to building elements regarded as needing urgent action to remove threats to the health, safety, security, and comfort of the occupants or to prevent further rapid deterioration in the building. In Scotland, urgent repairs are repairs to external or common parts and only those which are necessary to maintain the building in a wind and watertight condition or to remove a threat to safety, health or security. These definitions are broadly similar, but in Scotland they exclude internal repairs. In practice, the average level of urgent repairs is significantly lower in Scotland and the definitions are not comparable. This measure is not available for Wales.

b) *General repairs:* in England, Wales and Northern Ireland, this means all repairs needing action within five years, with replacement only if repair was impossible, more expensive than replacement, or would not last for the five-year period. In Scotland the nearest equivalent is *any repairs* but this excludes items not currently needing repair but likely to do so within the next five years. Again these standards appear similar but crucial differences, such as the exclusion of works needed within five years in Scotland, make comparisons unsafe.

c) *Comprehensive repairs:* in England and Northern Ireland this means all repairs together with the replacement of any elements judged to have less than 10 years life. This measure is not available in Scotland or Wales.

Information on disrepair is less readily available in other European countries than in the UK, and indicators of house conditions, such as the standard of heating insulation and the presence of central heating, are more widely used. The age of the dwelling stock is also widely used as a proxy indicator for poor housing conditions, although the emergence of problems in the 1919-45 housing stock, and in post-war dwellings built with non-traditional methods or materials, makes this increasingly less valid.

More detailed information on the definitions used in the national house condition surveys can be found in the individual survey reports (see References). The variety of definitions used makes accurate comparisons between countries in the UK impossible. Some differences arise because of variations in legislation, but England, Wales and Northern Ireland operate within the same legal framework. In relation to measures of amenities and disrepair no obvious reason presents itself to justify differences in standards, or the absence of at least one common standard. There is now increasing cooperation between those responsible for the national house condition surveys and it is to be hoped that this produces more consistency between countries in the 1996-97 round of surveys in order to eliminate or reduce definitional differences to a minimum.

Table 2.1: The standard of fitness for human habitation and the tolerable standard

The standard of fitness for human habitation in England, Wales and Northern Ireland	The tolerable standard for Scotland
The fitness standard is defined in Section 83 of Schedule 9 to the 1989 Local Government and Housing Act and the Housing (Northern Ireland) Order 1992. A dwelling house is fit for human habitation unless in the opinion of the local housing authority it fails to meet one or more of the following requirements and, by reason of that failure, is not reasonably suitable for occupation.	The tolerable standard is defined in Section 86(1) of the 1987 Housing (Scotland) Act.
Common elements	
The dwelling should – be structurally stable – be free from dampness prejudicial to the health of the occupants – have satisfactory facilities for preparing and cooking food including a sink with a satisfactory supply of hot and cold water – have an adequate piped supply of wholesome water – have adequate provision for lighting, heating and ventilation – have a suitably located WC exclusively for the use of the occupants – have an effective system for the drainage of foul, waste and surface water	– be structurally stable – be substantially free from rising or penetrating damp – have satisfactory facilities for the cooking of food within the house – have a sink provided with a satisfactory supply of both hot and cold water within the house – have an adequate piped supply of wholesome water within the house – have satisfactory provision for natural and artificial lighting, for ventilation, and for heating – have a WC available for the exclusive use of the occupants of the house and suitably located within the house – have an effective system for the drainage and disposal of foul and surface water
Different elements	
The dwelling should – have a suitably located bath or shower and wash hand basin, each provided with a supply of hot and cold water – be free from serious disrepair	– have satisfactory access to all external doors and outbuildings

Source: DoE (1993); Scottish Homes (1993)

Chapter 3

Housing conditions in the United Kingdom

Unfit dwellings or dwellings below the tolerable standard

As Chapter 2 indicated, the standard of fitness for human habitation and the Scottish equivalent, the tolerable standard, are the most important indicators of poor housing conditions. The latest information available on unfitness relates to 1991 in England (DoE, 1993) and Northern Ireland (Northern Ireland Housing Executive [NIHE], 1993), and to 1993 in Wales (Welsh Office, 1994). For Scotland data on BTS dwellings relates to 1991 (Scottish Homes, 1993).

Table 3.1 and Figure 3.1 show overall levels of unfitness/BTS (see Chapter 2). In total, some 1,638,000 occupied dwellings were unfit/BTS for human habitation. This represented about 7% or one in 14 dwellings in the UK in 1991. Comparisons between countries are relatively safe on this indicator, which suggests that the problem of unfitness was most severe in Wales, where 13.3% of dwellings were unfit. The exclusion of disrepair from the tolerable standard has reduced the apparent scale of the problem in Scotland.

Figure 3.1: Housing conditions in the UK (1991/93)[a]

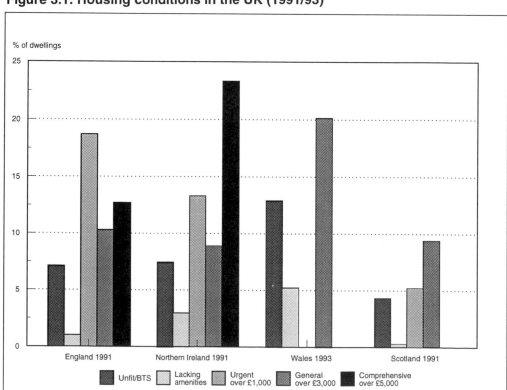

Table 3.1: Housing conditions in the UK (1991/93) (1)

	Unfit	Lacking amenities	Repair costs		
			Urgent over £1,000 (2)	General over £3,000 (3)	Compre-hensive over £5,000
Number of dwellings (000s)					
England 1991	1,354 (1,498)	205	3,573 (3,802)	1,960 (2,113)	2,417 (2,592)
Northern Ireland 1991	41 (50)	16 (19)	74 (92)	45 (59)	127 (146)
% of dwellings					
England 1991	7.1 (7.6)	1.0	18.7 (19.3)	10.3 (10.7)	12.7 (13.1)
Northern Ireland 1991	7.5 (8.8)	2.9 (3.3)	13.6 (15.9)	8.3 (10.2)	23.3 (25.5)

	Unfit	Lacking amenities	Repair costs over £1,500 (4)
Number of dwellings (000s)			
Wales 1993	151	61	230
% of dwellings			
Wales 1993	13.4	5.4	20.4

	BTS	Lacking amenities	Repair costs	
			Urgent over £1,000 (2)	General over £3,000 (3)
Number of dwellings (000s)				
Scotland 1991	92	13	107	189
% of dwellings				
Scotland 1991	4.7	0.6	5.2	9.3

Notes: (1) Figures in brackets include vacant dwellings; otherwise figures relate to occupied dwellings only. It is emphasised that figures are generally not comparable between countries because of differences in definitions, briefings, interpretation, repair costings, and survey methodology. See Chapter 2 for further details. (2) The definition of 'urgent repairs' differs between England and Northern Ireland, and Scotland. See Chapter 2. (3) The definition of 'general repairs' varies between Scotland, where general repairs are 'any repairs' as used in the published SHCS report (Scottish Homes, 1993) and England and Northern Ireland (see Chapter 2). (4) The 1993 WHCS identifies only 'repair costs' and this column shows dwellings with repair costs over £1,500.

Sources: 1991 EHCS, 1991 SHCS, 1991 NIHCS: analysis of data; 1993 WHCS: special tabulations.

Table 3.2 shows the main reasons for dwelling unfitness or BTS. Dwellings in Northern Ireland and Wales failed the standard, on average, on just over three items, compared with just over two items in England, and 1.5 items in Scotland, but the distribution was very skewed, with 54% of unfit dwellings in England, for example, being unfit on only one item, and a further 22% unfit on two items. In England, disrepair, food preparation, bath/shower/ wash hand basin facilities, and dampness were the main reasons why dwellings failed the fitness standard. In Northern Ireland the same reasons were also prominent, but the proportions of dwellings failing on each was much higher, with 64% of unfit dwellings failing on the grounds of disrepair, for example, compared with only 39% in England. In Wales, ventilation and drainage were also major reasons for unfitness. In Scotland, differences between unfitness and the tolerable standard make comparisons difficult. Dampness (found in 50% of BTS dwellings) stands out above all others as the main reason for failing the tolerable standard in Scotland. Some form of dampness was found in 13.2% of the Scottish dwelling stock, often in combination with condensation and mould.

Table 3.2 Reasons for unfitness/BTS, UK (1991/93)

Reason	England	Northern Ireland	Wales	Scotland
		% of unfit/BTS dwellings		
Repair	39.0	63.7	43.2	na
Food preparation	39.0	44.0	36.0	14.7
Bath/shower/whb	24.7	36.6	26.5	na
Dampness	22.2	51.4	38.2	49.2
WC	18.6	30.8	24.6	13.2
Lighting	8.1	13.4	22.6	
Ventilation	18.2	14.9	43.0	}16.9
Heating	12.3	16.1	29.6	
Stability	9.8	9.3	13.4	13.4
Drainage	8.9	27.8	36.4	4
Water supply	2.7	10.6	4.0	10.8
Water to sink	na	na	na	9.7
External access	na	na	na	10.4

Note: whb: wash hand basin

Sources: 1991 EHCS, 1991 SHCS, 1991 NIHCS: analysis of data; 1993 WHCS: special tabulations

Missing amenities

The proportion of dwellings lacking one or more basic amenities follows a similar pattern to unfitness (see Table 3.1, p 13), with Wales having the most severe problems (5.4% of dwellings lacking one or more basic amenities), followed by Northern Ireland (2.9%). In Scotland only 0.6% of dwellings lacked all five amenities but this excludes dwellings with an external WC.

Disrepair

As Chapter 2 indicated, comparisons between all four components of the UK are not possible in relation to this indicator. For England and Northern Ireland, definitions are generally similar. Table 3.1 suggests in contrast to the situation on unfitness that the dwelling stock in Northern Ireland is in better condition in relation to urgent repairs than that in England, but in worse condition when measured against the most comprehensive standard. In England, almost one in five dwellings had urgent repair costs of more than £1,000 in 1991, while in Northern Ireland, a quarter of dwellings had comprehensive repair costs (to reach the standard acceptable for a typical mortgage) of more than £5,000. However, differences arising from the updating of the price base for repair costs used in 1991 mean that prices in Northern Ireland are on average 20% lower than those for equivalent work in England (Northern Ireland Housing Executive, 1993) and this may account for the apparently greater level of disrepair in England.

In Scotland 5.3% of dwellings failed to meet the less stringent urgent repair standard. However, on the 'any repair' indicator, which was most similar to

England and Northern Ireland, the proportion of dwellings with costs over £3,000 was similar to that in the other two countries, at about 10%.

In Wales, the repair cost standard used in 1993 was not comparable with those used elsewhere. However, 20% of dwellings had repair costs of more than £1,500 and 4% had costs in excess of £5,000.

Mean repair costs per dwelling

Figure 3.2 shows mean repair costs per dwelling for urgent, general and comprehensive repairs, and the costs of repairs to dwellings which were unfit or fell below the tolerable standard (see also Table A3.1). Data in Figure 3.2 are for occupied dwellings. In England, the mean

cost of urgent repairs (averaged across the whole stock) was almost £700. The average general repair cost was £1,100 and comprehensive repair costs averaged £2,200. As Table A3.1 shows, the same costs for vacant dwellings were substantially greater. The final column in the chart shows the average general repair cost for unfit dwellings alone. This was almost £4,000 for occupied unfit dwellings and £9,000 for vacant unfits. The distribution of repair costs on all indicators was highly skewed, with most dwellings having nil or low costs and a smaller number having very high costs indeed. The median urgent repair cost for occupied dwellings in England, for example, was only £260. Only 30% of dwellings had urgent repair costs of more than £500 and only 10% had urgent repair costs over £1,800.

Figure 3.2: Mean repair costs, UK (1991/93)[a]

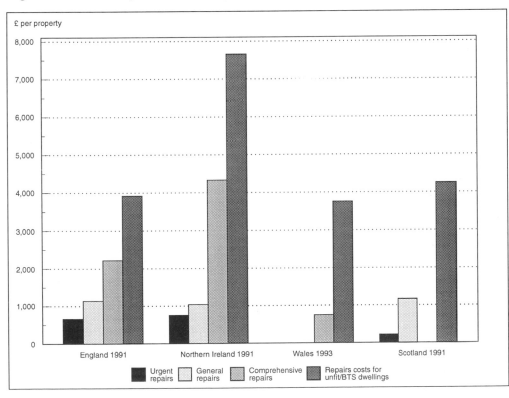

Mean costs in Northern Ireland for urgent and general repairs were similar to those in England, except in relation to vacant properties, where they were much greater. Mean comprehensive repair costs, and the costs of dealing with unfit dwellings, were substantially higher.

Mean costs in relation to general repairs ('any repairs' in Scotland) were similar in England, Scotland and Northern Ireland.

The pattern of unfitness in the private sector stock

Map 3.1 (p 18) shows variations in the proportion of privately owned dwellings which were unfit in England at district level in 1986. Table 3.3 shows authorities with the highest levels of unfitness and data for all authorities is shown in Appendix B. For English authorities these estimates are based on 1986 data produced by the Department of the Environment (DoE) for which no update is available. Estimates are required because the sample size of the EHCS does not provide data below regional level, while data from LA Housing Improvement Programme (HIP) submissions is incomplete and inconsistent because of the variety of approaches which LAs use to produce this information. In Wales, the 1993 WHCS did not provide district level estimates of unfitness so 1986 figures have again been used. Estimates are better used in a relative way to make comparisons between districts rather than as absolute measures of unfitness levels.

Areas with extremely high levels of unfitness include a large group of rural or industrial districts in the north of England – notably, North East Lancashire, northern cities or urbanised districts such as Manchester, Liverpool and Calderdale, parts of rural Wales and the South Wales valleys, a group of cities or industrial areas in the Midlands, including Leicester, Nottingham, Birmingham, Bolsover, and Amber Valley, and in the south, Bristol and

Bath and a small number of London boroughs, including Hackney, Islington, Hammersmith and Fulham, and Kensington and Chelsea.

Other areas with above average unfitness levels include a large number of rural areas in the south west, Yorkshire and Humberside, and the north Midlands, together with a few southern coastal districts, especially those in Kent. There are relatively few areas anywhere in England and Wales with a very low proportion of unfit dwellings but the area south of the Wash-Bristol Channel line stands out clearly as an area with below average unfitness levels compared with Wales and the north of England.

Map 3.2 shows the distribution of BTS dwellings in Scotland in 1995. Again there are differences in the approaches used by LAs which make comparisons with the 1991 SHCS difficult. The problem of poor conditions in rural areas (see below) is well illustrated, with areas such as the Western Isles, Argyll, Skye and Lochalsh, Ross and Cromarty, Lochaber and Orkney having between 20% and 30% of their privately owned stock below the tolerable standard. Glasgow also shows a very high level of private sector dwellings below the tolerable standard (10%), but the equivalent figure for Edinburgh is much lower (4%).

Contrasts between urban and rural areas

In all areas (except Northern Ireland) there are many more unfit dwellings in urban areas than in rural areas (Appendix Table A3.2). The proportion of dwellings which are unfit is similar in urban and rural areas in England and Wales, but in Scotland and Northern Ireland levels of rural unfitness are markedly higher (Figure 3.3). The problem of rural unfitness is particularly marked in Northern Ireland, where three times as many dwellings are unfit in rural areas as in urban areas.

Table 3.3: Authorities in England and Wales with the highest proportion of unfit private sector dwellings (1986)

Local authority	Unfit private sector dwellings (per 1,000)	Local authority	Unfit private sector dwellings (per 1,000)
Cynon Valley	139.6	Manchester	104.0
Pendle	131.0	Preseli	103.9
Ceredigion	130.2	Barrow-in-Furness	103.2
Rhondda	129.1	Leicester	103.2
Dinefwr	121.6	Bath	103.0
Hyndburn	121.1	High Peak	102.3
Dwyfor	120.1	Allerdale	101.9
Blaenau Gwent	117.7	Craven	100.1
Burnley	113.1	Bristol	99.7
Teesdale	112.2	Hackney	99.4
Blackburn	111.1	Bolsover	98.6
Eden	108.7	Calderdale	98.5
Wear Valley	107.4	Hammersmith	98.1
Rossendale	106.5	Derwentside	97.7
Islington	104.9	Nottingham	97.3

Source: DoE estimates and Welsh Office (1988)

Figure 3.3: Unfit housing by urban/rural location, UK (1991/93)[a]

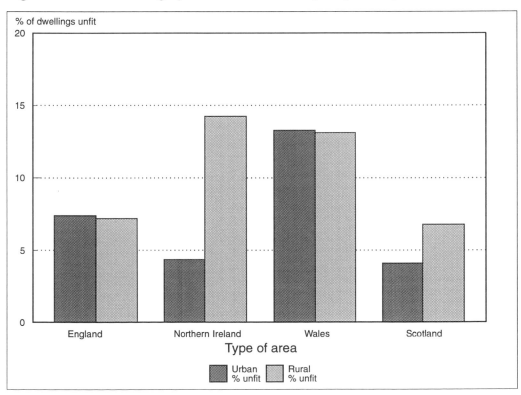

17

Map 3.1: Unfitness per 1,000 privately owned dwellings, England and Wales (1986)°

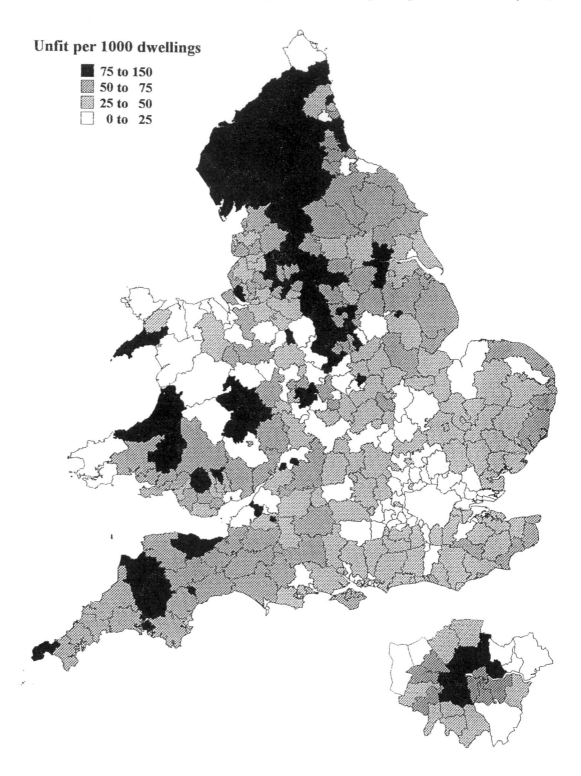

Unfit per 1000 dwellings

- 75 to 150
- 50 to 75
- 25 to 50
- 0 to 25

Map 3.2: Below tolerable standard per 1,000 privately owned dwellings, Scotland (1995)[p]

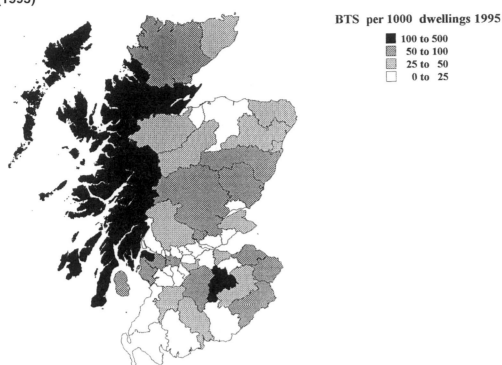

BTS per 1000 dwellings 1995

- ■ 100 to 500
- ▨ 50 to 100
- ▧ 25 to 50
- □ 0 to 25

Trends in house condition

Trends in house condition are difficult to assess because of differences in the interpretation of standards and changes in the definition of house condition indicators between surveys. In England, the number of dwellings lacking one or more basic amenities declined from almost three million in 1971 to only 205,000 in 1991. Trends in unfitness between 1971 and 1986 were more constant, although conclusions are based on reinterpretations of the results of previous surveys. Between 1981 and 1986, unfitness was estimated to have fallen from 6.3% to 5.6% of the stock under the old pre-1989 standard, while disrepair fell from 6.5% to 5.9% (DoE, 1988). The change in the fitness standard in 1990 made further comparisons difficult, but modelling of 1991 EHCS data suggested that levels of unfitness had fallen slightly since 1986 from 8.8% to 7.6%.

In Wales, the proportion of dwellings lacking basic amenities fell sharply over the 1981-91 period as in England. The level of unfitness also declined, from 8.8% to 7.2% under the old standard between 1981 and 1986, and from 19.5% to 13.3% under the new standard between 1986 and 1991. However, the 1993 report stresses that these results are subject to considerable statistical uncertainty (Welsh Office, 1993).

In Northern Ireland, the proportion of dwellings lacking one or more basic amenities fell from 120,000 to 20,000 between 1974 and 1991. The level of unfitness also appears to have declined over this period. Under the new fitness standard, unfitness fell from about 11% to 9% between 1987 and 1991. The increase in disrepair identified in Northern Ireland between 1979 and 1984 has now been compensated for by a continuous period of reduction since that point in time.

In Scotland comparisons over time are not possible as the 1991 survey was the first to be carried out.

Chapter 4

Housing conditions and the dwelling stock

Physical factors, in particular, the quality of the initial construction of dwellings and the extent and effectiveness of subsequent repair and maintenance, are the main influences on the condition of the majority of dwellings. Dwelling type and age are reasonable, although obviously far from perfect, proxies for these factors. These basic influences on house condition are, in turn, subject to a large number of other important influences, such as the prevailing technologies and legislative controls at the point of construction, the resources available to social rented sector landlords at this stage, or to those seen as potential clients by a speculative builder, and subsequently the resources of those who own and/or occupy the dwellings and the extent to which they are prepared to invest them in repair and maintenance. In this chapter we firstly examine the age and type profile of the dwelling stock and the extent to which variations in condition are associated with these factors. We then move on to look at variations in condition by tenure. Although there are distinct variations in conditions by tenure, and clear differences in the way in which owners in different tenures approach the task of investment in their upkeep, variations in condition by tenure are obscured by the large scale tenure transfers of this century, firstly of dwellings built for private renting into the owner-occupied sector, secondly of dwellings from the council sector in home ownership, and thirdly the more small-scale transfer of private rented and some owner-occupied dwellings into housing association (HA)

ownership in specific, mainly inner-city locations.

Age of the stock

There are significant differences in the profile of dwellings by age in the UK. In England and Wales almost half the housing stock was built before 1944 with 26% and 33% respectively built before 1919 (Figure 4.1; Table A4.1). Scotland's housing stock is slightly newer on average, but in Northern Ireland the stock is much more recent, with only a third built before 1944. The age of the stock has a significant impact on condition, as the following sections will show.

Dwelling type

The dwelling type profile also varies within the UK (Figure 4.2; Table A4.2). In England, semi-detached and terraced houses are the most common types of dwelling, each accounting for about 30% of the stock. About a fifth of dwellings are detached houses. Of the remaining 20% of dwellings, almost three quarters (14% of the total) are purpose-built flats, with the remainder being flats produced by conversion from other dwelling types. In Wales, terraced houses form over one third of the stock, with semi-detached houses accounting for 32%, and detached houses 24%. Only about 10% of dwellings in Wales are flats, the majority purpose-built.

Figure 4.1: Age of housing stock, UK (1993)[b]

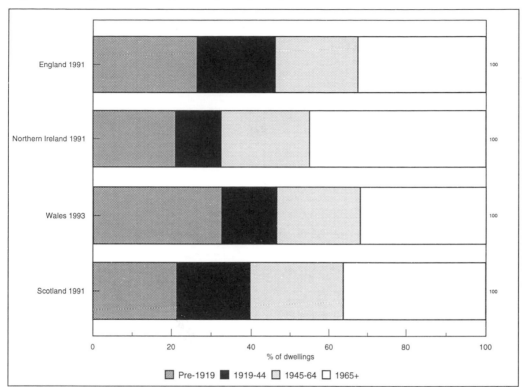

Figure 4.2: Type of dwelling stock, UK (1993)[b]

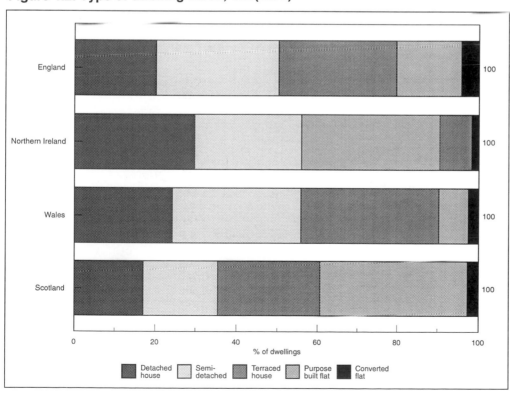

In Scotland, the stock profile is substantially different. Only 60% of dwellings are houses. Semi-detached houses (23% of all dwellings) are the most common type, followed by terraced houses (20%) and detached houses (17%). Purpose-built flats (including both older tenements and more modern LA flats) are by far the most common dwelling type (38%).

The Northern Ireland dwelling stock is more similar to that in England and Wales, with relatively few flats (8%, of which the majority are purpose-built). Terraced dwellings are the most common (37%), followed by detached houses (31%) and semi-detached houses (24%).

Age and type of dwelling

Figure 4.3 shows the composition of the housing stock in the UK by a number of key dwelling age/type categories. Appendix Table A4.3 shows detailed figures by country. Post-1945 dwellings make up more than half the stock, with semi-detached dwellings forming the largest group (19% of the stock), followed by detached houses (13%), terraced houses (13%) and purpose-built flats (11%). The only other significant groups are pre-1919 terraced houses which account for 11% of the stock, and inter-war semi-detached houses which form 10%. Purpose-built and converted pre-1919 flats form only 4% of the total stock. Pre-1919 dwellings, together with post-1945 purpose-built flats, form only about a third of the stock overall but, as following sections will show, this is where the majority of house condition problems lie.

Figure 4.3: Components of housing stock by age and type, UK (1991/93)[a]

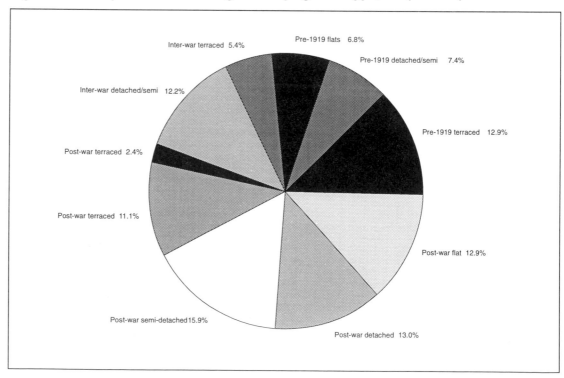

The pattern of older private sector properties

Although older housing is found in all districts the greatest concentrations of privately owned older housing are found in the north of England, Wales and parts of the South West (Map 4.1). Four areas stand out as having very high levels of older properties. These include: a band across Cumbria and into the west of County Durham, which is mainly rural but also includes old mining settlements (Allerdale, Eden, Teesdale and Wear Valley); a cluster of towns in north east Lancashire (Pendle, Burnley, Hyndburn, Rossendale, and Blackburn); a group of South Wales valleys (Cynon Valley and Rhondda); and parts of inner London (Islington, Hackney, Hammersmith and Fulham, Camden, Kensington and Chelsea, Westminster). Table 4.1 below shows those authorities with the highest proportion of pre-1919 stock and data for all authorities is shown in Appendix B.

Table 4.1: Authorities in England and Wales with the highest proportion of pre-1919 private sector dwellings (1986)

District	% private sector stock pre-1919	District	% private sector stock pre-1919
Islington	96.1	Eden	65.7
Hackney	88.5	Burnley	65.2
Hammersmith	88.3	Blackburn	63.8
Rhondda	78.8	Wear Valley	63.4
Camden	77.2	Waltham Forest	61.6
Kensington	76.9	Rossendale	61.4
Pendle	75.9	Allerdale	61.2
Hyndburn	70.2	Cynon Valley	60.2
Westminster	69.6	Barrow-in-Furness	59.2
Lambeth	69.0	South Shropshire	58.5
Wandsworth	68.7	Craven	58.1
Lewisham	68.4	Manchester	56.8
Newham	68.3	Penwith	55.6
Teesdale	68.0	Brighton	55.4
Haringey	66.1	Calderdale	55.2

Source: DoE estimates and Welsh Office (1988)

Dwellings in poor condition by age

Poor housing conditions are closely related to the age of the dwelling stock. Table 4.2 shows the proportion of dwellings in different age groups which are unfit, or in disrepair. (Appendix Table A4.4 shows fuller details.) It should again be noted that figures cannot be compared between countries. The post-1964 stock has the lowest level of unfitness/BTS in all cases, and the proportion of dwellings in each age band which are unfit increases steadily with age before rising sharply for the pre-1919 stock. However, there are significant levels of unfitness in the inter-war stock in Wales and Northern Ireland.

Map 4.1: Percentage of pre-1919 privately owned dwellings, England and Wales (1986)[i]

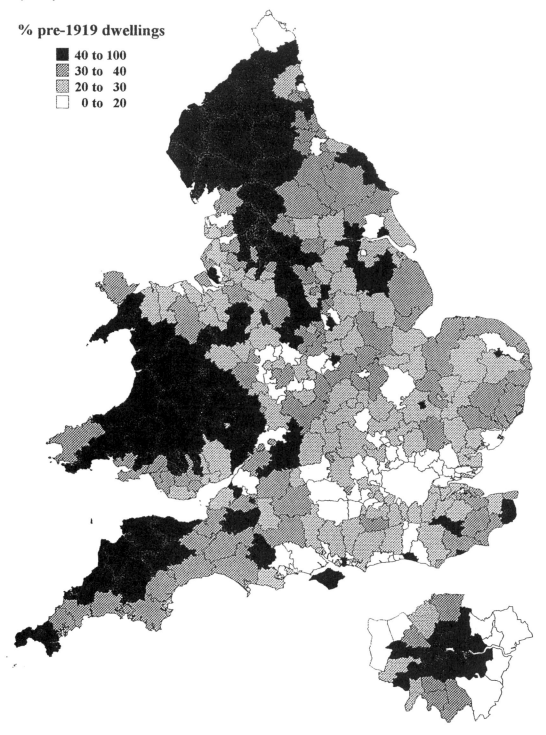

% pre-1919 dwellings

- 40 to 100
- 30 to 40
- 20 to 30
- 0 to 20

In terms of disrepair, the pre-1919 stock is again consistently most likely to be in the worst condition, with the proportion of dwellings in disrepair decreasing in the newer stock. The scale of the difference between newer and older dwellings is the worst in Northern Ireland, where pre-1919 dwellings are 20 times as likely to be in poor repair as those built after 1964. In England the same ratio is 13, in Scotland 11, but in Wales only 5, suggesting that disrepair in Wales is spread more evenly across the stock.

Table 4.2: Dwellings in poor condition by age, Britain (1991/93)

		% of dwellings in each age group			
Unfit/BTS		Pre-1919	1919-44	1945-64	1964+
England 1991	All	15.4	8.4	5.3	2.2
	Occupied	14.6	8.2	5.0	1.9
Northern Ireland 1991	All	29.5	11.3	4.0	0.8
	Occupied	26.2	11.5	3.5	0.8
Wales 1993	Occupied	20.3	16.9	11.6	6.0
Scotland 1991	Occupied	11.8	4.5	3.7	1.2
Disrepair					
England 1991 (1)	All	38.9	24.3	12.4	4.6
	Occupied	38.3	24.2	12.3	4.2
Northern Ireland 1991	All	45.7	25.4	10.6	2.3
(1)	Occupied	40.0	23.8	9.9	2.2
Wales 1993 (2)	Occupied	33.8	23.4	18.2	6.8
Scotland 1991 (1)	Occupied	13.7	6.4	2.9	1.3

Notes: (1) Dwellings with urgent repair costs over £1,000. Note, however, that comparisons cannot be made between countries on this indicator. (2) Dwellings with repair costs over £1,500.

Sources: 1991 EHCS, 1991 SHCS, 1991 NIHCS: analysis of data; 1993 WHCS: special tabulations

Figures 4.4 and 4.5 (and Table A4.5) show how unfit/BTS dwellings and dwellings in disrepair are split between the four dwelling age groups (in contrast to Table 4.2, which shows the proportion of dwellings in each age group in poor condition). The figures do not take account of the overall number of poor condition dwellings, which is much greater in England because of its larger dwelling stock (see Table 3.1).

Not surprisingly, the majority of unfit/BTS dwellings were built before 1919. The proportion is highest in Northern Ireland (71%), followed by England (56%). In Scotland and Wales a much higher proportion of unfit properties are newer, with more dwellings built in the period 1945-64 being unfit or BTS than those built in the 1919-44 period. Unfitness in newer dwellings has increased proportionately since the change in the fitness standard introduced in England and Wales in 1990 and in Northern Ireland in 1992. Evidence from the 1991 EHCS shows that there was a significant reduction in the level of unfitness (as measured by the old standard) in the pre-1919 stock during this period, offset by small increases in unfitness levels in the newer stock. Nevertheless, unfitness remains predominantly a problem of the pre-1919 stock.

The majority of disrepair is also consistently found in pre-1919 housing, despite differences in the standards used in each country. The share of disrepair accounted for by each age band declines steadily with age, except in Northern Ireland, where the 1945-64 stock accounts for a greater share than the inter-war stock, but this is partly explained by the relatively low level of building between 1919 and 1945 in comparison with the post-war period. Houses lacking amenities were also predominantly built before 1919 but significant numbers date from the inter-war period.

Figure 4.4: Unfit/BTS dwellings by age, UK (1991/93)[a]

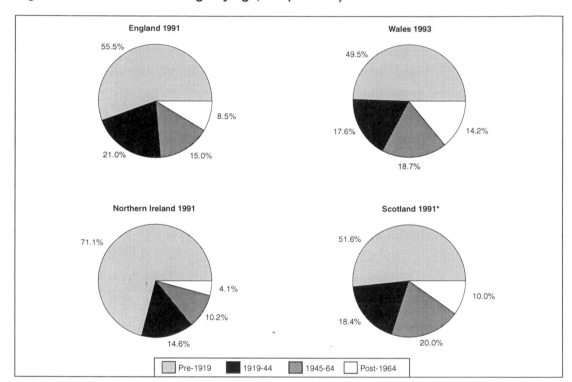

* Scottish data for dwellings below tolerable standard.

Dwellings in poor condition by type

Table 4.3 shows the proportion of dwellings of different types which are unfit, or in disrepair. (Table A4.6 shows fuller details.) Without placing too much emphasis on the actual proportions of dwellings in poor condition, which cannot be compared between countries, there are some interesting variations. In England, converted flats and terraced houses are the most likely types of dwellings to be unfit. Terraced houses also have high repair costs but purpose-built flats, most of which are in the LA sector, have higher repair costs than converted flats. In Wales, terraced houses stand out as more likely to be in poor condition than any other dwelling type. In Scotland, converted flats are the most likely dwelling type to be in poor condition, although tenements also have relatively high repair costs. In Northern Ireland, detached houses stand out as being the most likely dwelling type both to be unfit and to have high repair costs – this is due to the high incidence of poor conditions on isolated dwellings in rural areas.

Figure 4.5: Dwellings in disrepair by age, UK (1991/93)[a]

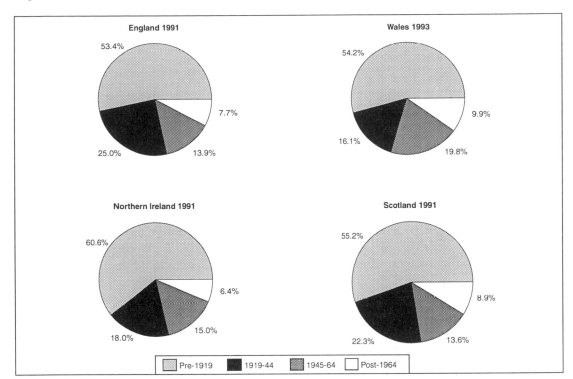

Table 4.3: Dwellings in poor condition by type, Britain (1991/93) (1)

| Unfit/BTS | % of dwellings in each type of category | | | | | |
	Terraced house	Semi-detached house	Detached house	Converted flat	Purpose-built flat	All types
England	10.6	6.5	3.9	12.9	6.7	7.6
Northern Ireland	8.4	5.4	12.1	3.0	15.6	8.8
Wales	16.1	13.8	8.6	13.3		13.4
Scotland	3.3	2.5	5.6	14.0	5.3	4.5
Disrepair						
England	37.6	17.9	11.3	10.3	25.2	19.4
Northern Ireland	17.8	12.2	18.6	7.1	18.2	16.0
Wales	37.4	18.8	13.0	9.8		20.4
Scotland	3.9	4.0	9.0	11.6	4.5	5.2

Notes: (1) Figures for England, Northern Ireland and Scotland are for 1991; figures for Wales are for 1993. Data for Wales and Scotland are for occupied dwellings only. Comparisons cannot be made between countries. See Table 4.2 for definition of disrepair.

Sources: DoE (1993); Scottish Homes (1993); NIHE (1993); Welsh Office (1994)

Figure 4.6 (and Table A4.7) shows the proportion of unfit/BTS dwellings accounted for by each dwelling type by country. The proportions shown in Table 4.3 are significantly modified as a result of differences in the size of the stock of dwellings of each type. In England, terraced houses account for over 40% of all unfit dwellings and semi-detached houses a further 26%. Only one in 10 unfit dwellings is a converted flat. A similar picture is found in Wales. In Scotland, purpose-built flats, and particularly tenements, are the most frequent sub-standard dwelling type (43% of all BTS dwellings), followed by detached houses. This dwelling type dominates the picture in Northern Ireland, where over 50% of all unfit dwellings are detached houses, with a

further 30% being terraced houses. The picture in relation to disrepair is similar.

Some of the differences in condition between the different dwelling stock types are accounted for by their age. Older dwellings are generally in poorer condition and where different countries have different age distributions by dwelling type this will account for some of the differences in condition.

Figure 4.7 (and Table A4.8) shows the distribution of unfit/BTS dwellings by a range of dwelling type/age categories. This can be compared with Figure 4.3 which shows the proportions of the dwelling stock as a whole in each category. Pre-1919 terraced dwellings are more than twice as likely to be unfit as their frequency in the dwelling stock as a whole would suggest.

Figure 4.6: Unfit/BTS dwellings by type, UK (1991/93)[a]

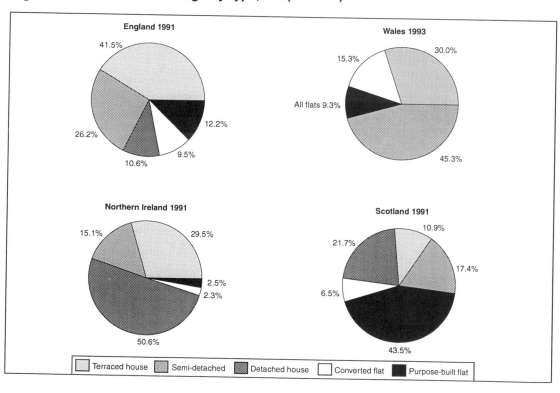

Figure 4.7: Unfit/BTS dwellings by age and type, UK (1991/93)[a]

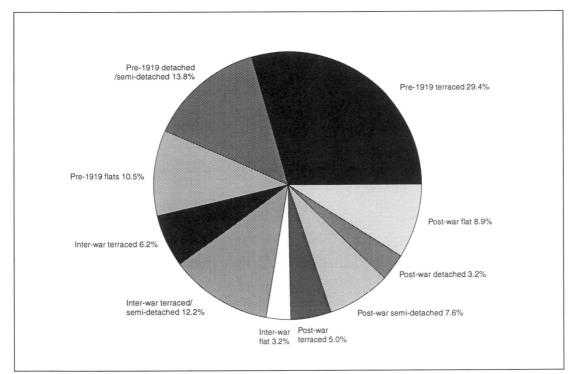

Pre-1919 detached /semi-detached 13.8%

Pre-1919 terraced 29.4%

Pre-1919 flats 10.5%

Post-war flat 8.9%

Inter-war terraced 6.2%

Post-war detached 3.2%

Inter-war terraced/ semi-detached 12.2%

Post-war semi-detached 7.6%

Inter-war flat 3.2%

Post-war terraced 5.0%

Tenure

Owner-occupation is the majority tenure throughout the UK but it is highest in Wales (72% of households), similar in Northern Ireland (69%) and England (68%), but still substantially lower in Scotland (56%) (Figure 4.8; Table A4.9). About 17-18% of dwellings in England and Wales are rented from LAs, with the remainder rented from HAs, and private landlords. In Northern Ireland, the proportion of housing rented from the public sector (exclusively the NIHE) is higher (26%) and the private rented and HA sectors are very small (4% and 2% respectively). In Scotland there is a much larger proportion of dwellings rented from public sector landlords (33%) than in the remainder of the UK, with relatively little private renting (7%).

Tenure and age of dwelling

Figure 4.9 shows the breakdown of dwellings in each tenure by age in 1993 for Britain as a whole. (Table A4.10 provides fuller details.) In total, just under a third of all dwellings date from after 1964, with the remainder split evenly between the other three age bands. Dwellings owned outright are split more evenly across tenures, with slightly more in the older pre-1919 age group. Dwellings being bought with a mortgage are more likely to have been built either before 1945 or after 1964. The LA sector reflects the history of this form of provision, with only 4% of dwellings dating from before 1919 and over three quarters built since 1945. The HA sector reflects a more complex development, with a quarter of dwellings dating from before 1919 (a mix of dwellings built by the 19th century associations and dwellings acquired more from private owners). Relatively few dwellings date from the 1919-64 period, but more than half have been built since then, reflecting the active HA new build programme since the 1960s. The private rented sector is characterised by older dwellings, with 49% built before 1919, and only 10% dating from after 1964.

Figure 4.8: Tenure of dwellings, UK (1994)[c]

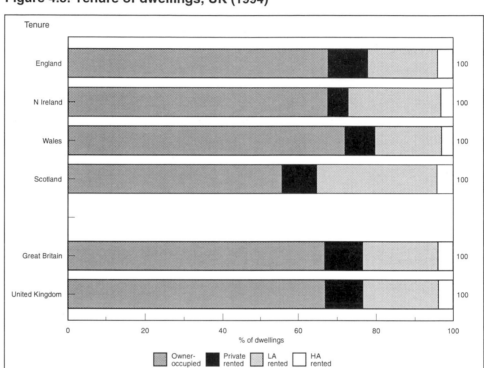

Figure 4.9: Age of dwelling by tenure, Britain (1993)[b]

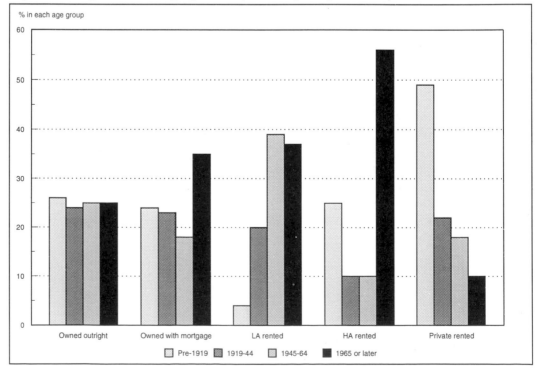

Tenure and dwelling type

Figure 4.10 shows the breakdown of dwellings in each tenure by type in 1993 for Britain as a whole. (Table A4.11 provides detailed figures.) Overall, semi-detached and terraced dwellings were the most common (accounting for about 30% of the stock each in 1993), followed by detached houses (19%), purpose-built flats (15%), and converted flats (6%). In the stock which is owned outright, detached and semi-detached houses are strongly over-represented (31% and 35% respectively). The other dwelling types, especially purpose-built flats, are under-represented, the latter reflecting the predominance of LA ownership of this type of dwelling. Owners still buying with a mortgage are more likely to live in terraced or semi-detached houses, but again less likely to occupy a flat. Detached houses are a rarity and semi-detached houses are under-represented in the LA and HA sectors, where houses are most likely to be terraced. However, despite over 15 years of sales under Right to Buy, 60% of LA dwellings and 39% of HA dwellings are houses. Nevertheless, purpose-built flats are strongly over-represented in these sectors. In the private rented sector, the most notable feature is the concentration of converted flats (26% compared to only 6% in the stock as a whole). Otherwise, terraced houses and purpose-built flats are found in this sector in about the same proportions as for the stock as a whole, while detached and semi-detached houses are less common.

Figure 4.10: Dwelling type by tenure, Britain (1993)[b]

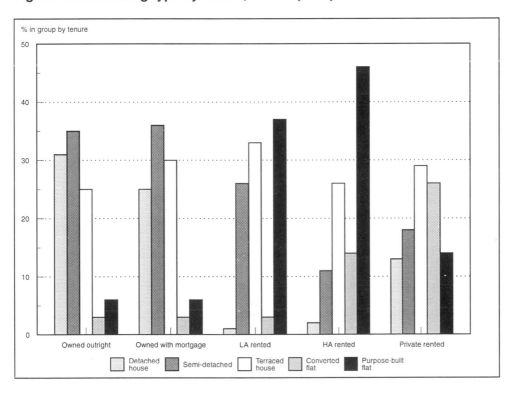

Dwellings in poor condition by tenure

There are distinct variations in housing conditions by tenure (Table 4.4; Table A4.12), although these can be masked by transfers between tenures. Vacant dwellings are the most likely to be in poor condition, but in the occupied stock the private rented sector has the highest proportion of dwellings in poor condition. In the remaining stock, conditions vary, with owner-occupied dwellings more likely to be in poor condition than the social rented sectors in Northern Ireland, but the reverse being the case in England and Wales. In Scotland the remaining tenures have generally similar proportions of dwellings BTS or in disrepair.

Table 4.4: Dwellings in poor condition by tenure, Britain (1991/93) (1)

| | % dwellings in each tenure group | | | |
	Owner-occupied	Private rented	LA rented	HA rented
England				
Unfit	5.5	20.5	6.9	6.7
Urgent repairs over £1,000	17.3	41.0	15.1	12.7
Northern Ireland				
Unfit	8.5	27.9	2.0	2.1
Urgent repairs over £1,000	15.5	38.9	5.6	1.4
Wales				
Unfit	11.9	25.6	15.8	6.0
Repairs over £1,500	19.9	34.3	18.7	8.4
Scotland				
BTS	3.5	15.0	4.3	3.7
Urgent repairs over £1,000	5.1	16.6	3.9	0.6

Notes: (1) Figures for England, Scotland and Northern Ireland are for 1991; figures for Wales are for 1993. Excludes vacant dwellings. Comparisons cannot be made between countries.

Sources: DoE (1993); Scottish Homes (1993); NIHE (1993); Welsh Office (1994)

The much larger owner-occupied stock means that in numerical terms the majority of occupied unfit dwellings are found in the owner-occupied sector (Figure 4.11; Table A4.13). This concentration is greatest in Northern Ireland (72% of all unfit dwellings owner-occupied), while in Scotland, with its smaller owner-occupied sector, almost as many LA rented dwellings are BTS. The HA sector has significantly fewer unfit/BTS dwellings because of its small size. The picture in relation to disrepair is very similar.

An overview of dwellings in poor condition

Figures 4.12-4.15 combine information on tenure and age of the dwelling stock in each country to provide a profile of unfit/BTS dwellings (see also Table A4.14). In England the pre-1919 owner-occupied stock forms the largest single group of unfit dwellings, comprising more than 400,000 properties. There are a further 260,000 unfit pre-1919 privately rented dwellings. Inter-war owner-occupied dwellings make up another substantial group of poor condition properties (12% or 177,000). The next largest group of unfits is the post-1945 LA stock (11% or 157,000 dwellings). Together these dwellings make up about two thirds of the poor condition stock.

In Wales, unfitness is more concentrated in pre-1919 owner-occupied dwellings (38% of all unfits), with post-war LA dwellings, and post-war owner-occupied dwellings forming the next largest groups of unfit dwellings (17% and 15% respectively) (Figure 4.13). In Scotland,

pre-1919 owner-occupied dwellings also form the largest BTS group (32%), followed by the post-1945 LA stock, and the pre-1919 privately rented stock (Figure 4.14). In Northern Ireland, 42% of the unfit stock is pre-1919 owner-occupied. The next largest category is the vacant owner-occupied stock of all ages, followed by the pre-1919 privately rented stock (Figure 4.15). (Table A4.15 shows the age and tenure breakdown of dwellings in disrepair.)

Figure 4.11: Unfit dwellings by tenure, UK (1991/93)[a]

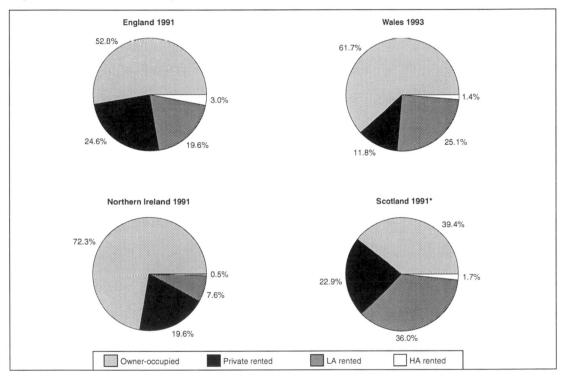

Figure 4.12: Unfit dwellings by age and tenure, England (1991)[d]

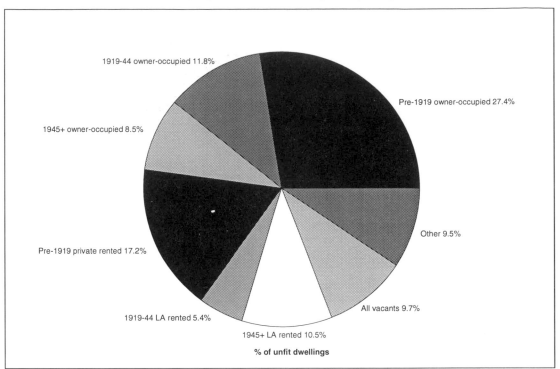

1919-44 owner-occupied 11.8%

Pre-1919 owner-occupied 27.4%

1945+ owner-occupied 8.5%

Other 9.5%

Pre-1919 private rented 17.2%

All vacants 9.7%

1919-44 LA rented 5.4%

1945+ LA rented 10.5%

% of unfit dwellings

Figure 4.13: Unfit dwellings by age and tenure, Wales (1993)[e]

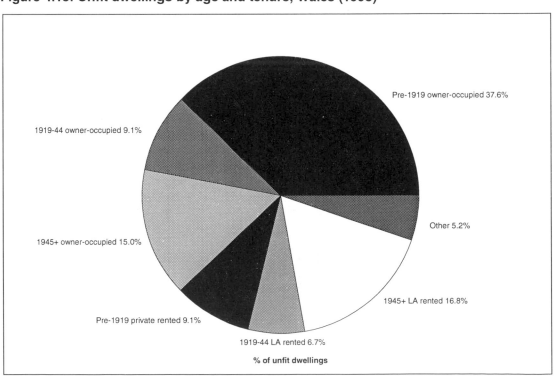

1919-44 owner-occupied 9.1%

Pre-1919 owner-occupied 37.6%

1945+ owner-occupied 15.0%

Other 5.2%

1945+ LA rented 16.8%

Pre-1919 private rented 9.1%

1919-44 LA rented 6.7%

% of unfit dwellings

Figure 4.14: BTS dwellings by age and tenure, Scotland (1991)[f]

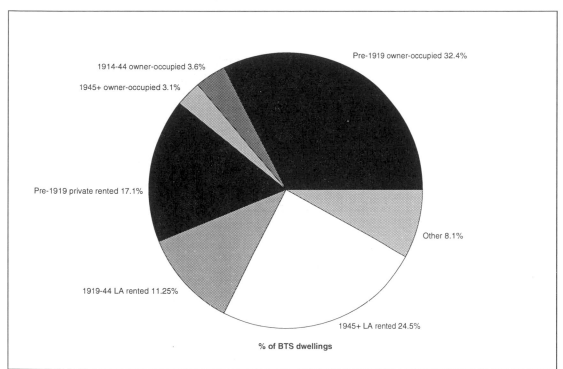

1914-44 owner-occupied 3.6%

1945+ owner-occupied 3.1%

Pre-1919 owner-occupied 32.4%

Pre-1919 private rented 17.1%

Other 8.1%

1919-44 LA rented 11.25%

1945+ LA rented 24.5%

% of BTS dwellings

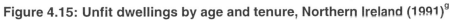

Figure 4.15: Unfit dwellings by age and tenure, Northern Ireland (1991)[g]

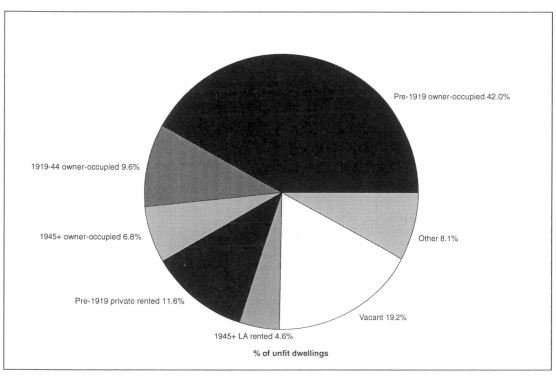

Pre-1919 owner-occupied 42.0%

1919-44 owner-occupied 9.6%

Other 8.1%

1945+ owner-occupied 6.8%

Pre-1919 private rented 11.6%

Vacant 19.2%

1945+ LA rented 4.6%

% of unfit dwellings

Heating, insulation and energy efficiency

Figure 4.16 shows the percentage of dwellings in the UK which have central heating (data not available for Wales).

Owner-occupied dwellings are most likely to have central heating, with HA stock in Northern Ireland also well catered for. Private rented dwellings are least likely to be provided with this amenity.

Figure 4.16: Central heating by tenure, England, Northern Ireland and Scotland (1991)[h]

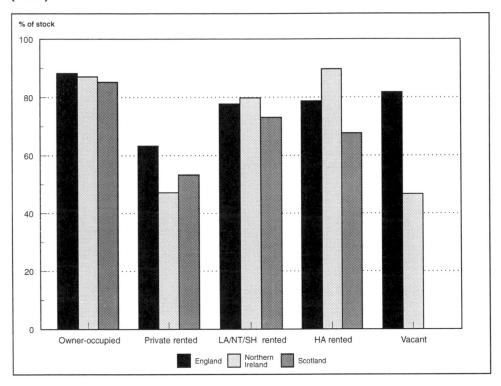

Figure 4.17 shows that there was, not surprisingly, an increase in the proportion of dwellings with some form of loft insulation from 1982 to 1992. Again, private rented dwellings are least likely to be insulated, although there are indications that this sector is catching up. Owner-occupiers with loft insulation also appear to insulate to a greater extent than local authorities or private landlords (Figure 4.18).

The Standard Assessment Procedure (SAP) rating was introduced by the government to provide a common measurement of the energy efficiency of a dwelling unit on a standard heating regime.

The SAP ratings are calculated both from heat loss from the dwelling and on efficiency and price of fuel for heating, with ratings normally falling between 1 and 100. Figure 4.19 compares estimated SAP ratings for owner-occupied, LA and private rented dwellings in England. Local authority dwellings are slightly less energy efficient than owner-occupied stock (average ratings of 34.4 and 37.2 respectively), but private rented dwellings are significantly less energy efficient (average rating of 21.7). Generally, higher ratings are due to superior insulation, while lower ratings result from poor heating systems.

Figure 4.17: Incidence of loft insulation, UK (1982 and 1992)[h]

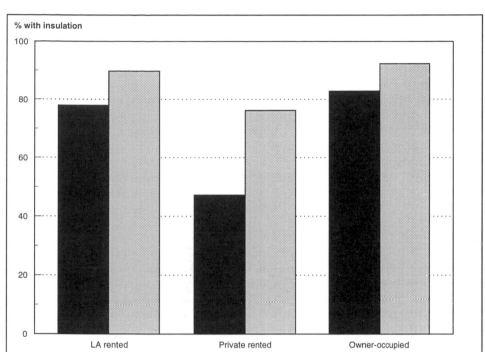

Figure 4.18: Depth of loft insulation, UK (1982 and 1992)[h]

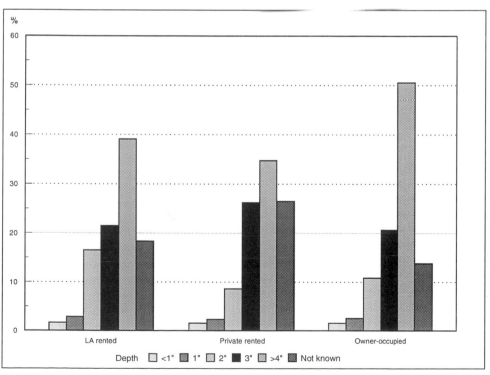

Figure 4.19: SAP ratings by tenure, England (1991)[h]

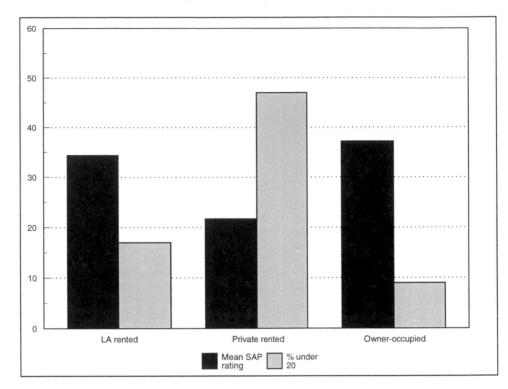

Data on National Home Energy Rating (NHER) scores is available from the 1991 SHCS. The Scottish average rating was 3.3 (out of 10), below the UK average of 4.5. Dwellings in the LA and HA sectors had the highest average rating (3.5), Scottish Homes stock had an average rating of 3.4, and homes in the owner-occupied sector averaged 3.3. Dwellings in the private rented sector were by far the worst, with an average rating of 2.2.

Chapter 5

People living in poor conditions

Social surveys linked to the national house condition surveys provide information on the characteristics of people living in poor conditions. It was argued in the previous chapter that characteristics such as dwelling age or type were factors which, directly or indirectly, influenced dwelling condition. Household characteristics such as income, economic status, length of residence, age of head of household, and household composition are also strongly associated with housing conditions, but the relationship between these factors and physical conditions is often complex. Some characteristics, for example, low income, may, to some extent, be contributory causes of poor conditions, by making it difficult for an owner to afford to carry out repairs. Others, such as age of head of household, have no obvious direct impact on condition but may be associated with variations in income, for example, the reduction in resources associated with retirement. Others (eg, length of residence) may be associated with attitudes to repair and maintenance which may, in turn, influence investment levels. But often cause and effect are difficult to disentangle, as low income households living in poor condition housing may have occupied this housing because its poor condition made it cheap to buy or rent.

Income

People on low incomes are generally more likely than those with higher levels of resources to live in poor housing conditions (Figures 5.1-5.4; Table A5.1). In England, for example, more than one in 10 households with an income of less than £4,000 per annum lived in unfit dwellings compared with only one in 35 of those with an income of £24,000 or more. In Scotland the same pattern applies in relation to BTS dwellings, but there is less differentiation by income group in relation to disrepair. (As Table A5.2 shows, most of those living in poor conditions have low incomes.) At least three quarters of those living in unfit housing or housing in serious disrepair had incomes below £12,000 in 1991. Nevertheless, this still leaves a minority of more affluent households living in poor conditions. This phenomenon is more common in England, where in 1991 almost 100,000 households with incomes of £20,000 per annum or more, and a similar number with incomes of between £16,000 and £20,000, lived in unfit dwellings.

Employment status

In England, households where the head is unemployed are more likely to live in poor conditions than other groups (Figure 5.5; Table A5.3). Almost 12% of unemployed households live in unfit housing compared with only 7% of all households. Households where the head is working are the least likely to live in poor conditions, while retired household heads fall in between.

Figure 5.1: Households living in poor conditions by income group, England (1991)[d]

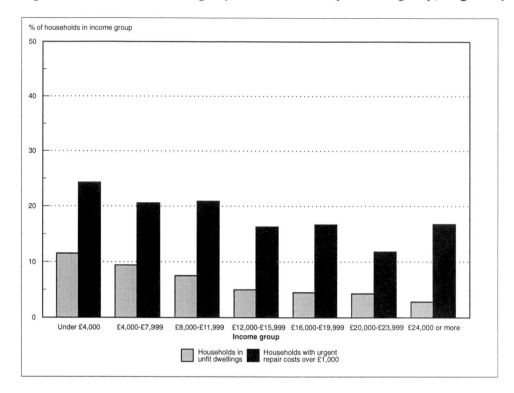

Figure 5.2: Households living in poor conditions by income group, Wales (1993)[e]

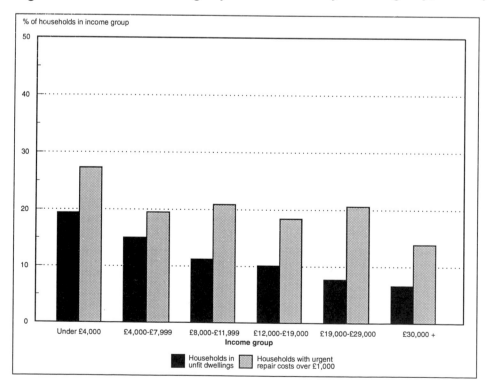

Figure 5.3: Households living in poor conditions by income group, Scotland (1991)[f]

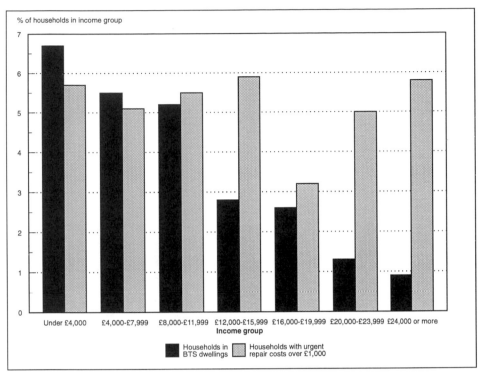

Figure 5.4: Households living in poor conditions by income group, Northern Ireland (1991)[g]

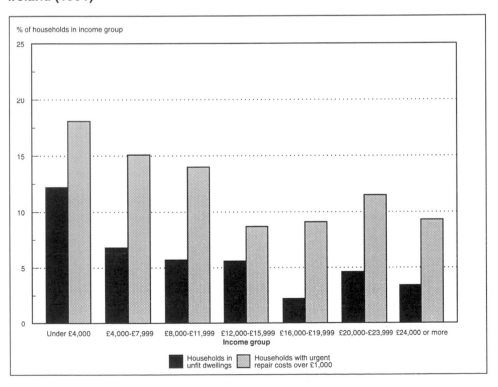

Figure 5.5: Households living in poor conditions by employment status, England (1991)[d]

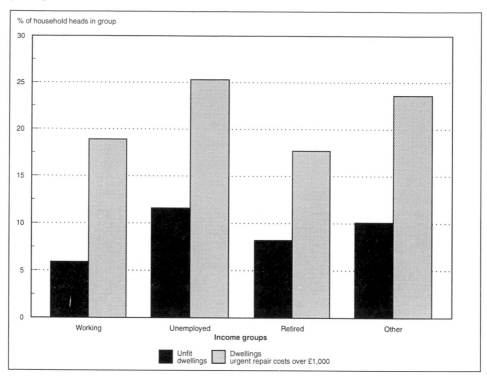

The pattern in Scotland is broadly similar, but the differences in the housing conditions between employment status groups are smaller (Figure 5.6; Table A5.3). In Northern Ireland the picture is different, with retired households still the most likely to live in poor condition property, followed by those who are unemployed (Figure 5.7; Table A5.3). Data for Wales is not available for 1993, but in 1986 the position was similar to that in Northern Ireland. This may be accounted for by the high proportion of older people living in poor condition housing in rural areas and in the Welsh valleys.

Household characteristics

The types of household which experience poor conditions are very similar throughout the UK (Figures 5.8-5.11; Table A5.4). Generally both younger and older single people are most likely to experience unfitness or live in BTS dwellings. In Scotland, lone parent households are also more likely to be living in BTS dwellings. The picture in Wales differs with less differentiation by household type.

The picture in relation to disrepair is less clear-cut. Lone person households are again very likely to experience problems, but in England, large families and multi-adult households are also more likely to live in dwellings with a high level of disrepair, and in Northern Ireland, pensioner couples appear more likely to experience disrepair in their homes than single pensioners. Otherwise, older couples are generally better housed than older single people. Two adult households and small families are the best housed.

Figure 5.6: Households living in poor conditions by employment status, Scotland (1991)[f]

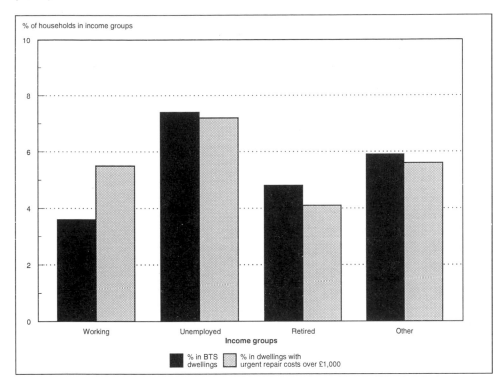

Figure 5.7: Households living in poor conditions by employment status, Northern Ireland (1991)[g]

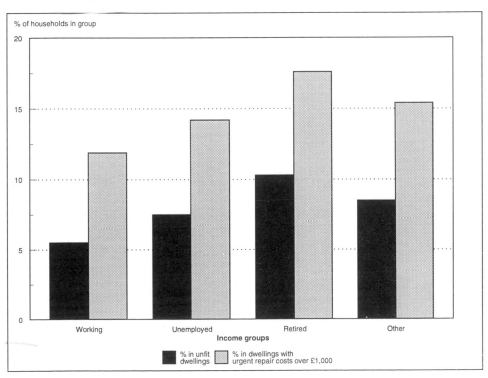

Figure 5.8: Households living in poor conditions by type, England (1991)[d]

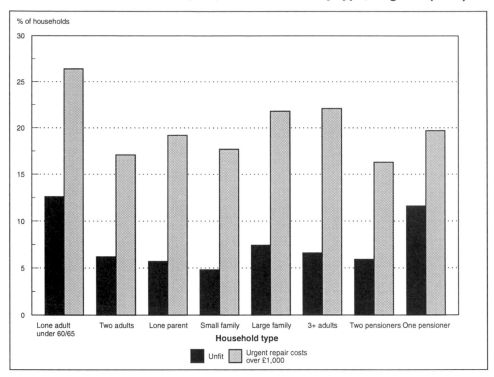

Figure 5.9: Households living in poor conditions by type, Wales (1993)[e]

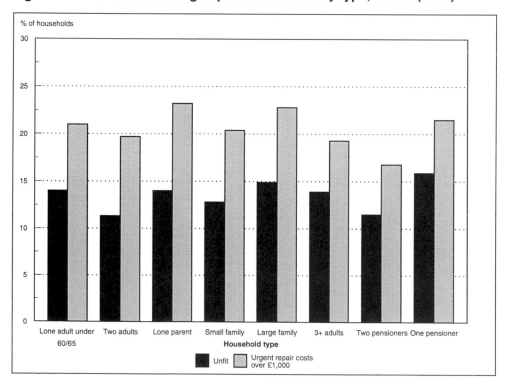

Figure 5.10: Households living in poor conditions by type, Scotland (1991)[f]

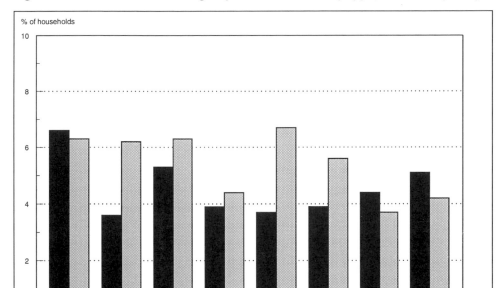

Figure 5.11: Households living in poor conditions by type, Northern Ireland (1991)[g]

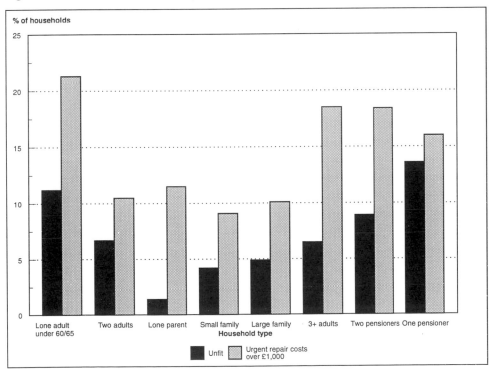

Age group

Older people and younger people just starting their housing careers are the groups most likely to live in poor conditions, with middle-aged people generally better housed (Figures 5.12-5.15; Table A5.5). Within older age groups the tendency to live in poor conditions is much greater after the age of 75. A detailed analysis for England shows an increase in the proportion of households living in unfit housing from 6.6% for households headed by a person aged between 60 and 64 to 13.2% for households headed by a person aged 85 or more (Table 5.1).

Figure 5.12: Households living in poor conditions by age group, England (1991)[d]

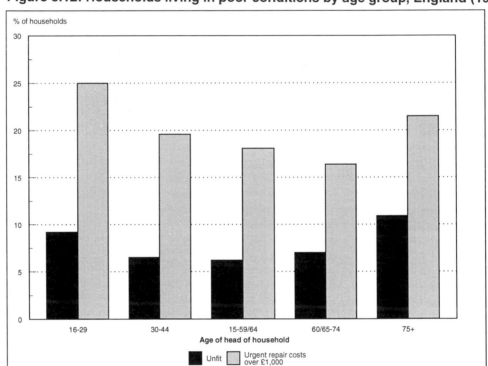

Table 5.1: Older households in unfit dwellings, England (1991)

Age of head of household	In fit dwellings (000s)	In unfit dwellings (000s)	% in unfit dwellings
60-64	1,499	106	6.6
65-69	1,369	108	7.3
70-74	1,451	102	6.6
75-79	1,083	126	10.5
80-84	632	69	9.9
85+	470	72	13.2
All households	17,697	1,414	7.4

Source: 1991 EHCS: analysis of data

Figure 5.13: Households living in poor conditions by age group, Wales (1993)[e]

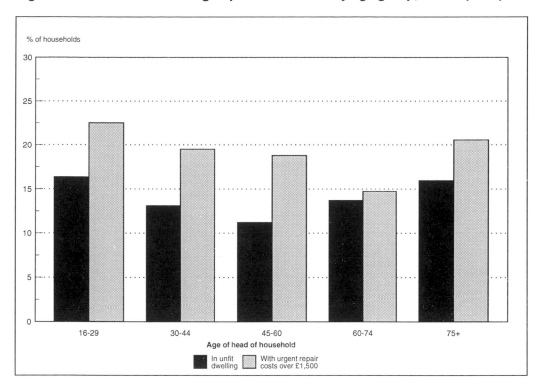

Figure 5.14: Households living in poor conditions by age group, Scotland (1991)[f]

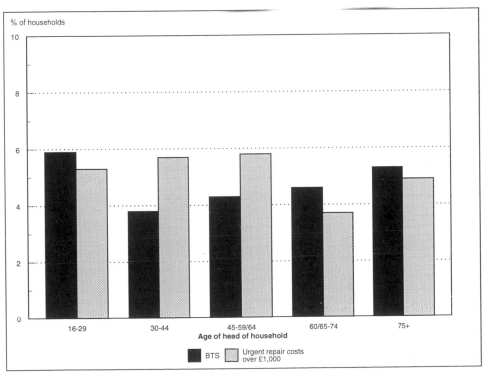

Figure 5.15: Households living in poor conditions by age group, Northern Ireland (1991)[g]

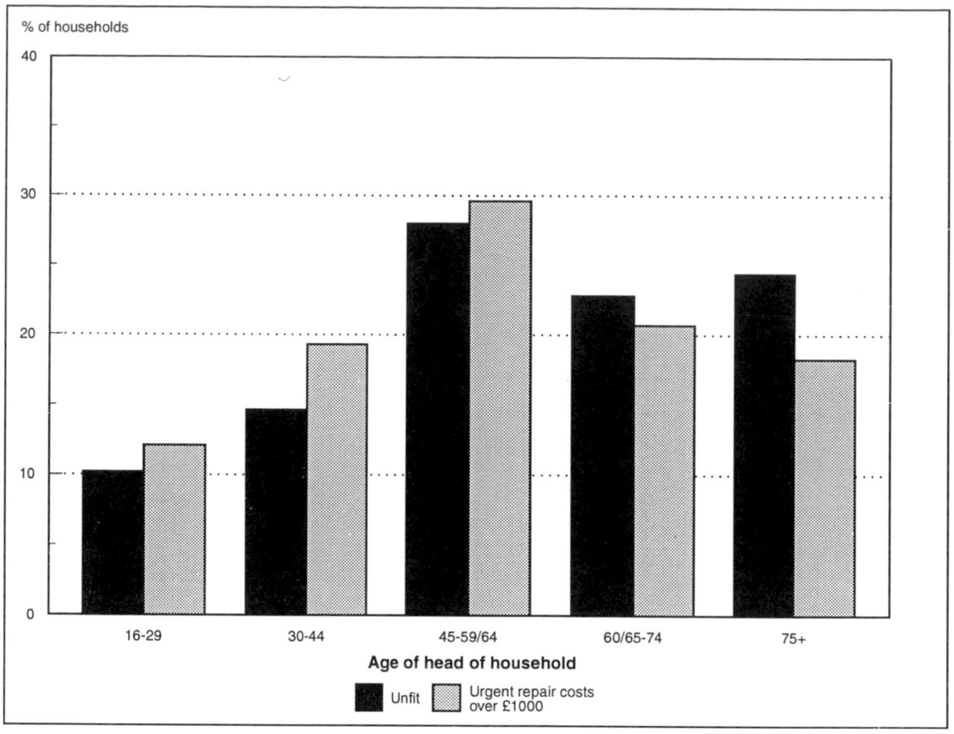

Gender of household head

Table 5.2 shows the proportion of households living in unfit dwellings by the age and gender of the head of household for England in 1991. Younger men are more likely to live in unfit dwellings than younger women, but from the age of 30 onwards households headed by women are more likely to experience unfit living conditions, with 13.6% of households headed by women in the 40-59 age band falling into this category. In the older age groups the differential narrows again but female headed households remain the most likely to experience unfitness. (Table A5.6 shows fuller details.)

Table 5.2: Households in unfit dwellings by age and gender of head of household, England (1991)

Age of head of household	Male head of household			Female head of household			Balance (% female minus % male)
	In fit dwellings	In unfit dwellings	% in unfit dwellings	In fit dwellings	In unfit dwellings	% in unfit dwellings	
15-29	1,417	160	10.1	527	38	6.7	-3.4
30-44	4,385	296	6.3	698	58	7.7	1.3
45-59	3,666	199	5.1	500	79	13.6	8.5
60-74	3,258	210	6.1	1,060	106	9.1	3.0
75+	1,087	125	10.3	1,098	143	11.5	1.2
All	13,815	989	6.7	3,883	424	9.8	3.1

Source: 1991 EHCS: analysis of data

Length of residence

Figure 5.16 shows that house conditions are closely linked to length of residence with those living in the same property for up to 2 years or 20 years and over being the most likely to experience poor housing conditions (see also Table A5.7). The same picture holds for households in Northern Ireland. In Scotland differences in levels of BTS or disrepair are relatively small. In England these differences are broadly the same across all tenures (Table A5.8). The association between length of residence and poor condition in the owner-occupied sector may be explained by age factors. The majority of households resident in their homes for a long period are older

people who in general are more likely to live in poor conditions, as shown above. It may also be the case that some home owners buy dwellings in relatively poor condition, invest heavily during the early years of residence in a particular dwelling, and subsequently neglect repair, improvement and maintenance.

In other tenures the cause of the link between length of residence and poor conditions is more difficult to explain, although it may simply be that older dwellings, which tend to be in poorer condition, are more likely to have long-standing residents than newer ones, and that in the social rented sector, households allocated to poor condition dwellings do not stay in them for a very long period.

Figure 5.16: Households living in poor conditions by length of residence, England (1991)[d]

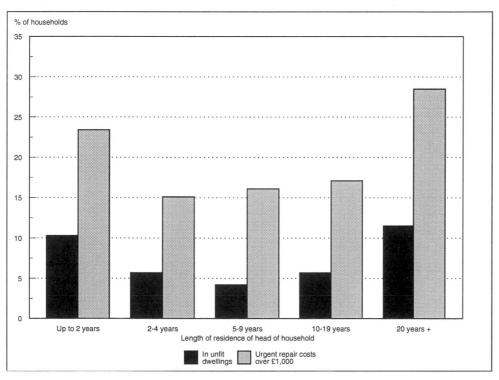

Ethnic origin

Data on ethnic origin and poor housing conditions is only available for England and Scotland (Figures 5.17 and 5.18; Table A5.9). In both countries, households with a head from a minority ethnic community were generally more likely to live in poor conditions than those from the white community. Sample numbers are too small to permit further analysis.

Figure 5.17: Households living in poor conditions by ethnic origin, England (1991)[d]

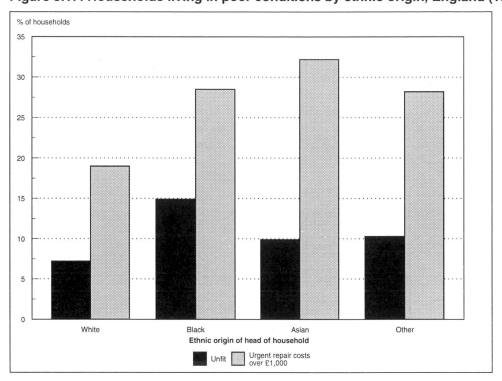

Figure 5.18: Households living in poor conditions by ethnic origin, Scotland (1991)[f]

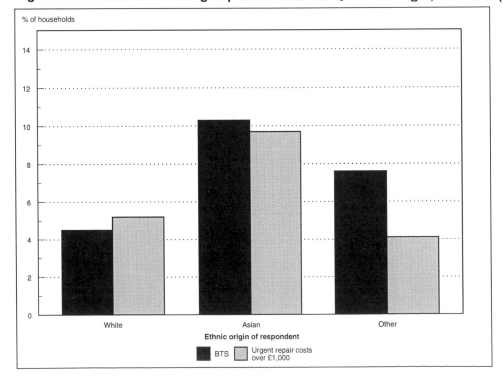

An overview of households living in poor conditions

Figures 5.19-5.22 (Table A5.10) combine information on tenure and household income in England to provide a profile of households living in unfit or BTS housing. (Similar data on disrepair is included in Table A5.11.)

Low income home owners (with incomes of under £8,000 per annum at 1991 prices) form the largest group in England, Wales and Northern Ireland. In England, this group accounts for over a fifth of all those in unfit housing, but this rises to a third in Wales and over half in Northern Ireland. In Scotland, about a fifth of households in BTS dwellings are low income owner-occupiers, a similar proportion to that for unfit housing in England, but the largest group of households in BTS dwellings is low income LA tenants, who account for 28% of the total. This is also the second largest group occupying unfit dwellings in Wales (25%). England and Northern Ireland differ, with low income households in the private rented sector forming the next largest group of occupants of unfit housing.

However, low income households do not account for all those in unfit or BTS housing. In all four countries there is a significant group of middle income owners in poor conditions (between 13% and 18%) and a smaller group of high income owners (10% in England, 5-6% elsewhere).

Figure 5.19: Households living in unfit dwellings by income and tenure, England (1991)[d]

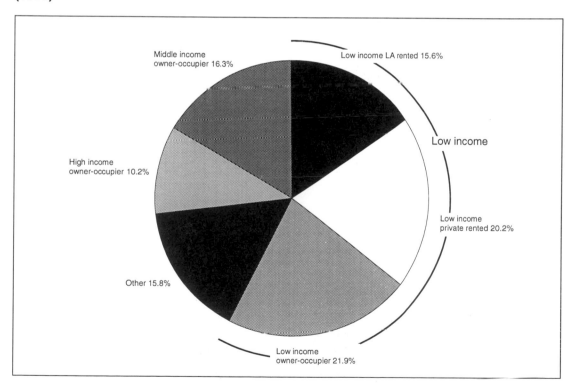

Figure 5.20: Households living in unfit dwellings by income and tenure, Wales (1993)[e]

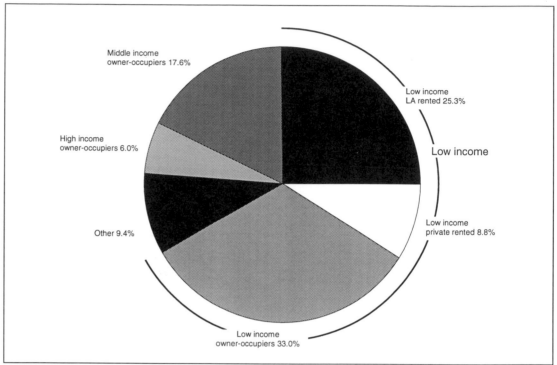

Figure 5.21: Households living in unfit dwellings by income and tenure, Scotland (1991)[f]

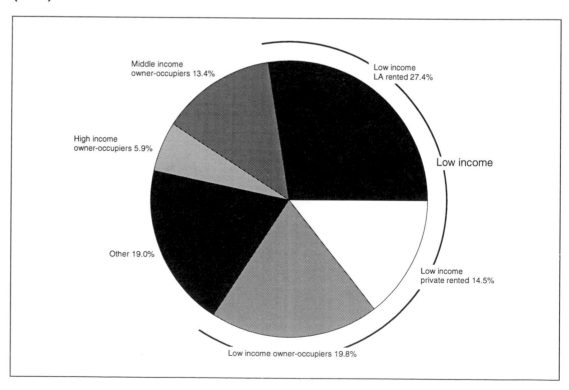

Figure 5.22: Households living in unfit dwellings by income and tenure, Northern Ireland (1991)[g]

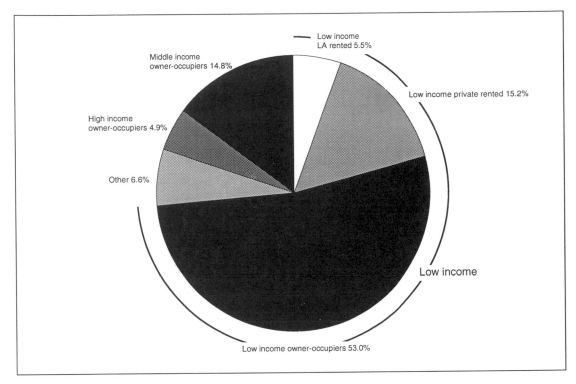

Chapter 6

Housing renewal policies

It is not practical to provide a detailed historical account of the development of housing renewal policies in the UK in a report of this size. A fuller account can be found in Leather and Mackintosh (1992).

In England, demolition and rehabilitation have been the two main programmes of public sector investment in poor condition housing in the post-war period. Rehabilitation policies in the private sector have been pursued through the provision of a range of grants to owners and tenants, and through area (or neighbourhood) renewal policies. From the mid-1960s onwards, there was increasing interest in renovation as a complement and eventually as an alternative to clearance. National house condition surveys revealed that there were many more sub-standard dwellings than had previously been thought and it was clear that even at the then high rates of clearance it would take many decades to deal with the backlog. Resident opposition to clearance also grew stronger as programmes moved from dwellings which were mainly privately rented into areas with higher levels of home ownership where the limited compensation provisions of the time, and the prospect of rehousing into the council sector were less attractive. The 1969 Housing Act extended the range of grants previously available to include more generous assistance with improvement as well as the installation of missing basic amenities. It also provided LAs with powers to declare General Improvement Areas (GIAs) where renovation efforts were focused.

The 1969 Housing Act envisaged renovation as a complement to clearance, with action taking place in areas of basically sound housing with high rates of home ownership which would not have been included in clearance programmes for many years. However, it soon became clear that opposition to clearance was forcing LAs to use renovation powers in areas of poorer condition housing, with high levels of social deprivation, as an alternative to clearance. The 1974 Housing Act provided additional powers, including a new repair grant, higher grant rates, and an additional type of improvement area, the Housing Action Area (HAA). There was more emphasis in HAAs in the involvement of LAs and HAs in acquiring and renovating poor condition properties. Despite this emphasis the majority of grants were, in practice, provided to individual properties outside HAAs and GIAs.

During the 1980s, emphasis shifted towards the renovation of the publicly owned housing stock, including not only the oldest public sector houses built mainly during the 1919-45 period, but also a substantial number of flats and maisonettes built during the 1960s and 1970s in high or medium rise estates. The Estates Action programme, which provided earmarked allocations to specific LA estates from resources top-sliced from the overall LA capital programme, expanded rapidly during the late 1980s and early 1990s, but from 1995 Estates Action resources in England were subsumed into the new Single Regeneration Budget, which amalgamated resources from a large number of programmes under a new heading, with uncommitted resources allocated by competition. It is feared that the emphasis on economic regeneration, and on funding partnerships between public and private sectors, will lead to a sharp decline in the level of LA estate renovation funded from this programme in the future.

In the HA sector, involvement in the acquisition and rehabilitation of private sector dwellings declined in the late 1980s and 1990s. One cause for this was the introduction of a new Housing Association Grant (HAG) regime which relied on attracting an increasing element of private funding and which placed the risk element in the renovation process on HAs. Rehabilitation projects became less attractive. Research also suggested that the supply of low cost formerly private rented dwellings in inner-city areas also declined, and that LAs looked to HAs more to provide new accommodation for rehousing needs.

In the private sector in the 1980s there was a move away from grants for improvement towards repair grants. In 1990, the whole system of renovation grants was revised. Tests of the applicant's resources were introduced for all types of grant. Improvement, repair and inter-mediate grants were merged into a single renovation grant (with variations for work in houses in multiple occupation [HMOs] and to the common parts of dwellings). For the first time a dedicated disabled facilities grant (DFG) was introduced to assist with adaptations. Finally, the minor works assistance (MWA) grant was introduced to cover a variety of small jobs. Renovation grants for work to make dwellings fit for human habitation, and DFGs for most adaptation work to dwellings to assist with mobility and access to facilities, were made available as of right, subject to the test of resources.

Over the 1990-96 period it became clear that the demand for grant aid exceeded the resources which the government was prepared to make available in England. Demand management mechanisms in-cluded the introduction of a maximum grant level and the lowering of this level to £20,000. To resolve this crisis, the 1996 Housing Grants, Construction and Regen-eration Act abolished mandatory renovation grants, and replaced MWA with the home repair grant, a similar grant but with a higher cost limit, broader purposes, and wider eligibility.

In Wales, the legislative framework was as for England. Renewal policies in Wales were also generally similar to those in England until the mid-1980s. However, the shift in resources in favour of public sector renovation which occurred in England did not take place in Wales, and levels of funding for private sector grants and related programmes have continued at a consistently higher level (pro rata to the size of the dwelling stock) than in England, reflecting the high priority given to private sector housing renovation by the Welsh Office. Although the 1989 Local Govern-ment and Housing Act changes to the grant system were applied in Wales, there were differences in the allocation and ear-marking of grant resources, and the maximum limit for grant in Wales is higher than in England. The changes to grant provision introduced in the 1996 Housing Grants, Construction and Regeneration Act will apply to Wales.

In Scotland, the predominance of the tenement dwelling in the poor condition privately owned stock has shaped housing renewal policy. As in England and Wales, there was a shift of emphasis from clearance to renovation which led to new legislation in 1969. As well as extending grant provision as in England, LAs were given powers to declare Housing Treatment Areas (HTAs) in neigh-bourhoods with a high proportion of unfit housing. Local authority powers to compel owners to carry out repairs, especially in HTAs, were stronger than in England and Wales. Use of HTA powers was, however, more limited than the use of GIA powers in England and Wales. Again, paralleling developments in England and Wales, new legislation in 1974 introduced HAAs, although there were marked differences from the English equivalent. The main emphasis was on dwelling eligibility criteria rather than social factors, and powers of compulsion were much stronger than in England, reflecting the need for co-ordinated action to deal with the problems of improving and repairing tenement buildings. In some parts of Scotland, particularly Glasgow, there was also a strong emphasis on the acquisition of poor condition dwellings by community-based HAs on a much greater scale than in England. The 1989 Act grant system changes in England and Wales were not applied in Scotland, which has continued with the earlier powers, subject only to minor amendment. In Northern Ireland, the 1989 Act changes to the grant system were introduced in 1992, with the addition of a new replacement grant.

Table 6.1 shows some key stages in the development of housing renewal policy over the 1954-96 period.

Table 6.1: Key stages in the development of housing renewal policy, Britain

1954	Beginning of post-war clearance programme
1967	First national house condition surveys in England and Wales
1965-68	Reappraisal of policy
1969	Housing Act: boost to grants as complement to clearance; area renewal via GIAs; in Scotland parallel legislation introduced HTAs
1974	Housing Act: grants for repair introduced; HAAs as an alternative to clearance; capital grant (HAG) to HAs to finance acquisition and rehabilitation; in Scotland 1974 Housing (Scotland) Act introduced HAAs
1979	Introduction of Priority Estates Project in England to target funds on poor condition public sector estates
1980	Housing Act: extension of repair grants to all pre-1919 dwellings
1982-84	Boom in grant take-up throughout UK due to increase in grant percentages; development in England and Wales of enveloping (form of simultaneous block renovation)
1985	Review of policy in England and Wales proposes targeting of grants via a means test and introduction of equity-sharing loans; launch of Estates Action programme in England to target resources on poor condition public sector estates
1987	Further consultation papers; government funding for experimental home improvement agencies in England and Wales to help older owners with renovation
1989	Local Government and Housing Act in England and Wales: new renovation, disabled facilities and minor works grants; means-testing of grant aid; new fitness standard; GIAs and HAAs replaced by Renewal Areas; reduction in government subsidy for grant payments
1990	1989 Act comes into operation in England and Wales
1991	Longer term funding for 120 home improvement agencies
1992	1989 Act system introduced in Northern Ireland; first review of 1989 Act system in England and Wales
1993	Second review of 1989 Act system in England and Wales and publication of consultation papers
1996	Housing Grants, Construction and Regeneration Act in England and Wales providing for abolition of mandatory renovation grants, replacement of MWA with home repair grant, and introduction of relocation grants

Chapter 7

Tackling poor housing conditions

Clearance

Figure 7.1 shows the number of dwellings demolished under slum clearance powers in Britain for each year since 1969 (see also Table A7.1). The level of demolition has declined sharply from more than 80,000 dwellings per annum in the early 1970s to some 4,200 in 1992. This represents an annual replacement rate of less than one in every 4,750 dwellings. Since 1992 the level of reported clearance in Scotland has been greater than in England. Overall there was a small increase in slum clearance levels in 1993 throughout Britain after many years of decline but the only factor likely to lead to any sustained recovery in demolition levels would be the provision of additional capital resources.

Figure 7.1: Dwellings demolished or closed, Britain (1969-93)[c]

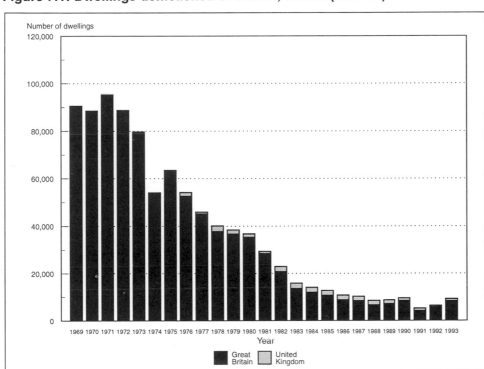

The rate of clearance since 1978 has been heavily skewed with 80% of authorities carrying out virtually no clearance during this period. As Map 7.1 shows, the highest rates of clearance (and the largest absolute numbers of cleared properties) are found in cities and metropolitan districts in the North West, North East, Yorkshire and Humberside and the Midlands. Table 7.1 shows authorities with the highest level of clearance relative to the size of the privately owned dwelling stock in their area. Only four authorities (Blackburn, Middlesborough, Hull and Sheffield) have cleared more than 100 properties per 1,000 private sector dwellings. Other authorities with high levels of slum clearance include Salford, Bolton, Sandwell, Oldham and St Helens.

Table 7.1: Authorities in England and Wales with the highest rate of demolitions and closures per 1,000 private sector dwellings (1978-93)

LA	Demolitions		LA	Demolitions	
	Number	Per 1,000		Number	Per 1,000
Blackburn	6,426	170.90	Burnley	1,525	52.85
Middlesbrough	4,741	132.07	Rochdale	2,670	49.11
Kingston-upon-Hull	6,448	107.12	Stoke-on-Trent	3,163	45.36
			Blaenau Gwent	871	44.82
Sheffield	13,395	101.07	Rotherham	2,769	42.05
Salford	5,106	96.36	Nottingham	2,652	40.20
Bolton	5,279	67.88	Tameside	2,513	39.93
Sandwell	4,297	65.69	Wigan	3,351	38.49
Oldham	3,969	64.63	Rossendale	773	38.41
St Helens	3,021	62.08	Derwentside	878	37.79
Southwark	2,087	58.53	Gateshead	1,806	36.85
South Tyneside	2,004	57.82	Newcastle on Tyne	2,418	36.78
Hartlepool	1,375	57.16			
Merthyr Tydfil	835	53.55	Leeds	6,792	35.49
Derby	3,518	53.28	Langbaurgh	1,424	34.43
Hyndburn	1,369	53.18	Bolsover	661	32.11

Source: *Local Housing Statistics* (various years)

The amount of dwelling clearance fell from the higher levels attained in the 1960s and early 1970s because of a shift in emphasis towards the renovation of the older housing stock. This came about for a number of reasons. In many areas the very poorest pre-1919 dwellings had, by this stage, been cleared. In some areas dissatisfied residents mounted successful campaigns of resistance to clearance. The government also promoted renovation, at first as a complement, and subsequently as a lower cost alternative, to demolition. The present level of clearance is widely regarded by professionals as too low but with a high proportion of older houses in individual ownership it is both difficult and expensive to provide appropriate re-housing. A recent pilot initiative in Birmingham offered 'rebuilding grants' to owners to persuade them to invest the compensation received from the clearance of their house in the purchase or part-purchase of another. This has led to the provision in the 1996 Housing Grants, Construction and Regeneration Act for 'relocation grants' which have the same objective. It is doubtful, however, whether this will lead to an increase in the overall level of slum clearance unless additional capital resources are made available.

Map 7.1: Dwellings demolished or closed per 1,000 privately owned dwellings, England and Wales (1978-91)[c]

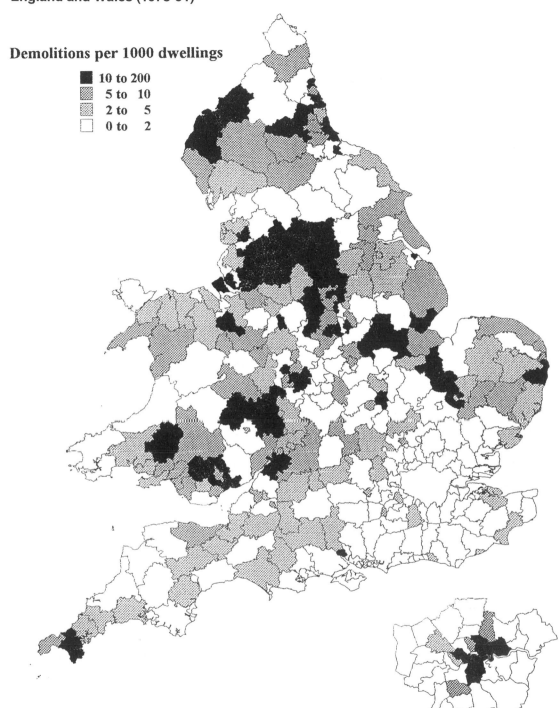

Demolitions per 1000 dwellings

- ■ 10 to 200
- ▨ 5 to 10
- ▨ 2 to 5
- □ 0 to 2

Grants to owners

Capital grants to assist home owners (and at times tenants) to improve, repair and adapt their homes have been available for almost 50 years, but the programme of grant aid began in earnest in 1969. In 1990, the grant system was substantially revised with further revisions in 1996 (DoE, 1996). Prior to 1990, *intermediate* (previously standard) grants were available to provide missing amenities and associated repairs. *Improvement* grants were for more substantial works including extensions, kitchen and bathroom facilities, attic conversions, and the subdivision of dwellings. They also included provision for repairs. *Repair* grants (available on a limited basis from 1975 and more widely after 1980) were exclusively for substantial repair work. Grant aid provided in any individual case was a percentage of the cost of qualifying work up to a set maximum (the eligible cost limit). Grant percentages and eligible cost limits varied. With the exception of grants to provide amenities, or those provided to assist with work carried out as a result of a *statutory notice* served by a local council, all grants were provided at the discretion of LAs.

The 1989 Local Government and Housing Act introduced a new system of grant aid which came into operation in England and Wales in 1990. The system was amended by the 1996 Housing Grants, Construction and Regeneration Act. A similar system was introduced in Northern Ireland in 1992, but in Scotland the old system remains in operation and is substantially similar to that described above.

Under the 1996 Act system there are three main types of grant:

■ *Renovation* grants cover all types of improvement and repair work. From 1990-96 renovation grants were available as of right to owner-occupiers in unfit dwellings but the 1996 Act removed this right and made the grant discretionary. The proportion of grant payable is assessed by a test of the applicant's financial resources and may vary from nothing to 100% of the qualifying costs of work.

■ *Disabled facilities* grants cover adaptations and other work to enable a disabled person to live in a dwelling. Like the renovation grant this grant is also subject to a test of resources. Grant for some types of work is mandatory.

■ *Home repair assistance.* Minor works assistance (usually a grant and always discretionary) was available to those on certain means tested benefits up to a maximum of £1,080 per grant from 1990-96. Most commonly the grant was provided to people aged 60 or more for work which would enable them to remain living independently or stay put in their own home. In 1996 minor works assistance was replaced with home repair assistance. This is a discretionary grant (or materials) to assist with small-scale works of repair, improvement or adaptation, including energy efficiency and crime prevention works. There is a limit of £2,000 per application and a maximum limit of assistance of £4,000 per dwelling in any three-year period. The grant is available to owner-occupiers and private tenants aged over 17 and in receipt of income support or certain other means tested benefits, or aged 60 and over, disabled, or infirm.

There is an upper limit on the amount of mandatory grant payable of £20,000 in England and £24,000 in Wales.

The overall level of grant provision

Figures 7.2 to 7.5 show the changing pattern of grant provision in the UK between 1969 and 1994 (and Tables A7.2-A7.5 provide detailed figures). In England, grant take-up grew slowly, but rose to a peak in 1973-74 when higher percentage grants were made available in certain economically depressed areas. After a lower level of take-up in the later 1970s there was a second boom in the 1982-84 period stimulated by another increase in grant rates. This applied particularly to repair grants for which the rate was increased to 90% of eligible costs for all owners of dwellings built before 1919. The level of take-up subsequently declined until 1990. Under the new system output initially declined further, even if the new DFGs which do not address renovation are included in the total. Since 1992 the total number of grants has again increased slowly but at about 60,000 per annum levels remain well below those achieved during the 1980s.

In Wales the pattern of take-up mirrored that in England, with a boom in improvement grants in the 1972-74 period and another in repair grants during the early 1980s. Although a decline followed in the mid-1980s this was less pronounced than in England and from the later 1980s, provision again picked up, reaching a level close to the all-time peak of 30,000 per

annum in 1990. Under the new grant system the overall level of output (including DFGs but excluding MWA) has declined from late 1980s levels to around 11,000 grants per annum.

In Scotland the level of grant provision was relatively low in the 1970s but Scotland again benefited from the repair grants boom of the 1980s. Although provision fell from the 60,000 grants provided in 1984, it has remained steady at a level above 20,000 per annum since 1990.

In Northern Ireland the data is less complete. There were relatively few grants provided until the newly formed NIHE took over this task early in the 1970s. The level of provision then built up very rapidly with a strong emphasis on repair grants and continued throughout the mid-1980s. Since 1986 there has been a fall in provision to around 7,000 per annum under the new grant system (including DFGs but excluding MWA).

Figure 7.2: Grants by type, England (1969-94)[c]

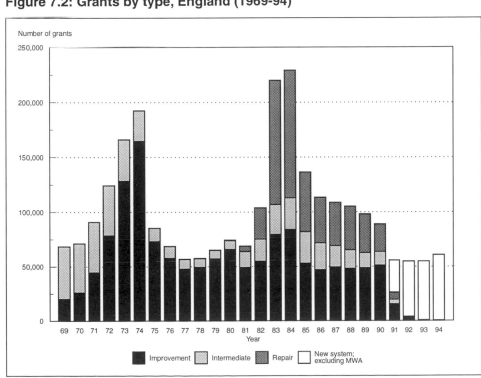

Figure 7.3: Grants by type, Wales (1969-94)^c

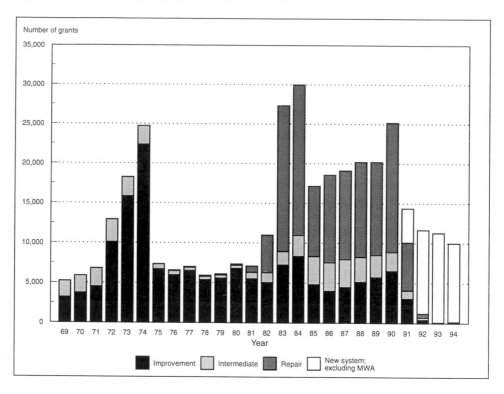

Figure 7.4: Grants by type, Scotland (1969-94)^c

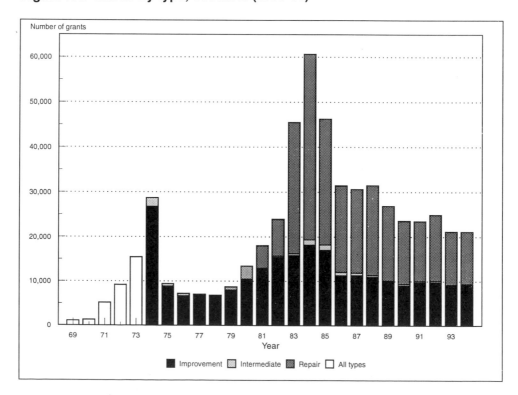

Figure 7.5: Grants by type, Northern Ireland (1977-94)[c]

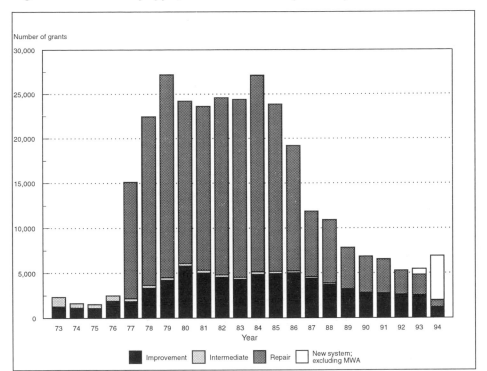

Grants per 1,000 dwellings

Figure 7.6 examines the number of grants in each country in comparison to the size of the housing stock (Table A7.6). This is difficult to estimate accurately because of changes over time in the nature of the dwelling stock eligible for grant, but accepting this limitation it is clear that until the late 1980s investment levels in Northern Ireland generally exceeded those elsewhere in the UK. For a 10-year period between 1977 and 1985 provision exceeded 70 grants per 1,000 private sector dwellings. After a slow start the number of grants in Scotland per 1,000 privately owned dwellings increased rapidly in the late 1970s and has generally remained above the level in England or Wales. Grant provision in Wales has exceeded that in England and in the late 1980s became comparable in terms of grants per 1,000 dwellings with Scotland and Northern Ireland. In England, provision has remained consistently the lowest, at less

than 10 grants per 1,000 private sector dwellings, except in the two boom periods in the early 1970s and early 1980s, despite the fact that the proportions of pre-1919 and inter-war dwellings exceed those in both Scotland and Northern Ireland. As a result, Glasgow, Belfast and Cardiff have received far higher levels of investment than many comparable cities in England.

Type of grant

Figure 7.7 shows details of the types of grant provided under the old grant system (in Scotland still the current system). In England, 58% of grants provided under the old system between 1969 and 1994 were improvement grants, with the residue evenly split between repair and intermediate grants. The profile varied, with improvement grants reaching a peak of around 80% of all grants in the late 1970s, becoming displaced by repair grants in the early 1980s, and regaining some ground to account for over 50% of grants at the end of the 1980s (Table A7.7). In Wales, there were fewer improvement grants under the old system (49%) and more repair grants (38%). Improvement grants accounted for 90% of all grants in the 1970s but declined to about 25% after the extension of repair grants to all pre-1919 properties in the early 1980s. In Scotland, information on grants by type was not available before 1974. In overall terms, 47% of grants over the 1974-94 period were improvement grants and 50% were repair grants. As in Wales, there was a strong focus on improvement grants in the 1970s, but these were subsequently displaced by

repair grants to an even greater extent than in Wales. The proportion of repair grants has declined during the 1990s from a peak of over 60% but still accounts for over 50% of grants provided. In Northern Ireland, repair grants account for three quarters of all grants provided under the old system over the 1977-94 period for which information is available. Such grants were available at an earlier stage than in the rest of the UK, accounting for 85% of grants in 1977. There was a steady decline in the proportion of repair grants to about 50% in 1992, the last year of the old system in Northern Ireland.

Figure 7.6: Grants per 1,000 privately owned dwellings, UK (1969-94)[c]

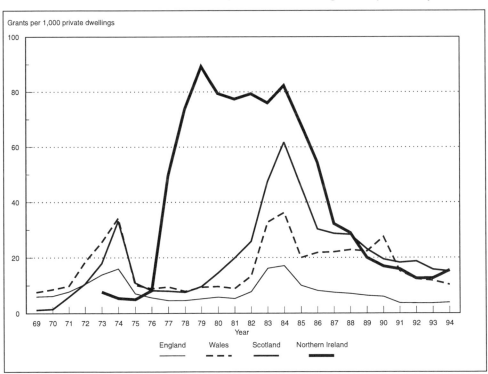

These findings reveal a different focus in renovation policy between England and the remainder of the UK under the old renovation grant system. In England there was emphasis on the more comprehensive improvement grants, while in Scotland, Wales and Northern Ireland grant aid

focused more on repair work. This may, in part, explain the higher per dwelling provision of grants outside England, as repair grants were typically worth far less than improvement grants. Average grant levels are examined further below.

Figure 7.7: Grants by type under the old system, UK (1969-94)[c]

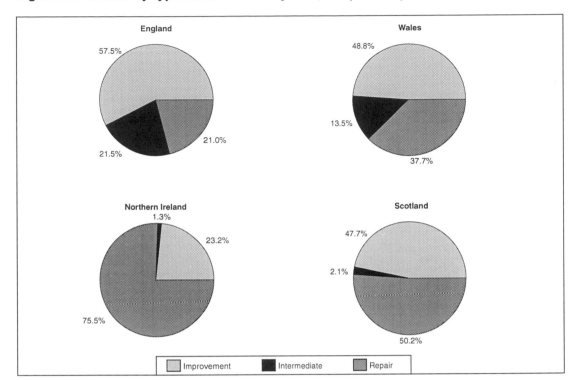

Mandatory renovation grants were the main type of grant provided under the new system in both England and Wales in 1994 (Figure 7.8; Table A7.8; Table A7.9). In England 54% of grants (excluding MWA) were of this type, with a further 8% discretionary renovation grants. In Wales the equivalent figures were 66% and 4% (Table A7.8; Table A7.10). Disabled facilities grants were the other main type of grant provided, accounting for 34% of grants in England and 27% in Wales. Almost all DFGs were mandatory. HMO grants formed only 3% of all grants provided and there were very few common parts grants. If MWA were to be added into the total, these grants would form 34% of all grants provided in England and 31% in Wales. (Table A7.11 shows the breakdown of grant provision in Northern Ireland for 1993 and 1994, the first two years of operation of the new system.)

Looking specifically at MWA, Table 7.2 shows the split in provision between the types of grant available (see also Table A7.12). Staying put grants to assist older people to continue living independently at home have been consistently the most significant type of assistance, accounting for 84% of all MWA provided in 1993/94 in England. Thermal insulation has been the other main purpose (36% of MWA in 1990/91, declining to 14% in 1993/94). The other three types of MWA have only rarely been provided.

The local pattern of grant provision

There have been substantial variations in the numbers of grants paid by individual LAs, as a result of differences in size, variations in housing conditions, and differences in the enthusiasm with which renewal policies were pursued. Map 7.2 shows the number of grants of all types provided under the old grant system per 1,000 private sector dwellings in the period 1978-91 in England and Wales. There are no clear patterns in the distribution but there are concentrations of authorities, especially in Wales, but also in the South West, East Anglia, the Midlands, North East Lancashire and the North East with high levels of grant activity. The authorities with the highest rates of grant provision overall are predominantly Welsh, including both urban and rural districts (Table 7.3). In England the majority of authorities with high levels of provision are rural and few large urban authorities have given a large number of grants relative to the size of their stock.

Figure 7.8: Grants by type under the new system, England and Wales (1994)[c]

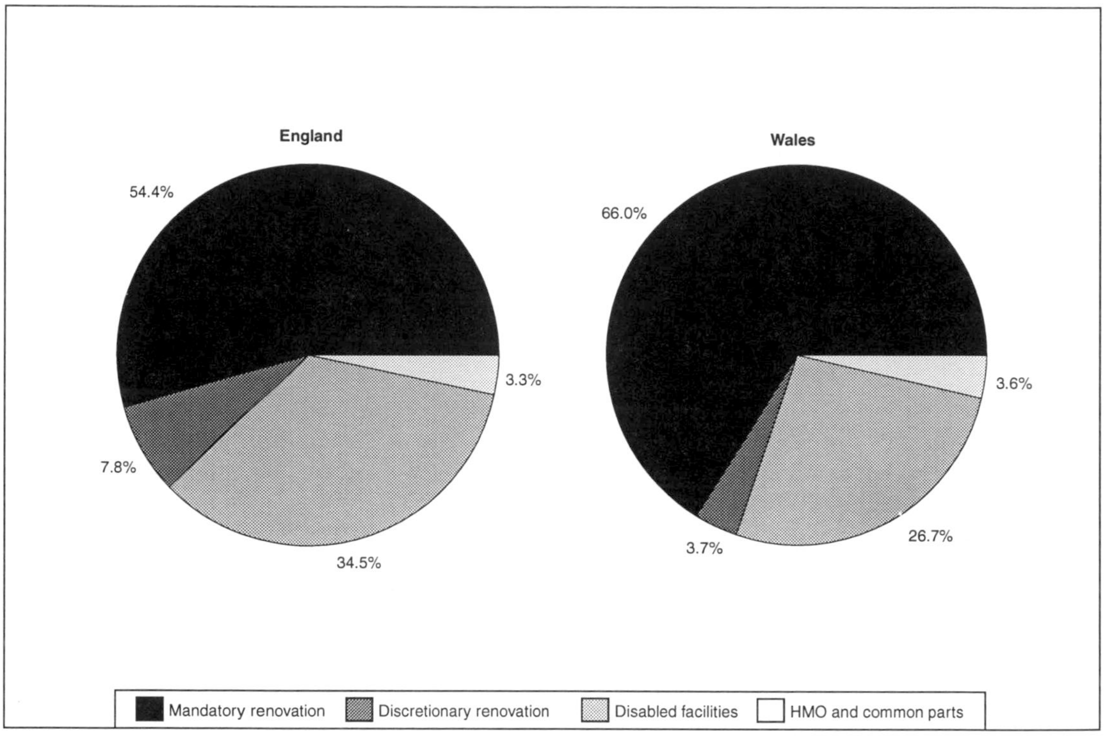

Table 7.2: Minor works assistance by type, England (1990-94)

Year	Thermal insulation		Patch and mend (1)		Staying put (2)		Elderly adaptation (3)		Lead pipes (4)	
	No	%	No	%	No	%	No	%	No	%
1990/91	5,512	35.9	1	0.0	9,454	61.5	407	2.6	–	–
1991/92	5,823	20.7	118	0.4	21,934	78.1	208	0.7	–	–
1992/93	5,309	19.3	21	0.1	21,749	79.2	384	1.4	–	–
1993/94	4,080	14.2	125	0.4	24,121	83.7	210	0.7	284	1.0

Notes: (1) Grant for a temporary improvement to a property which is in a clearance area or will be within 12 months. (2) Repairs, improvements or adaptations to properties owned or tenanted by a person aged 60 or more. (3) Adaptations to property to enable an older person, not the owner or tenant, who is or who proposes to be resident in the property to be cared for by a friend or relative. (4) Replacement of lead water service pipes (introduced from September 1992).

Source: *Housing and Construction Statistics* (various years)

Table 7.3: Authorities in England and Wales with the highest rate of 1985 Act grant payments per 1,000 private sector dwellings (1978-94)

LA	1985 Act grants		LA	1985 Act grants	
	No	Per 1,000		No	Per 1,000
Rhondda	19,599	772.80	Cardiff	25,676	293.06
Islwyn	10,831	571.00	Swansea	15,157	279.95
Cynon Valley	8,547	436.16	Port Talbot	4,005	279.32
Merthyr Tydfil	6,589	422.59	Blackburn	10,146	269.85
Blaenau Gwent	7,497	385.80	Bolsover	5,518	268.09
Carmarthen	6,667	384.51	Leicester	18,091	263.40
Neath	7,292	369.16	Brecknock	3,305	261.32
Llanelli	7,943	349.66	Hastings	6,848	256.31
South Pembs	4,532	345.22	Waveney	9,091	254.66
Arfon	5,315	340.74	Ogwr	10,152	248.84
Lliw Valley	6,416	330.50	Burnley	7,128	247.01
Taff-Ely	9,454	327.71	Allerdale	6,726	245.98
Meirionnydd	3,397	307.39	Preseli	5,085	244.22
Dwyfor	2,704	303.62	Wear Valley	3,940	230.26
Rhymney Valley	8,400	297.03	Wandsworth	17,861	228.37

Source: *Local Housing Statistics* (various years)

Data for Scotland at LA level is not available for an extended period, but Map 7.3 shows overall levels of grant activity per 1,000 households by area in Scotland over the 1990-93 period. Rural areas in north Scotland, such as the Western Isles, Skye and Lochalsh, Sutherland, Lochaber and Caithness, provided the highest number of grants per household, followed by some of the larger cities (Aberdeen, Edinburgh and Glasgow). Although providing far more grants in total these areas provide less grants per household than many more rural areas.

The pattern of grant provision under the new system

Map 7.4 shows the number of renovation grants provided per 1,000 private dwellings in England and Wales over the period 1990-94. As with grants under the old system the picture is dominated by Welsh authorities (Table 7.4), predominantly from South Wales but not exclusively so. In England authorities providing high numbers of grants relative to their stock include Hull, Middlesbrough, Barrow-in-Furness, Rugby, Leicester, Hastings, Derby, Stoke on Trent, Coventry, Liverpool, Salford, a group of North East Lancashire authorities including Blackburn and Pendle, areas of Teesside including Middlesborough and Stockton, Wansbeck and Blyth Valley, and a number of authorities in East Anglia and the South West. Relatively few grants have been given in London and the South East.

Map 7.2: Grants under the old system per 1,000 privately owned dwellings, England and Wales (1978-91)[c]

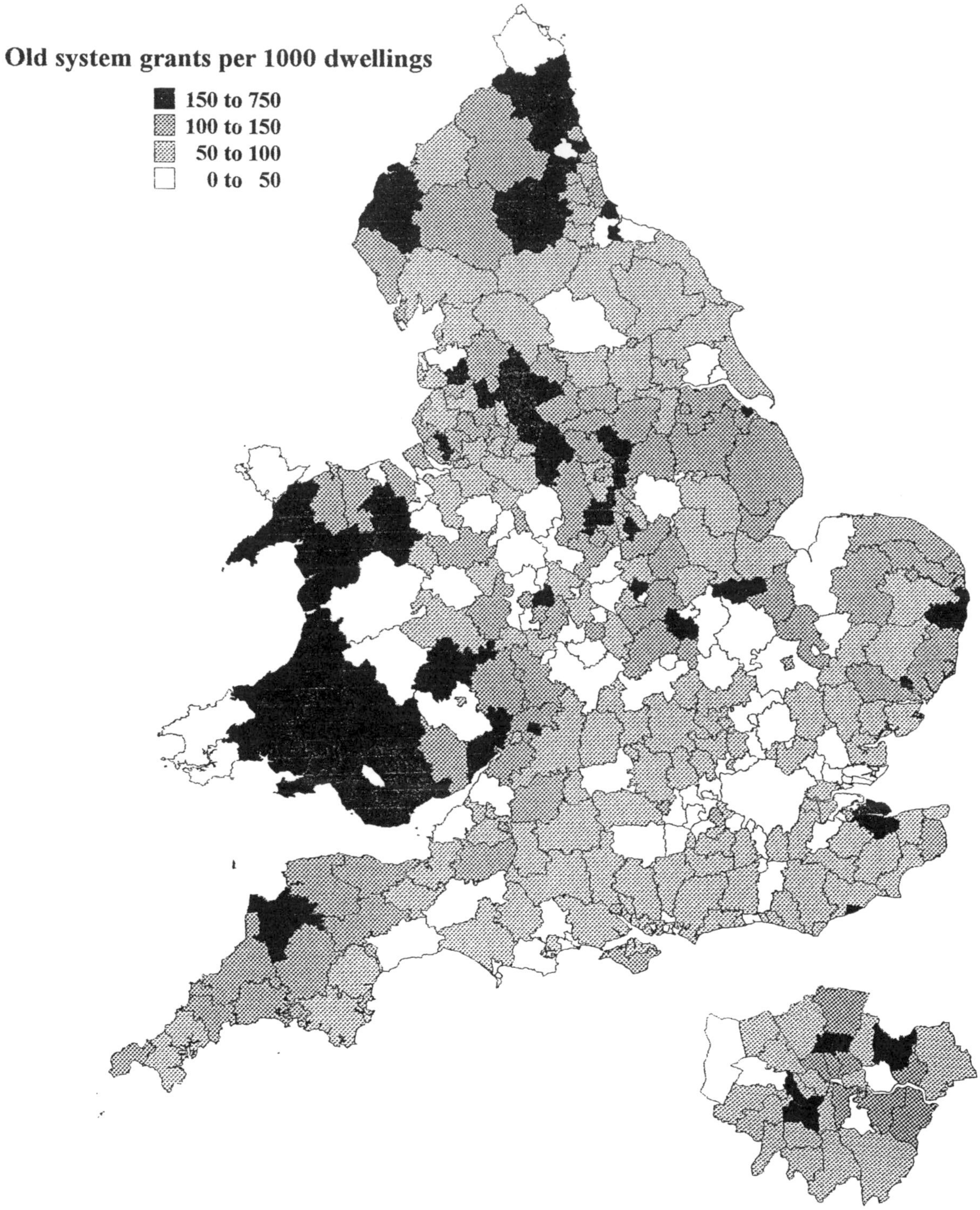

Old system grants per 1000 dwellings

- ■ 150 to 750
- 100 to 150
- 50 to 100
- □ 0 to 50

Map 7.3: Grants per 1,000 households by area, Scotland (1990-93)[p]

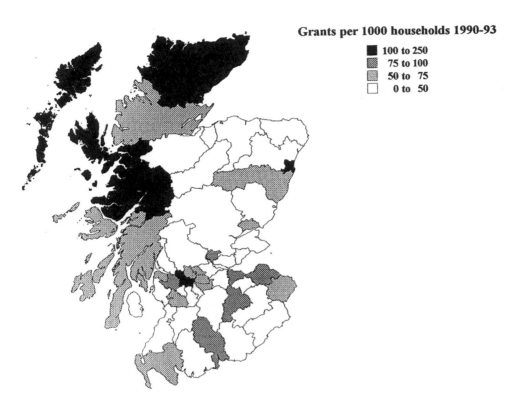

Grants per 1000 households 1990-93

■ 100 to 250
▨ 75 to 100
▨ 50 to 75
□ 0 to 50

Table 7.4: Authorities in England and Wales with the highest rate of renovation grant payments per 1,000 private sector dwellings (1990-94)

LA	Renovation grants		LA	Renovation grants	
	No	Per 1,000		No	Per 1,000
Islwyn	1,692	89.62	Cardiff	2,199	29.01
Cynon Valley	1,369	75.27	Barrow-in-Furness	724	28.76
Rhondda	1,768	71.29	Rugby	521	28.75
Port Talbot	801	58.86	Lliw Valley	546	28.69
Blaenau Gwent	1,011	54.34	Leicester	1,598	28.12
Neath	1,045	52.90	Ceredigion	549	28.01
Dwyfor	437	52.89	Swansea	1,459	27.78
Wansbeck	682	42.01	Carmarthen	393	27.68
South Pembs	533	41.67	Ynys Mon	404	27.25
Llanelli	736	40.94	Montgomery	346	26.92
Rhymney Valley	986	36.10	Ogwr	1,045	26.30
Arfon	521	34.11	Dinefwr	316	25.49
Preseli	489	30.55	Derwentside	590	25.39
Hull	1,596	29.62	Radnor	194	24.90
Middlesbrough	977	29.27	Colwyn	459	24.62

Source: *Local Housing Statistics* (various years)

Map 7.4: Renovation grants per 1,000 privately owned dwellings, England and Wales (1990-94)[c]

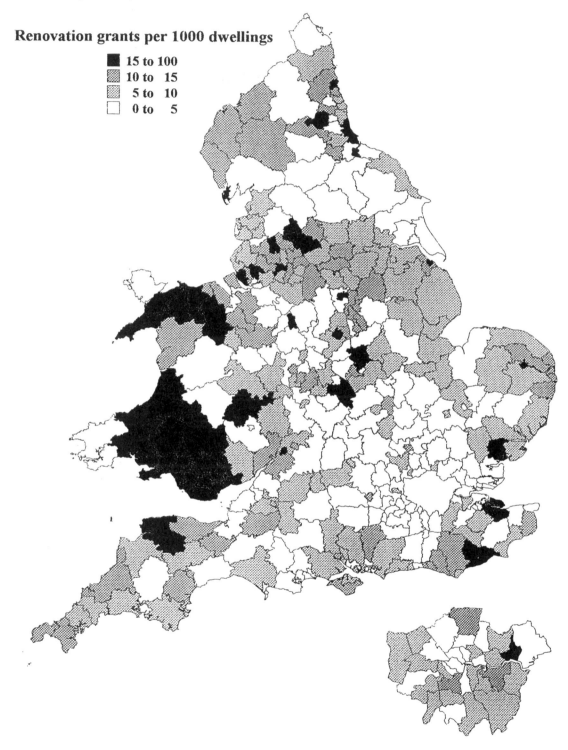

Renovation grants per 1000 dwellings

- ■ 15 to 100
- ▨ 10 to 15
- ▨ 5 to 10
- □ 0 to 5

Map 7.5 shows the number of DFGs given per 1,000 private dwellings over the same period. The level of provision is lower than for renovation grants. Table 7.5 shows the authorities providing the most grants of this type relative to their dwelling stock. Welsh authorities are again prominent, many being the same authorities as in Table 7.4. The English authorities differ from those in

Table 7.4 and include both metropolitan districts, such as Rotherham, Barnsley, Leeds, Manchester, Calderdale or Knowsley, towns such as Burnley, Norwich and Exeter, and more rural districts such as Caradon or West Oxfordshire. There is no spatial pattern to the distribution of authorities active in the provision of DFGs.

Table 7.5: Authorities in England and Wales with the highest rate of DFG payments per 1,000 private sector dwellings (1990-94)

LA	No	DFGs Per 1,000	LA	No	DFGs Per 1,000
Islwyn	1,217	64.16	Radnor	116	14.81
Rotherham	2,841	43.14	Newark	463	14.73
Ellesmere Port	617	27.09	Burnley	403	13.97
Swansea	1,381	25.51	Calderdale	852	13.91
Neath	454	22.98	Waveney	473	13.25
Caradon	569	22.64	Port Talbot	189	13.18
Vale of Glamorgan	773	21.68	Knowsley	379.5	11.99
Cardiff	1,825	20.83	Barnsley	687	11.81
West Oxfordshire	508	18.77	Rhondda	298	11.75
Preseli	365	17.53	Exeter	369	11.58
			Rhymney Valley	327	11.56
Stockton-on-Tees	798	16.23	Manchester	1,035	11.55
			Norwich	343	11.48
Torfaen	365	16.06	Braintree	391	11.37
Delyn	325	15.81	Leeds	2,087	10.90
Lliw Valley	292	15.04	West Somerset	114	10.76

Source: *Local Housing Statistics* (various years)

Map 7.6 shows the distribution of MWA. The level of provision is much higher. Again there are high levels of provision in South Wales but otherwise the pattern is scattered with more rural areas relatively active in providing MWA than renovation grants or DFGs (Table 7.6). There is some

limited evidence that areas with well-established home improvement agencies provide higher levels of MWA (see below for further discussion of the role of home improvement agencies in relation to MWA). Some 16 LAs appear never to have provided MWA since its inception.

Map 7.5: Disabled facilities grants per 1,000 privately owned dwellings, England and Wales (1990-94)[c]

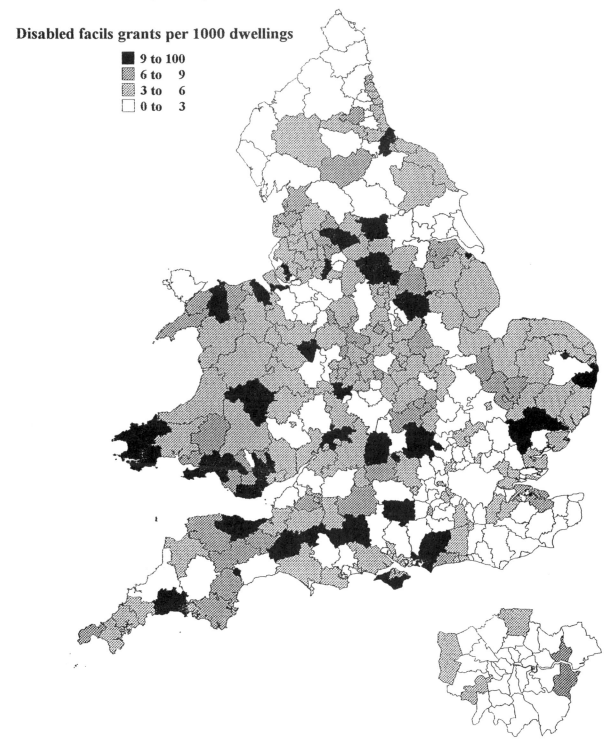

Disabled facils grants per 1000 dwellings

- 9 to 100
- 6 to 9
- 3 to 6
- 0 to 3

Map 7.6: Minor works assistance per 1,000 privately owned dwellings, England and Wales (1990-94)[c]

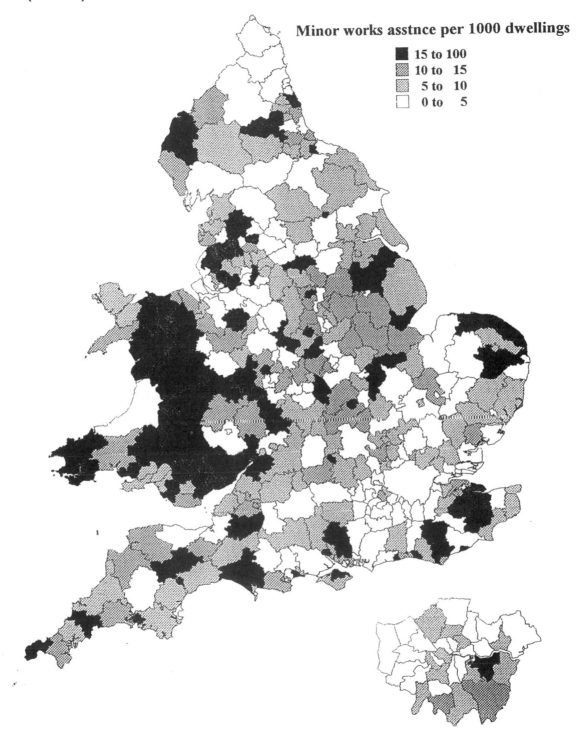

Minor works asstnce per 1000 dwellings

■ 15 to 100
▨ 10 to 15
▦ 5 to 10
□ 0 to 5

Table 7.6: Authorities in England and Wales with the highest rate of MWA payments per 1,000 private sector dwellings (1990-94)

LA	Minor works grants		LA	Minor works grants	
	No	Per 1,000		No	Per 1,000
Cynon Valley	1,484	75.73	Derwentside	767	33.01
Rhymney Valley	1,572	55.59	Exeter	1,051	32.93
Oxford	1,641	52.27	Maidstone	1,324	31.00
Grimsby	1,386	50.65	West Lindsey	715	30.33
Rhondda	1,216	47.95	Mid Devon	598	29.98
Blaenau Gwent	885	45.54	Islwyn	560	29.52
South Pembs	565	43.04	Llanelli	637	28.04
St Helens	1,985	40.79	Ribble Valley	481	28.01
Merthyr Tydfil	633	40.60	Great Yarmouth	763	27.73
Bournemouth	2,268	39.21	Preseli	575	27.62
Colwyn	742	38.13	Wealden	1,271	27.32
South Shropshire	455	36.00	East Staffordshire	827	27.30
Blackburn	1,327	35.29	Cardiff	2,366	27.01
Torfaen	786	34.58	Boston	377	24.30
Newport	1,282	33.46	Ogwr	987	24.19

Source: *Local Housing Statistics* (various years)

Average value of grant

Figure 7.9 shows the average value of grants of various types between 1979 and 1994 under both the old and new grant systems (see also Table A7.13). Average values have been updated to 1993/94 price levels. Average grant levels under the old system (an amalgamation of repair and improvement grants) were generally similar for England and Wales. Average values rose from about £4,000 in 1979 to almost £8,000 in the mid-1980s before falling again in the late 1980s. After the start of the new grant system in 1990, the average values of the residual completions under the old system rose as if in sympathy with the higher grants provided at the same time under the new system. Average renovation grant levels under the new system then increased sharply, from £5,000 in 1990 to about £10,000 in 1994 in England, and from £10,000 in 1990 to £18,000 in 1994 in Wales. All these values are expressed in constant price terms. In Scotland, grants have also increased but more steadily, rising from about £3,500 in 1979 to £7,500

in 1990. Since then there has been a slight fall in real terms. The average value of grants in Northern Ireland was higher than in the rest of the UK throughout the period, reaching almost £11,000 in the mid-1980s, but subsequently falling back to £10,000. It is too early to assess trends in Northern Ireland under the new grant system.

In part, the large increases in average grant levels under the new system are due to the higher grant percentages paid under the new system in England and Wales. Under the new renovation grant system, grant is not assessed as a fixed percentage, but covers the residual cost of work after the owner's contribution has been assessed. Table 7.7 shows that, on average, renovation grants covered 85% of the total costs of grant-aided work in 1993/94, with DFGs covering an average of 91%. Some 61% of renovation grants and 81% of DFGs covered 100% of the cost of works in 1993/94. For both types of grant the proportion which covered all the costs of work has remained fairly constant since the introduction of the new system. The absence of an upper limit on grant payments between 1990 and March 1993 also contributed to the increase in the average grant. A limit of £50,000 per grant was imposed from April 1993, and this was subsequently reduced to £20,000 (£24,000 in Wales) in January 1994. But it is also likely that the extent of work carried out with grant aid has increased because grant aid is being targeted on the properties in poorest condition.

Figure 7.9: Average value of grants, UK (1979-94)[c]

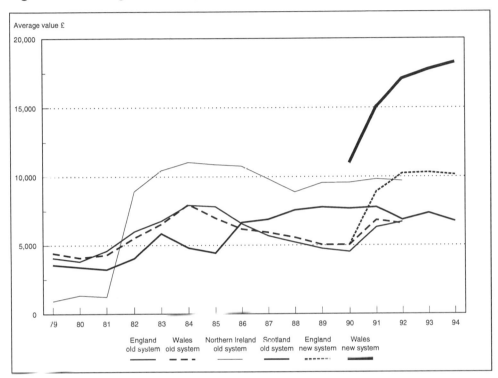

Table 7.7: 100% grants and average grant as % of costs of work, renovation grants and DFGs, England (1990-94)

| | 100% grants as % of all grants | | Aggregate grant as % of aggregate cost of works | |
	Renovation	DFG	Renovation	DFG
1990/91	56	79	89	93
1991/92	59	77	87	90
1992/93	57	77	90	85
1993/94	61	81	85	91

Source: *Housing and Construction Statistics* (various years)

However, average grant values conceal substantial local variations. Map 7.7 shows the average value of mandatory renovation grants by LA district in England and Wales in 1993/94. Almost half the authorities are Welsh, demonstrating the impact of higher levels of resources in Wales. Some 8% of authorities gave mandatory renovation grants with an average value of under £5,000 in 1994/95, 41% gave grants averaging £5,000-£9,999, 30% averaged between £10,000-£14,999, and a further 13% averaged between £15,000-£19,999. Only 8% (32) of authorities gave grants with an average exceeding £20,000 (Table 7.8). Variations of this magnitude suggest that there is considerable scope for the application of local discretion in identifying unfitness and determining appropriate solutions. In England the highest average grants occurred mainly in rural areas, where the number of grants was small.

Table 7.8: Authorities in England and Wales with the highest rate average payments for mandatory renovation grants (1994/95)

LA	Average mandatory renovation grant (£)	Number of grants	LA	Average mandatory renovation grant (£)	Number of grants
Preseli	33,183	131	Ribble Valley	23,714	14
Berwick-upon-Tweed	33,019	13	Sandwell	23,574	342
South Pembs	32,000	111	Kensington &	23,140	7
Merthyr Tydfil	31,303	109	Chelsea		
Alyn & Deeside	29,779	86	Meirionnydd	23,116	43
Carmarthen	28,252	119	South Ribble	22,572	27
Taff-Ely	28,019	158	Richmondshire	22,466	16
Wyre Forest	27,779	26	Torfaen	22,057	140
Dinefwr	26,224	58	Southwark	21,961	102
Blaenau Gwent	25,710	207	Bridgnorth	21,819	50
Bromsgrove	25,671	4	Mid Devon	21,006	39
Wrexham Maelor	25,515	103	Waltham Forest	20,875	57
Dwyfor	25,464	112	Llanelli	20,774	208
Oldham	24,204	37	South Lakeland	20,598	28
Montgomery	24,135	52	Brecknock	20,556	90
South Shropshire	23,806	20			

Note: data for Wales are for the calendar year 1994.

Sources: unpublished data supplied by the DoE; *Welsh Housing Statistics No 15* (Welsh Office, 1995)

Map 7.8 shows average values of DFGs in 1994/95 and Table 7.9 shows authorities providing the highest average value DFGs. Some 14% of authorities provided DFGs averaging under £2,500 in 1994/95. The largest group (53%) provided grants averaging between £2,500-£4,999. A further 22% averaged between £5,000-£7,499 and 7% averaged between £7,500-£9,999. Only 3% averaged £10,000 or more.

Map 7.7: Average value of mandatory renovation grants, England and Wales (1994/95)°

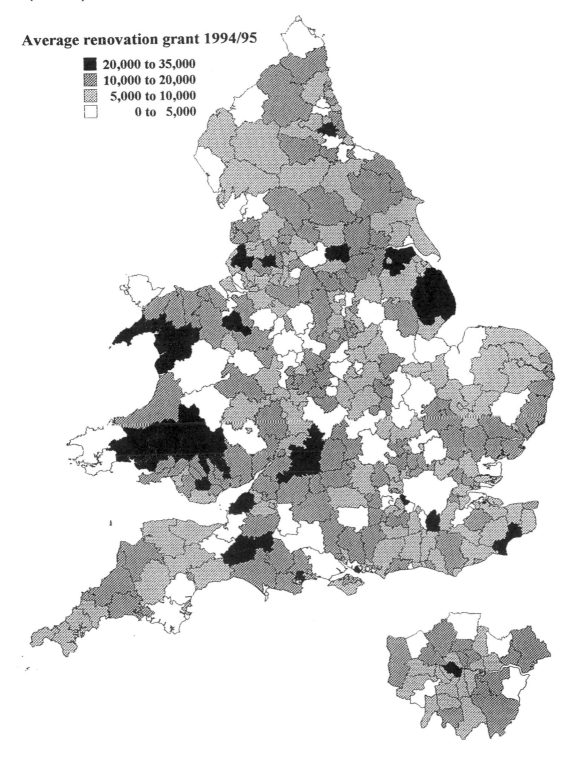

Average renovation grant 1994/95

■ 20,000 to 35,000
▨ 10,000 to 20,000
▧ 5,000 to 10,000
□ 0 to 5,000

Map 7.8: Average value of mandatory DFGs, England and Wales (1994/95)[c]

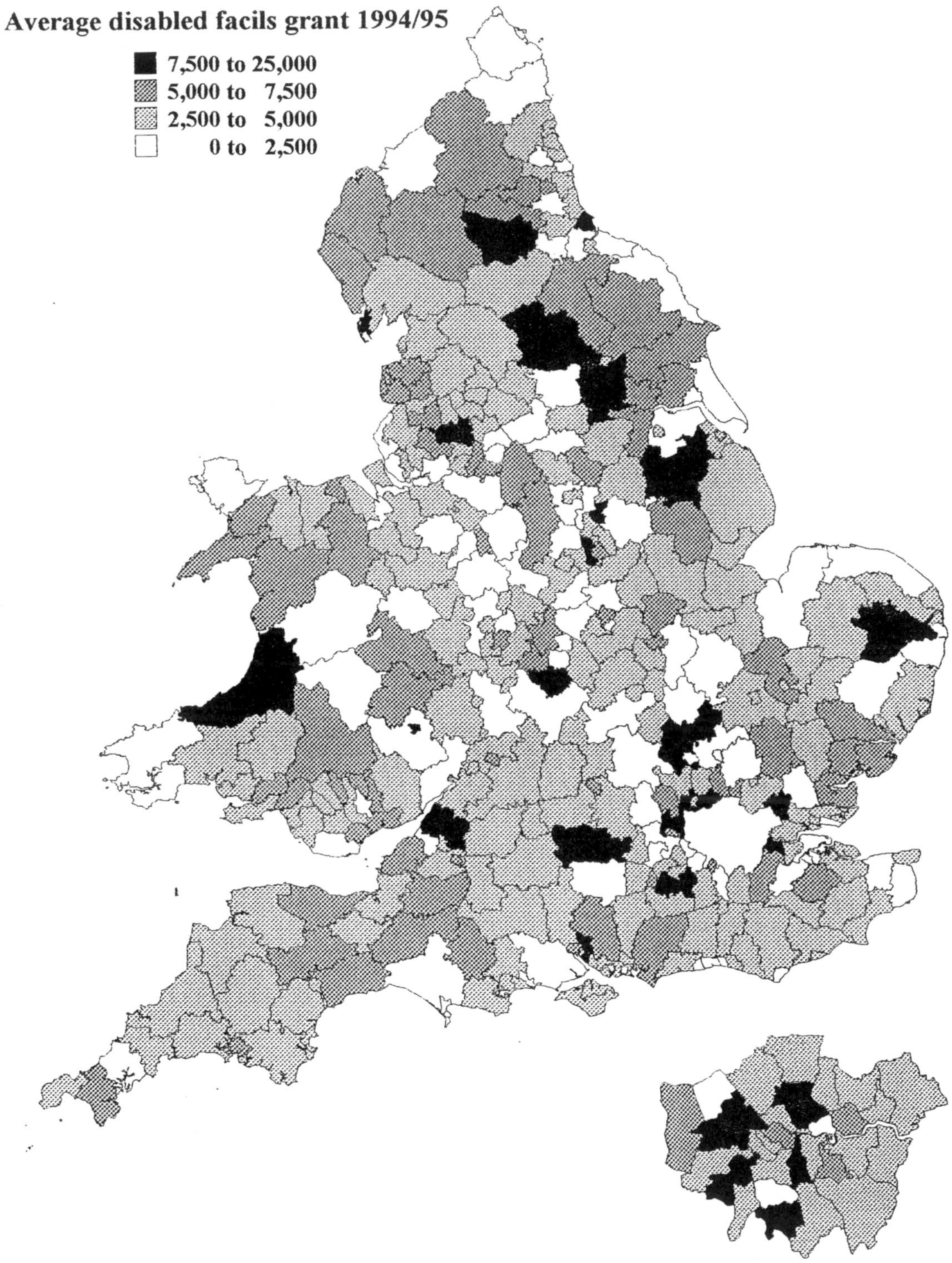

Average disabled facils grant 1994/95

- ■ 7,500 to 25,000
- ▨ 5,000 to 7,500
- ▧ 2,500 to 5,000
- □ 0 to 2,500

Table 7.9: Authorities in England and Wales with the highest rate average payments for mandatory DFGs (1994/95)

LA	Average mandatory DFG (£)	Number of grants	LA	Average mandatory DFG (£)	Number of grants
Islington	20,040	11	Barnet	9,237	68
Ealing	16,172	78	Hertsmere	9,081	10
Harrow	14,788	27	Redbridge	8,995	55
Coventry	14,414	45	Birmingham	8,870	419
Waltham Forest	13,853	21	Merton	8,783	26
Hackney	12,015	25	Enfield	8,681	123
Greenwich	11,561	52	Gravesham	8,595	26
Haringey	11,414	16	North Cornwall	8,563	11
Alyn & Deeside	11,278	36	Havering	8,533	31
Carlisle	11,056	11	Sutton	8,527	34
Lewisham	10,778	12	Elmbridge	8,483	15
Huntingdon	10,307	11	Walsall	8,427	24
South Pembs	9,548	42	Camden	8,333	16
Hounslow	9,389	35	North Wiltshire	8,305	33
Gillingham	9,274	9	Ashfield	8,209	24

Note: data for Wales are for the calendar year 1994.

Sources: unpublished data supplied by the DoE; *Welsh Housing Statistics No 15* (Welsh Office, 1995)

Map 7.9 shows average improvement grant levels by area in Scotland for 1993. There is substantial variation, with average grants exceeding £20,000 in three areas, but under £3,000 in 15 areas. A group of Highland districts such as Ross, Skye and Lochalsh, and Sutherland, have relatively high average grant values. There is substantial variation between the larger urban areas, with an average value of £15,000 in Dundee, Glasgow and Edinburgh averaging £7,000-£8,000, and Aberdeen averaging only £2,500.

Grants and poor conditions

It is difficult to measure the impact of grant investment on poor housing conditions. At national level there has been some improvement in the proportion of dwellings lacking amenities but unfitness and disrepair remain serious problems despite the small decrease in unfitness levels shown in the 1991 EHCS. At a local level data on changes in house condition is not available so it is impossible to demonstrate the impact of grant investment over a period of time. It has been shown that a high proportion of pre-1919 dwellings are in poor condition so it is to be expected that those authorities with large numbers of pre-1919 dwellings would have given more grants. Figure 7.10 indicates that this is generally the case, but there is a substantial amount of variation with some authorities with high levels of pre-1919 dwellings giving very low numbers of grants, particularly inner London boroughs, while at the other extreme some authorities have provided a much larger number of grants than might be expected, for example, Rhondda, Leicester and Wandsworth.

Map 7.9: Average value of improvement grants by area, Scotland (1993)[p]

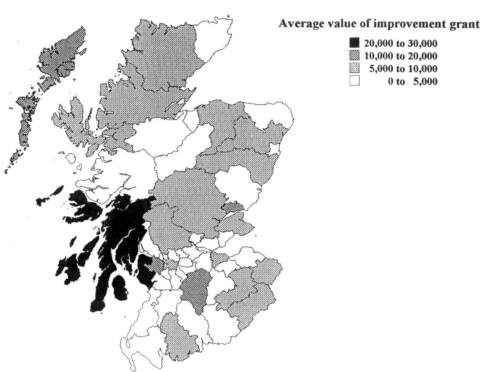

Average value of improvement grant

■ 20,000 to 30,000
▨ 10,000 to 20,000
▤ 5,000 to 10,000
☐ 0 to 5,000

Figure 7.10: Grant payments by number of pre-1919 dwellings, England and Wales (1978-94)[c]

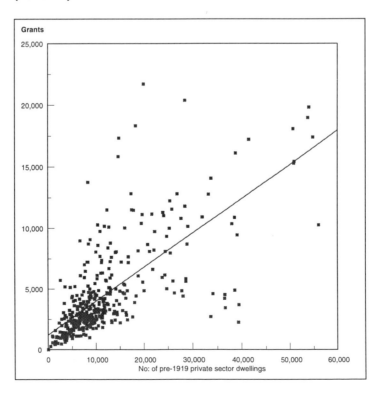

Note: each dot represents a LA.

Grant recipients

The 1986 EHCS provides information on grant recipients during the period 1981-86 when the old grant system was in operation. Some 82% were owner-occupiers and 15% were landlords. Households with incomes of under £3,000 per annum were under-represented, taking up 13% of all grants, while those with an income of between £3,000-£9,000 were over-represented, receiving 55% of all grants. Those with incomes of more than £12,000 received 33% of all grants. In terms of age, younger households aged between 17-39 received a disproportionate share of grants (46%). At the other extreme those aged 75 and over were under-represented (3% of grants).

Specific surveys into the distribution of grants undertaken over the same period also showed that households headed by older people were under-represented among those taking up grants. The socio-economic characteristics of grant recipients were very similar to the population as a whole with the majority of grants (59% in England and 57% in Wales) going to people in skilled manual or non-manual occupations. The average income of grant recipients (£7,000 in England and £5,200 in Wales) was similar to the national average in 1982, but those receiving improvement grants were better off than those receiving repair or intermediate grants. After 1982 the shift to higher percentage repair grants led to an increase in the number of recipients who were older or who had been resident for 10 years or more.

There has been no detailed monitoring of the characteristics of grant recipients under the new grant system apart from a study carried out for the DoE in the system's early period of operation. This showed that older people received a higher proportion of grants under the new system than under the old one. During the first two years of operation, 48% of renovation grant approvals were awarded to people over 60, a much higher proportion than under the old system. In addition, 75% of DFG approvals were awarded to those aged

60 or more. As a result of the test of resources, grants were closely targeted on those with low incomes. In total, 60% of those who had grants approved were in receipt of some form of state benefit.

In terms of tenure, private landlords have fared badly under the new system compared with the old (Table 7.10). In 1990/91, 93% of renovation grants went to owner-occupiers and only 7% to landlords. Subsequent years have seen the proportion of renovation grants to landlords increase only slowly to reach 12% in England in 1993/94 and 7% in Wales. Disabled facilities grants are less focused on owner-occupiers but this group nevertheless received about two thirds of these grants in 1993/94 in England (about three quarters in Wales). Local authority tenants have been the next largest group of recipients (26% of DFGs in England in 1993/94, 20% in Wales). Tenants of private landlords in England have accounted for about 7% of DFGs. Private owners and HAs as land-lords have received insignificant numbers of DFGs, both in England and in Wales.

Properties receiving grants

Monitoring by the DoE has shown that in the first 18 months of the new grant system, three quarters of renovation grant approvals related to dwellings built before 1919. One fifth of approvals were for dwellings built after 1945. However, more than 80% of approvals related to properties which were unfit for human habitation. Grants under the new system are thus more closely targeted on the poorest condition properties than those under the old system, which placed more importance on dwelling age. As might be expected, DFG approvals were fairly evenly spread across the dwelling stock and only a quarter were unfit. For MWA, 39% of dwellings where a grant was approved were built before 1919, with 21% dating from the inter-war period and 39% from the post-war period. Almost 90% of MWA approvals were for dwellings which were fit.

Table 7.10: Grants by tenure of recipient, England and Wales (1990-94)

England		Owner-occupier	Private landlord	HAs	Private tenant	LA tenant	All recipients
				% of grants			
Renovation	1990/91	92.6	6.4	1.0	0.0	–	100.0
	1991/92	92.0	7.2	0.2	0.6	–	100.0
	1992/93	88.8	10.1	0.8	0.3	–	100.0
	1993/94	87.4	11.7	0.7	0.2	–	100.0
Disabled facilities	1990/91	67.5	0.2	0.2	5.1	27.0	100.0
	1991/92	63.2	0.4	0.9	5.1	30.4	100.0
	1992/93	66.2	0.5	0.3	6.5	26.5	100.0
	1993/94	65.4	0.5	0.9	7.4	25.8	100.0

Wales		Owner-occupier	Landlord (including HA)	Private tenant	LA tenant	All recipients
			% of grants			
Renovation	1990	100.0	0.0	0.0	–	100.0
	1991	97.9	2.0	0.1	–	100.0
	1992	95.7	4.1	0.2	–	100.0
	1993	93.6	6.0	0.3	–	100.0
	1994	92.9	6.8	0.3	–	100.0
Disabled facilities	1990	81.5	0.0	3.7	14.8	100.0
	1991	74.7	2.0	2.3	21.0	100.0
	1992	76.5	2.2	3.3	18.0	100.0
	1993	73.4	1.7	4.7	20.2	100.0
	1994	73.3	2.5	4.1	20.1	100.0

Note: Renovation grants not available to LA tenants. Grants to private tenants include grants to HA tenants. Separate information on grants to private landlords and to HAs as landlords is not available for Wales.

Sources: *Housing and Construction Statistics* (various years); *Welsh Housing Statistics* (various years)

Area renewal

General improvement areas and housing action areas

Since the 1960s, LAs have had powers to declare special areas where they will focus their housing renewal activities. In some circumstances, households in these areas have been eligible for additional types of grant or grants at higher rates. From 1969, LAs could declare GIAs, and from 1975, HAs. There are no comprehensive official statistics on the number of areas declared or the number of dwellings included within these areas in England and Wales, but Thomas (1985) estimated that

by 1982 just over 500 HAAs had been declared in England, containing around 173,000 dwellings, less than 10% of the potential level estimated from 1971 Census data. The 1981 EHCS estimated that only 408,000 dwellings fell within potential HAAs, but even on this lower estimate, less than a quarter of dwellings with potential for area action were included in current declared areas.

Figure 7.11 shows the number of grants provided to private owners in GIAs or HAAs over the period 1975-89 and the proportion of all grants which this represents. The number of grants in declared areas rose slowly from the mid-1970s to a peak of 35,000 in 1983 and declined thereafter to about 12,000 in 1989. As a proportion of all grants provided, grants in GIAs and HAAs were never very significant, reaching a peak of 22% in 1982, but rarely exceeding 15%. Area improve-

ment has never been a dominant element of renewal programmes in England except in a small number of local areas where these policies have been pursued more intensively.

Figure 7.11: Grants in HAAs and GIAs, England (1975-89)[c]

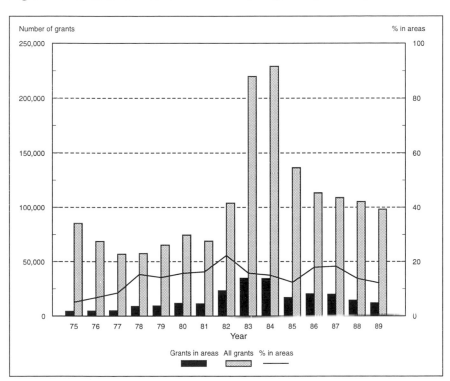

Renewal areas

Renewal areas replaced HAAs and GIAs as the statutory mechanism for area-based private sector housing renewal in July 1990. By March 1995, some 84 renewal areas had been declared in England, together with a

further 20 in Wales. (Table A7.14 lists renewal areas in England declared by March 1995, in order of declaration, together with the number of dwellings in each area. Table A7.15 shows equivalent information for Welsh renewal areas.) Map 7.10 shows the location of these areas.

Map 7.10: Location of renewal areas, England and Wales[i]

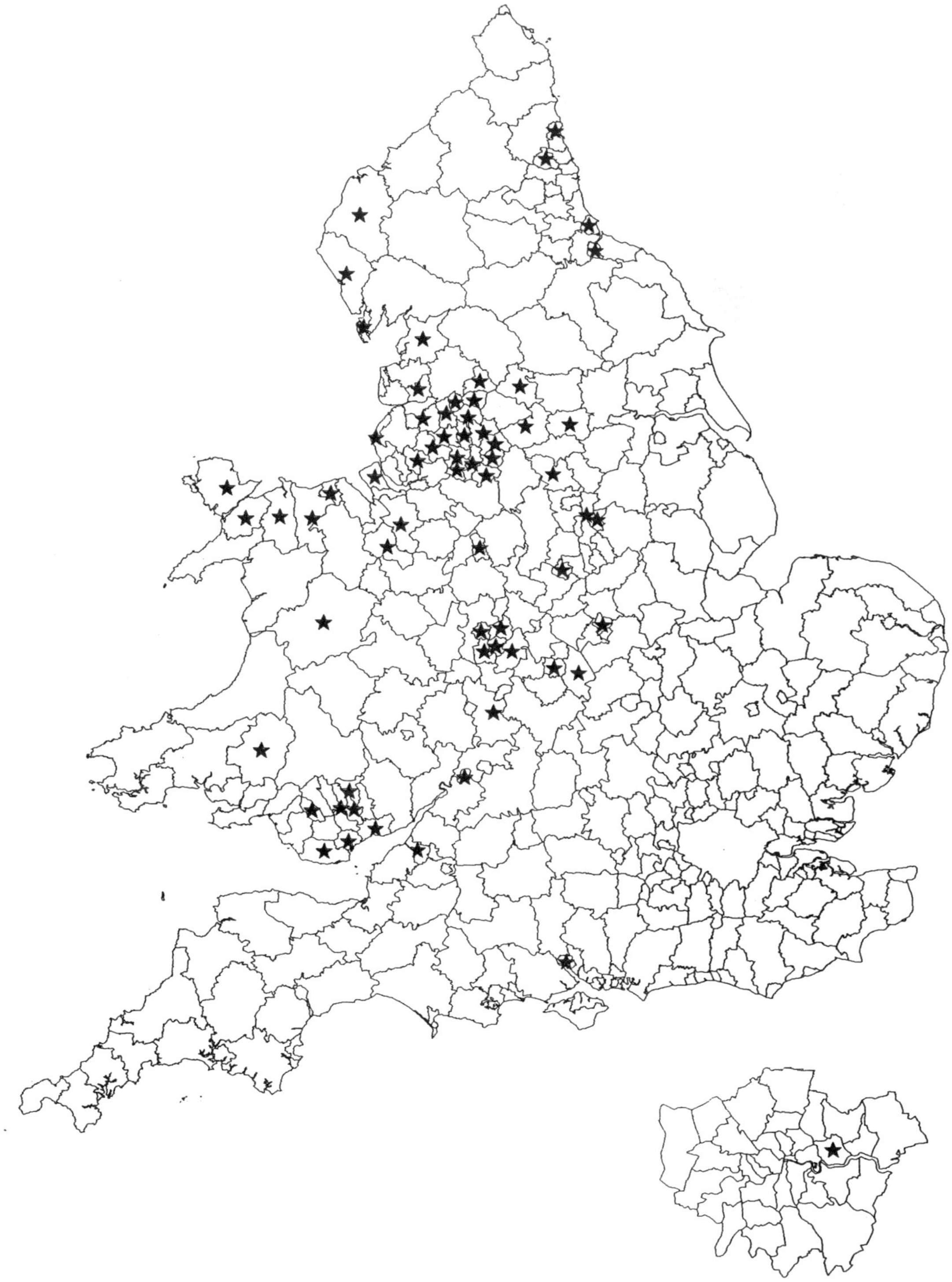

In total, some 126,000 dwellings were included in renewal areas in England, an average of just under 1,500 per area. In Wales, the total number of dwellings was 19,272, or 964 dwellings per area on average. It is difficult to form a judgement on whether this is a satisfactory level of renewal area activity. No explicit target for renewal area declarations has been set out, as this is a matter for individual LAs. The number of dwellings in declared areas in England is equivalent to 11% of unfit private sector dwellings in 1991, but of course not all unfit dwellings are in areas which would be eligible for renewal area status and not all dwellings in renewal areas are unfit or privately owned.

Table 7.11 shows the distribution of renewal areas in England by standard region. So far, renewal areas are pre-dominantly located in the north of England (60%) and the Midlands (32%). One region, the North West (excluding Cumbria but including Merseyside) had 40% of the declared renewal areas, with the West Midlands having the next largest proportion (18%). There were only seven renewal areas (9%) in the south of England and East Anglia had no declared areas.

Table 7.11: Renewal areas by standard region, England

Region	Renewal areas		LAs declaring renewal areas	
	No	%	No	%
North (including Cumbria)	8	10	7	13
Yorkshire/Humberside	8	10	4	8
East Midlands	12	14	5	10
East Anglia	0	0	0	0
Greater London	3	4	1	1
Rest of South East	1	1	1	1
South West	3	4	2	4
West Midlands	15	18	10	19
North West (including Merseyside)	34	40	22	42
Total	**84**	**100**	**52**	**100**

The average number of dwellings in renewal areas was 1,495, but the range was very wide, with the largest area having 4,535 dwellings and the smallest only 335. Figure 7.12 shows that in England the size distribution is skewed towards smaller areas, with the median (1,363 dwellings) well below the mean (Table A7.16). Over a third of declared areas had less than 1,000 dwellings, and 60% had less than 1,500 dwellings. However, there was a significant group of larger areas (18%) with more than 2,500 dwellings. In Wales renewal areas are significantly smaller, with no areas having more than 2,500 dwellings, and 50% of areas having less than 1,000.

Overall levels of activity in declared renewal areas for which data is available for the years 1990/91 to 1993/94 are shown in Figure 7.13. Total expenditure increased from £8.1m in 1990/91, to £47.7m in 1991/92, £86.0m in 1992/93, and £110.8m in 1993/94. Increasing the latter figure pro rata for missing data would boost total spend in 1993/94 to £123.4m. In terms of the source of investment, in 1993/94 59% of investment in renewal areas came from LA sources (including government subsidy where appropriate), 34% from HAs (including HAG and LAHAG), and 7% from private sources. Private spending has declined since 1991/92, while HA investment peaked in 1992/93.

Figure 7.12: Size distribution of declared renewal areas, England and Wales[i]

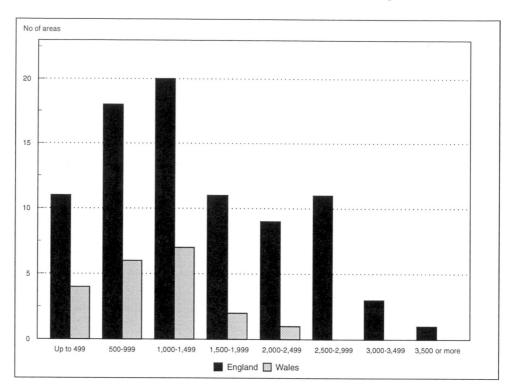

Figure 7.13: Changing proportion of spending in renewal areas by source[i]

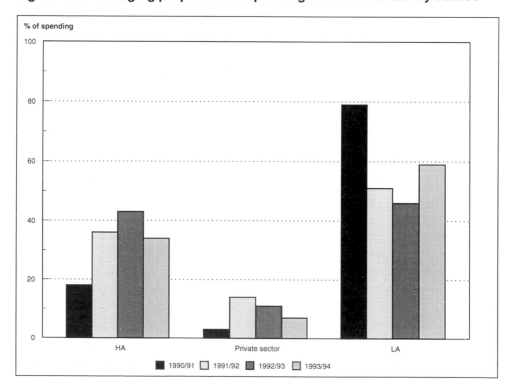

The breakdown of expenditure between programmes also changed over this period, with the proportion accounted for by grants steadily increasing over the period to reach 29% of the total by 1993/94 (Table A7.17). Since 1991, new build by HAs and the private sector has remained the largest component of renewal area investment, accounting for 38% of the total in 1993/94. In the same year, demolitions accounted for 13% of spending, followed by group repair (10%). If demolition costs are added to new build over 50% of renewal area expenditure was on new development, indicating the extent to which activities in these areas go beyond housing renovation.

The proportion of renovation, HMO and common parts grants provided in renewal areas was, as might be expected, small, increasing from 1% in 1990/91 but reaching only 6% in 1993/94. Just over 2,000 dwellings were included in completed group repair schemes in 21 authorities. About 1,400 minor works grants and 400 DFGs have been provided in renewal areas.

Group repair

Table 7.12 shows progress with group repair schemes in England since 1990. After a slow start, the number of dwellings in schemes started increased to over 2,000 in 1995. Completions have followed this trend, reaching over 1,900 in 1995. Despite this, the level of overall progress with group repair remains low, with only 5,250 dwelling completions under group repair since 1990.

Most group repair takes place in declared renewal areas. Some 40% of completions up to the end of 1995 were in the North West region, followed by Yorkshire and Humberside (26%). There has been almost no completed group repair work in the North region, and none in London or the South East. A small number of individual LAs (Wakefield, Mansfield, Rochdale, Bristol, Sheffield, Burnley, and Stockport) account for 60% of all group repair completions to date.

Table 7.12: Group repair schemes and dwellings in schemes, England (1991-95)

| Period | Starts | | Completions | |
	Schemes	Dwellings	Schemes	Dwellings
1991	47	721	11	170
1992	42	735	51	798
1993	127	1,526	57	706
1994	113	1,572	132	1,667
1995	141	2,091	132	1,904
Total dwellings		6,645		5,245

Source: DoE Building Stock Research Division, unpublished paper

Area renewal in Scotland

The mechanism for area-based renewal in Scotland has remained the HAA since 1974. A recent study by Robertson and Bailey (1996) provides some details of activity over the 1978-92 period. Unlike the position in England and Wales before 1990 there were three basic types of HAA: HAAs for demolition, HAAs for improvement, and areas with a combination of the two. By the end of 1994, about 1,700 HAAs had been declared, of which 257 were HAAs for demolition, with the majority of the remainder being HAAs for improvement (Table 7.13).

Table 7.13: Housing action area declarations and completions, Scotland (1978-94)

At end 1991/92	Completed		Outstanding		All		Average number dwellings
	No	Dwellings	No	Dwellings	No	Dwellings	
HAA for demolition	238	7,887	19	558	257	8,445	33
HAA for improve-ment	923	37,850	419	16,353	1,342	54,203	40
HAA for both	46	4,667	9	699	55	5,366	98
Total	1,207	50,404	447	17,610	1,654	68,014	41
At end 1994/95	1,333	na	333	na	1,666	na	na

Sources: Robertson and Bailey (1996); *Scottish Housing Bulletin* (various)

Declarations rose steadily from about 50 in 1981 to a peak of around 125 in 1987. New declarations remained at close to 100 per annum until 1991 after which there was a steep decline in activity. Housing action areas in Scotland typically contain far fewer dwellings than those in England and Wales. The average HAA over the 1978-92 period contained just 41 dwellings, and only 22% of HAAs for improvement contained over 200 dwellings. The size of HAA being declared has also grown smaller over time.

Figure 7.14 shows the contribution to improvement made by various sources in completed Scottish HAAs for improvement. Housing associations have been the dominant force for improvement, but their contribution was at its greatest in the early 1980s (Table A7.18). Since 1992, grant take-up by individual owner-occupiers, as in England and Wales, has come to dominate the profile of activity, although HAs still account for 26% of activity, a much higher proportion than in England and Wales. In general, area-based housing renewal in Scotland has been more significant as a proportion of all grant activity than area-based renewal in England and Wales, but has still accounted for a relatively small proportion of all renovation activity.

Improving the local authority stock

Chapter 4 showed that the overall condition of the housing stock owned by LAs in England, Wales and Northern Ireland was proportionately better than the privately owned stock. Nevertheless, substantial house condition problems were found to be present in the public sector. The 1991 EHCS showed that 265,000 LA dwellings (6.9% of the total) were unfit for human habitation, a figure only marginally below that for the dwelling stock as a whole. Similarly, in Wales 15.8% of the LA stock (38,000 dwellings) was unfit in 1993. In Scotland, the proportion of dwellings falling below the tolerable standard (4.3%) was second only to that in the private rented sector.

The majority of poor condition LA dwellings were constructed after 1945. In addition to the need for improvements to amenities and repairs in the traditionally built housing stock, there are substantial problems of repair in the non-traditional stock. An estimated 500,000 low rise dwellings of non-traditional construction using prefabricated reinforced concrete (PRCs) were built in Britain between 1945 and 1965, together with approximately one million dwellings built using industrialised or system building methods (Diacon, 1991). Many of the latter took the form of medium or high rise blocks of flats. Problems with non-traditional construction are particularly severe in Scotland.

Figure 7.14: Improvements in Scottish HAAs by source (1979-95)[j]

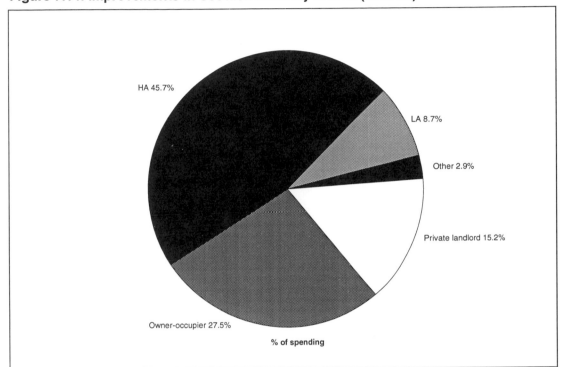

HA 45.7%

LA 8.7%

Other 2.9%

Private landlord 15.2%

Owner-occupier 27.5%

% of spending

Renovations to local authority stock

Figures 7.15-7.16 show the level of renovations to LA stock over the period 1969-94 (see also Table A7.19). England shows a minor peak in the 1972-74 period (when much investment was financed through the improvement grant system), and a substantial build up of expenditure during the 1980s. This reached a maximum in the late 1980s when many LAs made use of accumulated capital receipts to improve the condition of their stock. The number of LA dwellings renovated overtook the number of private sector dwellings renovated in 1978, and although the position was reversed for a short period during the grant boom of 1982-84, by 1990 LA renovation was running at almost three times the level of private sector renovation. After falling back from the 1990 peak of 230,000 renovations to about 175,000 in 1992, activity has risen again to an all-time high of almost 300,000 dwellings in 1994. The growth in LA stock renovation has not, however, been at the expense of private sector renovation, but as a result of a shift in resources from new construction by LAs.

In Scotland, there were similar peaks in the early 1970s and late 1980s. The level of LA renovation consistently exceeded the number of private sector grants, except during the 1982-84 period, with about 78,000 dwellings renovated in 1990 compared with 23,000 private sector grants. As in England, the level of activity has risen in the 1990s to a new all-time peak of almost 100,000 dwellings.

In Northern Ireland, the level of public sector renovation also generally exceeded the provision of grants in the limited period for which comparative data is available, but in contrast to England and Scotland, declined from over 50,000 dwellings in 1984 to less than 10,000 dwellings in 1991. The level then fell further to under 7,000, before rising to around 8,500 in 1994. Nevertheless, this is a historically low figure for Northern Ireland.

In contrast to the remainder of the UK, the level of LA renovation in Wales has generally been much lower than the level of grant provision to the private sector. In 1984 only 2,300 public sector dwellings were renovated while some 30,000 grants were provided to private owners. Since 1988, however, the level of public sector renovation has increased sharply, rising from around 10,000 dwellings per annum to over 20,000 in 1993 and 1994, while the number of private dwellings improved with a grant has fallen.

Figure 7.15: Renovations to LA stock, England (1969-94)[c]

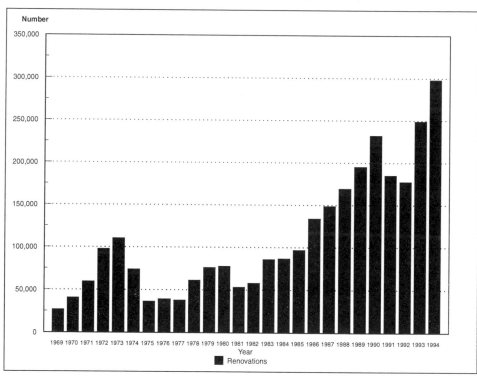

Average value of local authority renovation work

Figure 7.17 shows the average value of LA renovations in comparison with those carried out in the private sector with the assistance of a grant and those undertaken by HAs, all at constant 1993/94 prices (see also Table A7.20). Data limitations make it only possible to produce this information for England. In addition, experience with the collection of data on LA stock renovation in the EHCS suggests that LA records on dwelling stock renovation often record the number of dwellings in a renovation scheme and the total cost rather than the number of dwellings where work was carried out. This would lead the true average cost of work to be understated. During the 1970s the average value of LA renovations substantially exceeded grants to the private sector, although this difference was reduced when owners' contributions were also taken into account.

During the 1980s average private grant levels overtook LA renovation costs, although both declined steadily in real value at much the same rate. In the 1990s, however, the gap has widened rapidly as private sector grant values increased rapidly in real terms under the new renovation grant system. Housing association renovations are discussed below.

Figure 7.16: Renovations to LA stock, Wales, Scotland and Northern Ireland (1969-94)[c]

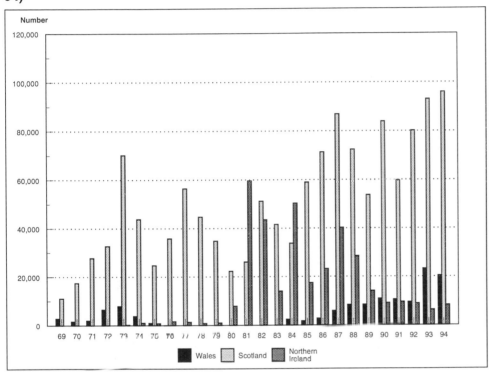

Figure 7.17: Average value per dwelling of LA, HA and private sector renovations, England (1979-94)[c]

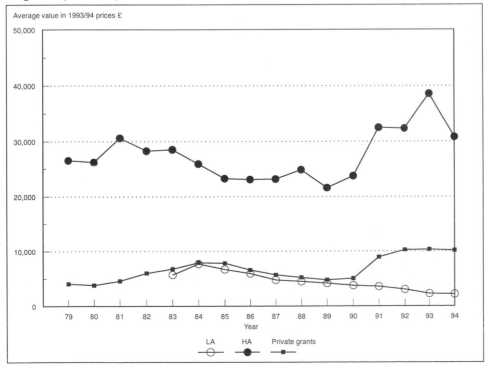

The pattern of local authority renovation

Map 7.11 shows the number of renovations carried out by LAs to their own stock between 1978-94 per 1,000 public sector dwellings, and Table 7.14 shows the authorities with the highest rate of renovation per 1,000 dwellings. Although the data should be treated with caution because of the variations in what constitutes a 'renovation', the map suggests that activity levels have generally been highest in the south east and the south west of England and in parts of the Midlands. It is notable that the majority of metropolitan districts with large public sector stocks have not been able to achieve as much renovation relative to the size of their stock as smaller districts.

Table 7.14: Authorities in England and Wales with the highest rate of renovation to their own stock per 1,000 council dwellings (1978-94)

| LA | LA renovations | | LA | LA renovations | |
	No	Per 1,000		No	Per 1,000
Elmbridge	15,278	3,082	St Albans	10,370	1,567
Solihull	39,748	3,051	Sunderland	68,393	1,554
Great Grimsby	18,969	2,726	Shepway	6,343	1,523
Woking	9,071	2,100	Bolsover	9,480	1,429
Kingston	11,856	2,090	Crawley	14,392	1,395
Enfield	32,545	2,061	Broadland	1,537	1,385
Bristol	68,393	1,968	Bolton	30,460	1,369
North Kesteven	8,956	1,927	Wyre Forest	9,111	1,353
Brecknock	4,776	1,888	Bournemouth	7,555	1,315
South Pembs	4,710	1,803	Stratford	8,338	1,313
Port Talbot	8,792	1,751	Mansfield	11,290	1,292
Charnwood	12,463	1,743	Chester-le-Street	7,669	1,260
Wansdyke	7,366	1,723	Dover	7,639	1,248
Rother	5,521	1,641	East Yorkshire	5,103	1,246
Ribble Valley	2,497	1,636	Bath	7,701	1,240

Source: *Local Housing Statistics* (various years)

Estates Action

The Estates Action initiative was developed in 1985 as a way of renovating run-down estates. Local authorities were able to bid for centrally allocated resources to improve estates which had higher than average levels of vacancies, arrears, tenant turnover, vandalism or other indicators of social and economic problems. The initiative aimed to improve the condition of the housing stock, to set up estate-based management in which tenants have greater input, and to develop new forms of management, such as tenants cooperatives and trusts. It also aimed to increase levels of private sector investment and to encourage diversification of tenure. Resources for this initiative increased steadily from the launch of the scheme to reach over £373m in 1994/95, or about 12% of total LA gross capital expenditure in England. Nearly 500,000 dwellings were improved under the Estates Action programme between 1987 and 1995. From April 1994 the Estates Action programme was incorporated into the Single Regeneration Budget.

Map 7.11: Renovations to LA stock per 1,000 publicly owned dwellings, England and Wales (1978-91)[c]

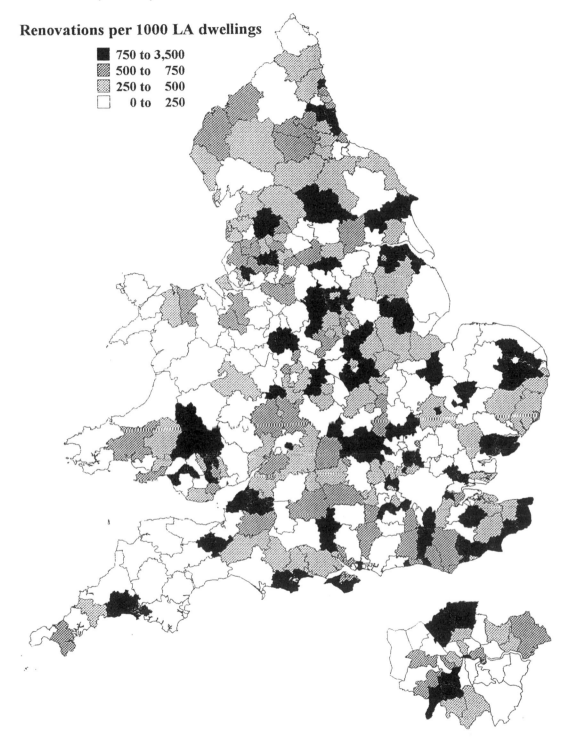

Renovations per 1000 LA dwellings

- ■ 750 to 3,500
- 500 to 750
- 250 to 500
- □ 0 to 250

The role of housing associations

Figures 7.18 and 7.19 show renovations by HAs in England, and in Wales, Scotland and Northern Ireland, over the period 1969-94 (see also Table A7.21). In England, there was a rapid increase in the level of renovations as a result of the introduction of HAG in 1975. The level of renovation activity fluctuated between 10,000 and 20,000 throughout the 1980s before falling to below 6,000 per annum for most of the 1990s. This decline has been partly attributed to the new arrangements for funding HAs introduced by the 1988 Housing Act. Lower levels of HAG and the requirement that associations should bear any cost over-runs in full have made rehabilitation much less attractive than new build schemes. A similar decline has occurred in the remainder of the UK.

Figure 7.18: Renovations to HA stock, England (1969-94)[c]

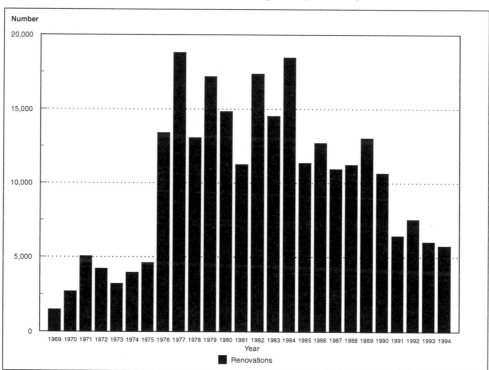

In the past the majority of HA renovation work has been undertaken on dwellings purchased from private sector owners, so this activity has made an important contribution to the alleviation of poor housing conditions in the private sector. In England, the level of HA renovation varied between 2% and 5% of the level of private sector renovation until 1975, after which it rose rapidly to a peak of 33% in 1977. It remained over 20% until 1982, but declined to between 7% and 12% in the later 1980s. However, as Table 7.15 shows, HA renovations have been heavily con-centrated in areas with a high proportion of private sector housing in poor condition. The impact of this investment was therefore much greater than this proportion would suggest. In Scotland, the level of HA involvement in rehabilitation was similar, reaching a peak equivalent to 31% of the private sector grant renovation programme in 1979, but subsequently declining to only 2-4% in the 1980s. In Northern Ireland and Wales HA invest-ment has been relatively insignificant in comparison to the programme of private grants.

Figure 7.19: Renovations to HA stock, Wales, Scotland and Northern Ireland (1969-94)[c]

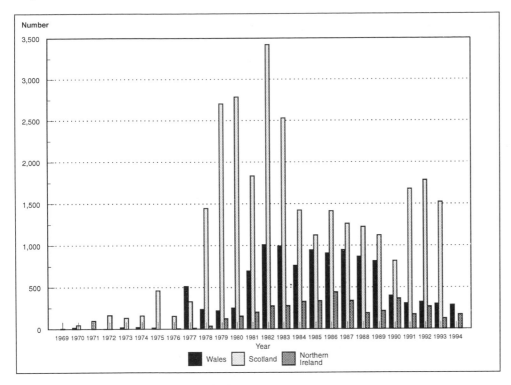

Table 7.15: Authorities in England and Wales with the highest rate of HA renovation per 1,000 private sector dwellings (1978-94)

LA	HA renovations		LA	HA renovations	
	No	Per 1,000		No	Per 1,000
Liverpool	15,851	115.76	Leicester	6,000	47.36
Kensington	8,923	106.86	Birmingham	20,948	40.34
Tower Hamlets	5,867	100.59	Salford	4,950	39.65
Islington	7,861	100.53	Copeland	2,167	39.41
Westminster	9,797	99.41	Newcastle on Tyne	5,792	38.94
Hackney	8,539	99.21	St Helens	2,441	38.68
Manchester	12,292	89.20	Allerdale	2,995	38.49
Hammersmith	7,722	83.49	South Tyneside	3,220	35.74
Camden	6,853	69.60	Sefton	4,720	32.38
Brent	6,784	64.30	Southwark	9,895	31.66
Winchester	898	57.84	Woking	700	30.17
Lambeth	11,066	55.08	Newham	5,090	27.56
Haringey	5,415	53.70	Wirral	4,680	27.14
Wandsworth	7,160	51.96	Coventry	4,289	25.35
Nottingham	6,179	48.31	Sutton	2,023	24.82

Source: *Local Housing Statistics* (various years)

Average value of housing association renovation work

Figure 7.17 shows that the average value of HA rehabilitation jobs in England has been much greater than the equivalent figures for LA or private sector renovation work. This partly reflects the fact that HAs have often purchased and improved dwellings which were in much poorer condition than those in the private sector, but in addition HA work has generally achieved much higher standards than the private improvement grant programme. It should also be noted that a small proportion of grants appearing in the figures for private sector renovation were awarded to HAs.

The pattern of housing association renovation

Map 7.12 shows the number of HA renovation jobs per 1,000 private sector dwellings for the period 1978-94 for districts in England and Wales. Housing association investment is heavily concentrated in urban areas, even taking account of the relative size of the private sector stock. Comparing the map with the distribution of improvement grants to private owners, it is clear that HA activity has been much more important in London than renovation by private owners, reflecting the high proportion of privately rented older housing in the capital which HAs have been able to acquire over the period covered by the data. Table 7.15 shows authorities where HA renovation has been proportionately greatest. Table 7.15 is heavily dominated by the London boroughs and the larger metropolitan areas or cities, indicating that the HA renovation programme was targeted on these areas to a much greater degree than the programme of grants to private owners.

Dealing with adaptations

Since the mid-1970s, grants have also been available to assist private owners with the costs of adapting dwellings to meet the needs of disabled people. Until 1990, this assistance was provided through the mechanisms of improvement and inter-mediate grants, but a separate grant, the DFG, now provides this form of help. Figures 7.20 and 7.21 show the number of grants provided for people with disabilities in England and Wales since 1975, and the proportion of all grants which this represents (see also Tables A7.22 and A7.23). In both England and Wales, the number of grants awarded has followed a similar pattern to the level of grant provision as a whole, with a peak in the 1982-84 period in both countries, paralleling the peak in other types of grant. There was a further boost in Wales in the late 1980s. In England, total spending in grants for people with disabilities rose to around £60m per annum at 1993/94 prices in the mid-1980s, and remained at that level before reaching a peak of almost £80m in 1990. It then fell under the new system of DFGs to about £55m in 1991, but subsequently continued to rise steeply in real terms to reach an all-time high of £85m in 1994. In comparison to total grant provision, the proportion of spending on grants for people with disabilities also rose, slowly in the 1970s and then more sharply in the 1980s, to reach a peak of 22% of all spending on private sector grants in 1990. The proportion fell again in the early 1990s under the new grant system, but rose again to reach 18% in 1994. In Wales, spending at 1993/94 prices rose from £6m in the early 1980s to around £10m in 1990. The increase resumed quickly after a slight drop under the new grant system in 1991, and reached £12m in 1993, before falling slightly in 1994. Spending on grants for disabled people as a percentage of all grant spending has been consistently lower in Wales than in England, peaking at around 10% in 1989, before falling to 6% in 1992 and rising again to 8% in 1994.

Minor works assistance grants can be used to meet the costs of adaptations and this is often thought to be a significant source of additional funding for minor adaptations. However, a special analysis of home improvement agency records revealed that only 10% of the MWA grants dealt with by agencies in 1994/95 were for adaptation work. If this proportion were applied across all MWA grants in England and Wales, this would add a further £2.5m to total spending on adaptations for people with disabilities.

Figure 7.20: Grants for people with disabilities, England (1979-94)[c]

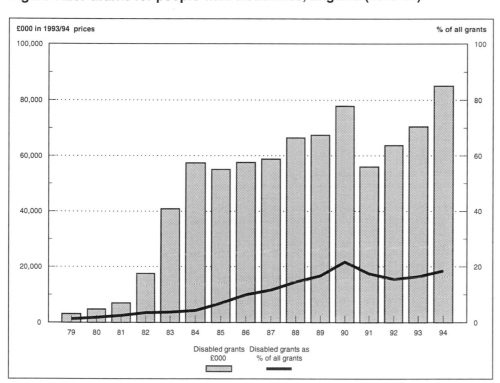

Total expenditure on adaptations for people with disabilities is not centrally recorded. In 1994, LAs in England and Wales provided grants to the value of £90m at cash prices, including MWA. Data for Scotland is not available, but assuming expenditure amounted to 8% of all grant provision, this would add a further £7m, bringing the total to £97m. Assuming an average grant rate of 90% would bring an additional £9m through contributions from private owners.

Map 7.12: Renovations to HA stock per 1,000 privately owned dwellings, England (1978-94)[c]

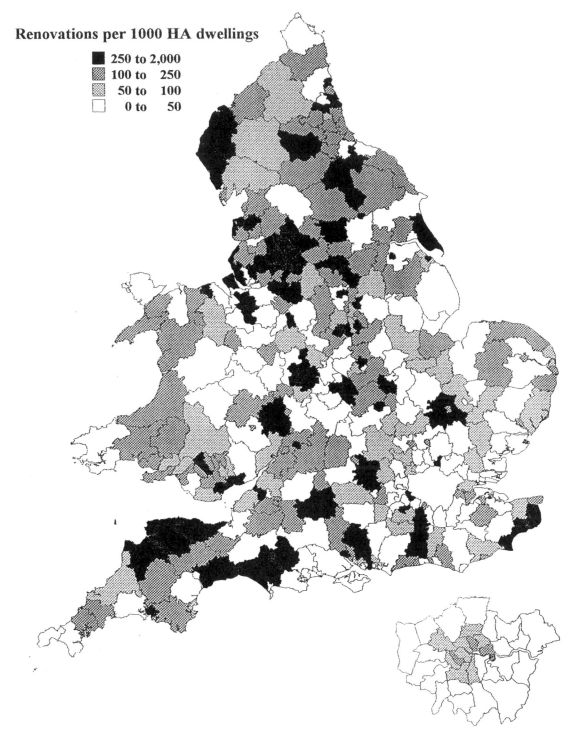

Renovations per 1000 HA dwellings

- 250 to 2,000
- 100 to   250
- 50 to   100
- 0 to   50

Figure 7.21: Grants for people with disabilities, Wales (1979-94)[c]

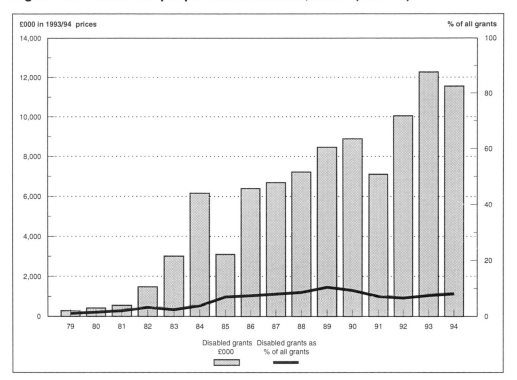

Expenditure on equipment and adaptations by social services departments in Britain is estimated at £75m (Laing and Buisson Ltd, 1993). Spending on adaptations undertaken by LAs from their housing revenue accounts (HRA) is not separately recorded, and the production of a reliable estimate is highly problematic. Most previous work has been based on small samples. The sums involved are potentially much greater than those spent through social services sources or through the renovation grant system. In most authorities minor adaptations for council tenants are funded from HRA, and in perhaps two thirds of authorities major adaptations are also funded from this source or from capital. In total, LAs in Britain spent around £2.75bn on the repair and maintenance of council dwellings in 1994/95, together with £2.4bn in capital expenditure. If only 2% of the total from each source is spent on adaptations, this would produce expenditure of around £100m. Housing associations also spend revenue resources on adaptations and the Housing Corporation provides an annual capital sum from its Approved Development Plan (ADP) budget. No estimate is available of the former but the latter provided about £11m in 1994/95, or about £12m if additional sums are assumed for HAs in Scotland (Tai Cymru in Wales does not provide capital funds for HA adaptations). Adding in revenue spending at about the same level as that assumed for LAs (2%) would produce a further £11m in HA spending, bringing the total to £23m. Finally, individuals also invest their own resources in equipment and adaptations. Published data from the annual Family Expenditure Survey (FES) does not permit the identification of spending on adaptations and equipment so no reliable estimate of this spending is possible.

A total of more than £300m in public resources was therefore spent on equipment and adaptations in 1994/95. Known private spending of £9m linked to grant aid, and additional private spending, must also be added to this sum. Table 7.16 summarises these estimates.

The pattern of grant provision for disabled people

Map 7.5 shows the local pattern of provision of DFGs in England and Wales; Table 7.9 shows the most active authorities; and Table 7.10 shows the distribution of DFGs by tenure.

Home improvement agencies

Home improvement agencies provide practical help to older, disabled and low income households with repair, improvement and adaptation work to their homes. They assist clients to diagnose house condition problems, obtain estimates from competent builders, raise finance to meet the costs of work, and ensure that work is carried out properly. The government, LAs, HAs, and a number of charities provide funding to meet the running costs of these organisations. Anchor Housing Trust, with 48 agencies, is the largest provider. In 1995/96, 201 home improvement agencies were in operation in England, together with 23 in Wales, and 18 in Scotland. In Northern Ireland, the Housing Executive takes a leading role in funding three projects. Map 7.13 shows areas in Britain with a home improvement agency. Overall, less than two thirds of LA districts have such projects. There are concentrations in urban areas of the North East, North West, Midlands, South Wales, and in south coast resorts in Kent, Sussex and Hampshire. The South West, East Anglia, Lincolnshire, Yorkshire and rural areas of northern England have relatively few projects.

Table 7.16: An estimate of spending on equipment and adaptations, Britain (1994/95)

Source	Estimated spending (£m)
Disabled facilities, minor works and other LA grants to private owners and tenants	97
Spending by social services authorities on equipment and adaptations	75
Spending by health authorities on equipment and adaptations	5
Capital and revenue spending by LAs on adaptations to their own stock	104
Capital and revenue spending by HAs on adaptations to their own stock	23
Total public/social rented sector spending	**304**
Private contributions to LA grants	9
Other private spending	not known

Sources: Authors' estimates, based on data from *Housing and Construction Statistics* (various years); Wilcox (1995); Laing and Buisson Ltd (1993)

Table 7.17 provides a profile of the clients helped by government-funded home improvement agencies in England and Wales in 1994/95 and the work which these clients carried out. A high proportion of clients helped are vulnerable because of age, illness, disability or low income. The majority of jobs carried out involve repairs to the structure or external envelope of the dwelling or the provision or renewal of basic amenities and services such as wiring or heating. An increasing proportion of jobs include adaptations for disabled people.

Home improvement agencies have played an important role in assisting LAs to target grants under the new renovation grant system, and a high proportion of their clients use funding from this source, particularly MWA for older people. In 1994/95, home improvement agencies in England dealt with about 7% of all renovation grants, 7% of DFGs and 49% of MWA.

Energy efficiency

The 1995 Home Energy Conservation Act places a duty on housing authorities to publish measures likely to significantly improve energy efficiency in their area. Programmes already underway include the Home Energy Efficiency Scheme (HEES), which provides grants for energy efficiency measures for those receiving benefit, and a network of Energy Advice Centres supported by the Energy Saving Trust.

Table 7.17: Output of government-funded home improvement agencies in England and Wales (1994/95)

	England	Wales
% clients aged 75 or over	47	48
% clients ill or disabled	65	75
% clients on low income	93	56
Number of clients helped with advice	48,466	4,356
Number of clients helped with building work	21,735	2,002
Total cost of work completed (£m)	38.46	5.68
% jobs involving adaptations	17	39
% jobs involving essential work	82	87
% jobs funded by renovation grant	12	12
% jobs funded by DFG	7	16
% jobs funded by MWA	49	35

Sources: Care and Repair England (1995); Leather (1995)

Figure 7.22 shows the uptake of HEES by tenure for the period October 1990 to March 1993. It shows that over 70% of recipients were in LA accommodation, owner-occupiers received 18% of grants, and less than 4% went to private rented dwellings, although this tenure is the least energy efficient. Figure 7.23 shows take-up grants by dwelling type with most grants going to terraced or semi-detached dwellings. Figure 7.24 shows that the majority of grants were split between the inter-war and the 1950-65 stock. Unfortunately HEES data does not utilise the commonly accepted dwelling age bands.

To encourage householders to undertake energy conservation measures, a three-year pilot scheme of local energy advice centres (LEACs) was set up by the Energy Saving Trust. Map 7.14 shows the location of LEACs.

Map 7.13: Location of government-funded home improvement agencies, Britain (1995/96)[q]

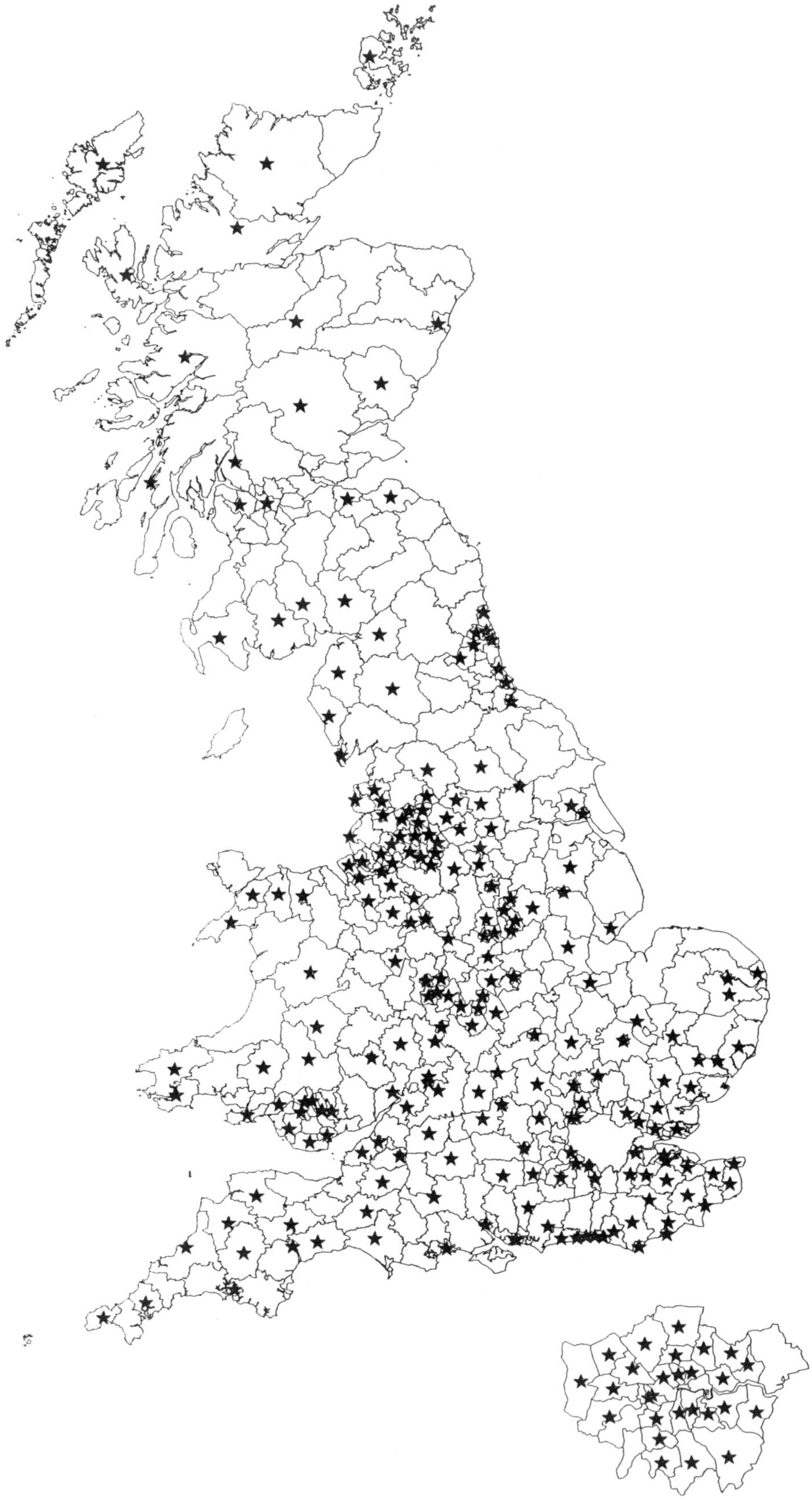

Figure 7.22: Take-up of HEES by tenure, England (1990-93)[h]

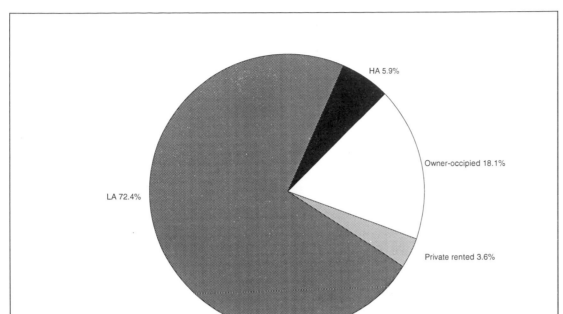

Figure 7.23: Take-up of HEES by dwelling type, England (1990-93)[h]

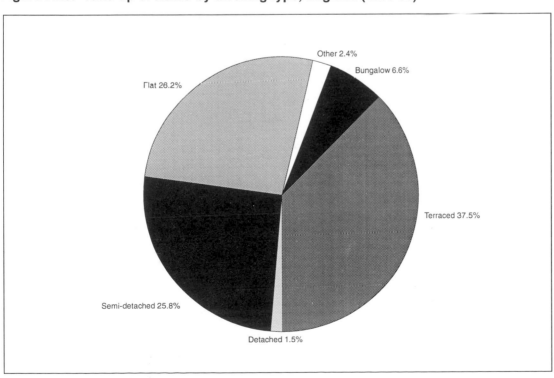

Figure 7.24: Take-up of HEES by dwelling age, England (1990-93)[h]

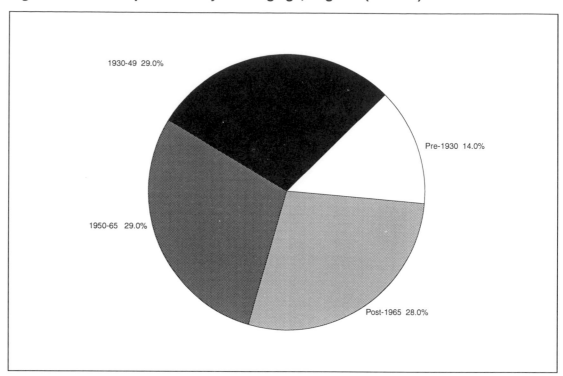

Map 7.14: Location of LEACs^r

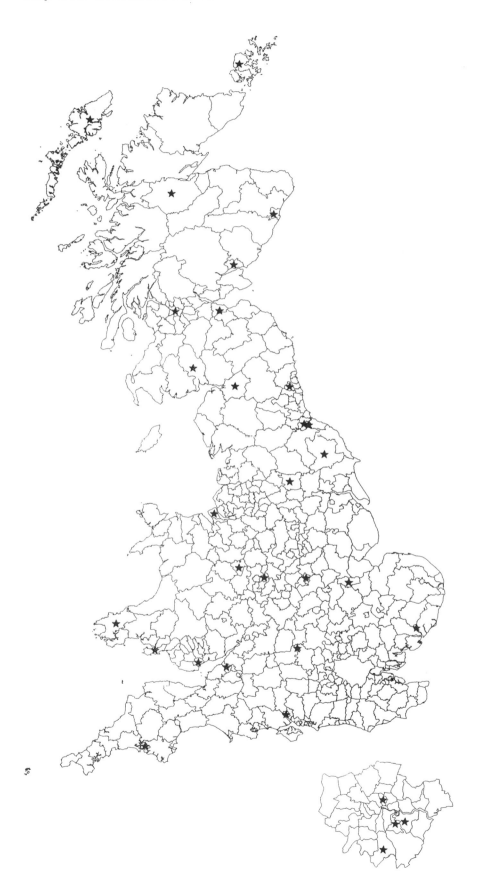

Chapter 8

Public investment in housing renovation

Renovation's share of public expenditure

Renovation took an increasing share of public expenditure during the 1980s while new building declined. In England, LA renovation increased from 20% in 1979/80 to almost 50% in 1989/90. After falling back slightly in subsequent years the programme increased again to account for 43% of capital spending in 1994/95. Expenditure on grants to private owners reached a peak of 24% in 1983/84, and remained at around 15% before falling to 10% in 1989/90 (Figure 8.1; Table A8.1). During the 1990s the programme's share of spending has risen slightly as a result of the need to meet mandatory demand and earmarking of resources through specified capital grant. The Housing Corporation programme, although in decline since 1993, accounts for a third of total capital spending on housing. An increasing proportion of this is for new build rather than renovation activity, but despite this, renovation is likely to continue to dominate LA investment programmes.

Figure 8.1: Percentage shares of public expenditure on housing by programme, England (1979-93)[k]

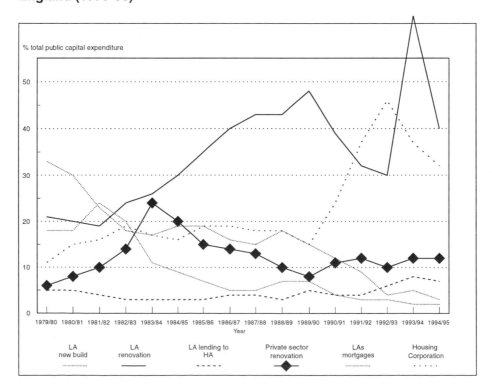

In Wales (Figure 8.2; Table A8.2) new building fell even more dramatically than in England. Local authority renovation also increased its share of total expenditure from 20% to 40% during the 1980s, but was overtaken in importance by grants to private owners which reached 41% of total investment in the early 1980s and returned to this level at the end of the decade. As in England, the Tai Cymru programme has recently increased in significance.

Figure 8.2: Percentage shares of public expenditure on housing by programme, Wales (1981-95)[k]

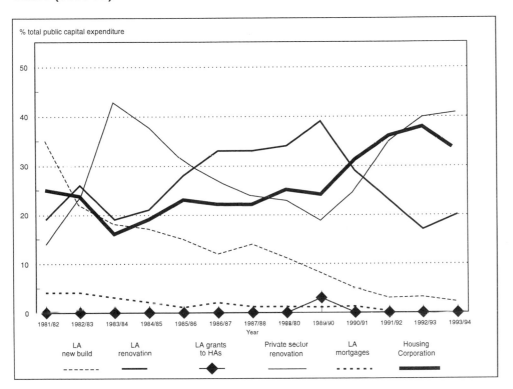

Detailed data on expenditure within the housing programme is not available for Scotland. In Northern Ireland, data is only available for the latter part of the 1980s. As in England and Wales, public sector renovation (of NIHE stock) has increased to about 40% of the programme, but expenditure on grants to private owners declined to less than 20% of the total (Figure 8.3; Table A8.3). New building by the NIHE has also declined to about 25% of the total programme, but this level of expenditure remains substantially higher than in England or Wales. Support for the voluntary sector has historically been low in Northern Ireland, at around 20% of total expenditure.

Renovation expenditure

Figures 8.4 to 8.6 show expenditure on the renovation of LA, HA, and private stock in England, Wales and Northern Ireland since 1979. In England, expenditure increased from £1.1bn in 1981/82 to a peak of £3.6bn in 1989/90, before falling back sharply to under £2bn in the 1990s. Expenditure on LA renovation has taken the main share of spending throughout the 1979-95 period, accounting for over half of all renovation expenditure in most years (Figure 8.4; Table A8.4). Private sector renovation spending only approached spending on the LA stock in the early 1990s during the repair grants boom. Investment in renovation by HAs remained consistently below both other programmes. When expressed in constant prices it is striking how consistent total spending by HAs and the

aggregate value of grants to private owners have been over a long period. However, as Chapter 7 showed, increases in HA unit costs and private grant levels have reduced the volume of output over the period by a substantial amount, while reductions in unit costs since 1990 have sustained the volume of LA renovation output (see Figures 7.9 and 7.17).

Figure 8.3: Percentage shares of public expenditure on housing by programme, Northern Ireland (1985-95)[k]

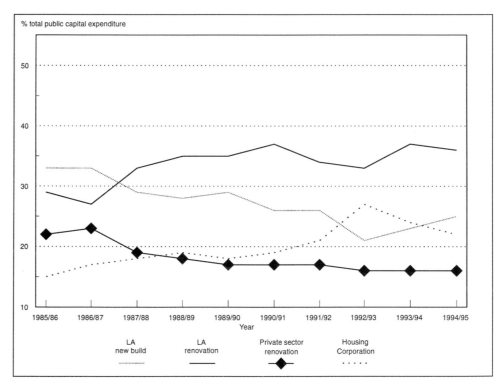

In Wales, expenditure increased from only £106m in 1981/82 at 1993/94 prices to £291m in 1993/94 (Figure 8.5; Table A8.5). As in England, renovation of the LA stock increased up to 1989 and has subsequently reduced, although it remains higher than in the early 1980s. Spending on grants to private owners has increased, and in the 1990s has exceeded levels achieved during the early 1980s boom in real terms. In contrast to England, spending on private

grants is almost 2.5 times that on renovation of the LA stock. Housing association renovation investment has been relatively insignificant. In Northern Ireland, expenditure on renovation has fallen since the mid-1980s from £142m to only £102m in 1991/92 (Figure 8.6; Table A8.6). Within this overall decline, renovation of NIHE stock has increased, while expenditure on grants to private owners has fallen sharply.

Figure 8.4: Public expenditure on housing renovation, England (1979-95)[k]

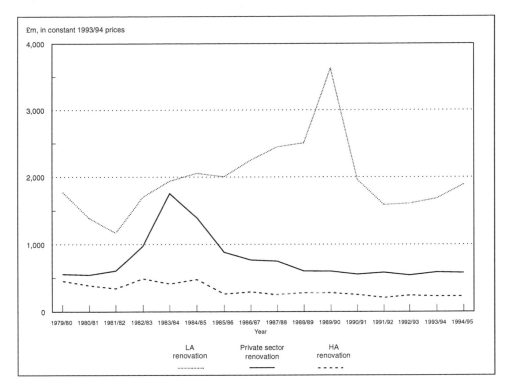

Figure 8.5: Public expenditure on housing renovation, Wales (1981-94)[k]

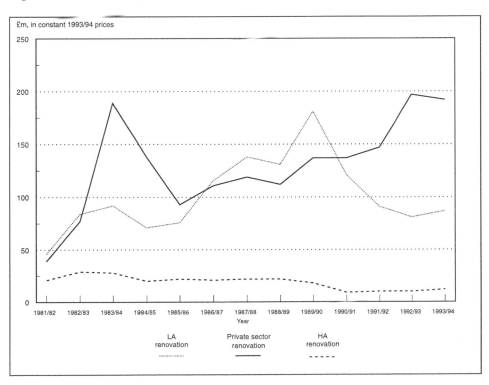

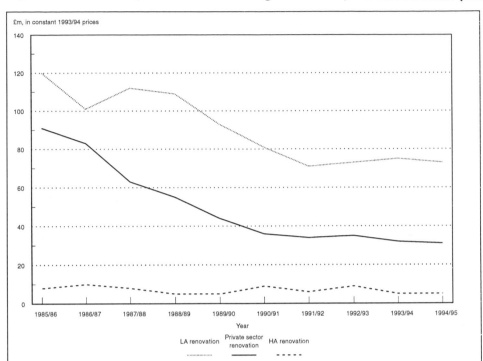

Figure 8.6: Public expenditure on housing renovation, Northern Ireland (1985-95)[k]

Chapter 9

Private investment in housing renovation

Private expenditure

In addition to public expenditure on renovation, there is a large volume of expenditure undertaken by individual households or owners using their own resources. Relatively little is known about this investment. The annual FES (see, for example, Central Statistical Office [CSO], 1992) records some details of expenditure on repair, maintenance and decoration but this information is incomplete as it excludes expenditure financed by borrowing. Accepting this limitation, Figure 9.1 (see also Table A9.1) shows variations in household expenditure over the period 1986-94. In cash terms this shows a steady increase over the period, from £253 per annum in 1986 to £386 in 1993, followed by a fall in 1994 to £343. Adjusting this spending to constant 1993/94 prices reveals a fall between 1986 and 1988. This was followed by an increase in spending between 1989 and 1991 when the average across all households exceeded £400. In subsequent years the total fell back to only £336 in 1994. These figures represent aggregate expenditure of about £8.1bn in 1994.

Figure 9.1: Household expenditure on repair, maintenance and decoration, UK (1986-94)[1]

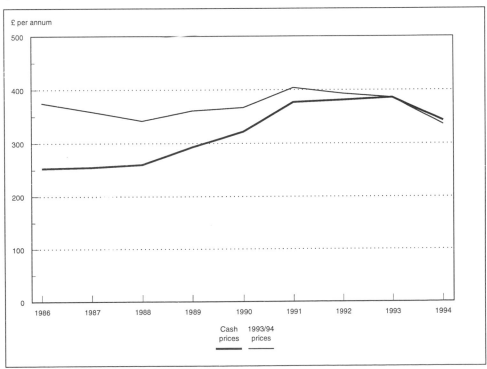

As might be expected, home owners spend more than those in other tenures on repair, maintenance and decoration (Figure 9.2; Table A9.1). On average, home owners spent about £470 per year in 1994 but those with a mortgage spent about £500 while outright owners spent £400. Private tenants in unfurnished accommodation spent about £110, LA tenants £75, HA tenants £40, and those renting furnished accommodation £31.

Figure 9.2: Household expenditure on repair, maintenance and decoration, 1986-94 by tenure, UK (1993/94 prices)[1]

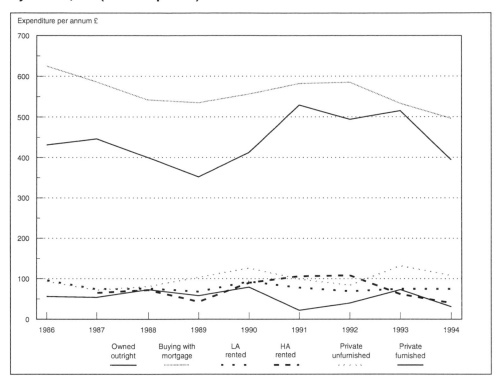

Expenditure in 1994 was greatest among the 30-49 and 50-64 age groups, at about £430 per annum, and least among those under 30 and over 75 (Table A9.2). Among home owners, spending was highest in Northern Ireland, Scotland, Wales, the North and Greater London, and lowest in East Anglia, the Midlands, the South East and the South West (Table 9.1). This may be related to the age profile of the dwelling stock, with expenditure lowest in the regions with the highest proportion of post-war stock.

Expenditure on repairs, maintenance and decoration generally increases with income (Table 9.2), both for households as a whole and for home owners, but the proportion of total income devoted to these items decreases as income rises (Table 9.3), with the exception of those in the highest income decile, where there is a sharp increase in spending which is reflected in the proportion of income devoted to repair work.

Table 9.1: Expenditure on repairs, maintenance and decoration by region, UK (1994-95)

Region	Owned outright	£ per annum Buying with mortgage	All owner- occupiers
North	320	600	494
Yorks/Humberside	295	580	483
East Midlands	467	352	397
East Anglia	289	310	301
Greater London	466	504	491
Rest of South East	416	511	480
South West	400	364	380
West Midlands	323	437	395
North West	424	504	472
England	390	477	446
Wales	258	736	535
Scotland	287	660	551
Northern Ireland	–	616	1,121
United Kingdom	402	506	469

Source: CSO (1995)

Table 9.2: Average weekly spending on repairs, maintenance and decoration by income, owner-occupiers, UK (1994-95)

Income decile	Lower boundary of decile	£ per week All tenures	Outright owners	Buying on mortgage	All owner- occupiers
Lowest	0	1.29	3.97	1.92	3.43
2	77	2.13	4.45	2.43	4.06
3	117	3.02	4.67	5.80	5.00
4	162	4.37	7.07	4.43	6.05
5	223	6.02	9.27	6.24	7.72
6	291	5.47	9.90	4.82	6.28
7	367	6.17	6.77	7.31	7.18
8	455	9.36	9.31	10.51	10.28
9	556	10.00	8.91	10.44	10.17
Highest	728	18.21	20.66	18.84	19.10

Source: CSO (1995)

Table 9.3: Average weekly spending on repairs, maintenance and decoration by income as a percentage of income, owner-occupiers, UK (1994-95)

Decile	All tenures	Outright owners	% Buying on mortgage	All owner-occupiers
Lowest	2.2	6.6	3.2	5.7
2	1.8	3.8	2.1	3.5
3	1.9	2.9	3.6	3.1
4	2.0	3.2	2.0	2.7
5	2.1	3.2	2.1	2.7
6	1.5	2.7	1.3	1.7
7	1.4	1.5	1.6	1.6
8	1.7	1.7	1.9	1.8
9	1.4	1.2	1.4	1.4
Highest	2.1	2.4	2.2	2.2

Source: CSO (1995)

Table 9.4 shows more detail from the FES on the nature of spending on repairs, maintenance, decoration and related matters in Britain in 1994-95. Some of the groupings seem rather idiosyncratic but this is the form in which the survey results are presented. The items are ranked in ascending order of expenditure, averaged not across all households but across those who incurred expenditure under each heading. Some 46% of all households did not undertake any spending at all on repairs, maintenance, decoration and related matters. Those who did spent on average £12 per week or £636 per annum. Roughly half of those spending on repairs, or a quarter of all households, invested in central heating repairs, investing £110 per annum on average. Some three quarters of households purchased home contents insurance, at an average cost of £117. Only 5% of households invested in tools, costing £242 where they did so. A total of 13% spent an average of £366 per annum on materials other than paint, wallpaper, plaster and wood, or in the hire of equipment. About 26% spent an average of £470 on home maintenance falling outside any of the other categories in Table 9.4. Only 8% of households invested resources on doors, or electrical and other fitting, but those who did so invested over £900 on average. Only 1.5% of households admitted to work on the somewhat heterogeneous grouping of DIY improvements to double glazing, kitchen units, or sheds, but those who did so invested £1,332. The largest average spend was incurred by those who carried out work on house extensions (16%), whose average spend was £2,350.

The 1991 EHCS and SHCS also obtained details of work undertaken by private owners. The 1991 EHCS recorded details of all building work carried out in 1991 and of major work carried out over the 1987-91 period. In 1991, three quarters of households in England carried out work to their dwellings. Owner-occupiers (84%) were the most likely group to do work (Table 9.5). The average value of work carried out during the year (allowing for the notional costs of DIY inputs) was £1,648. Work by owner-occupiers (including those who carried out no work) averaged about £2,200, while tenants carried out work averaging around £500. Figure 9.3 (Table A9.3) shows the distribution of households by the value of work carried out for each tenure.

Table 9.4: Spending on repairs, maintenance and decoration and related matters, UK (1994-95)

Spending category	% of all households with any spend	Average spend across all households	Average spend if spent at all under heading	
			Per week	Per annum
Total spend on repairs, maintenance and decoration	53.93	6.60	12.24	636.33
Sub categories				
Central heating repairs	24.08	0.51	2.12	110.14
Home contents insurance	76.26	1.72	2.26	117.28
Tools	5.36	0.25	4.66	242.37
Other materials, hire of equipment	12.92	0.91	7.04	366.24
House maintenance	26.63	2.40	9.01	468.71
Paint, wallpaper, plaster and wood	10.36	1.07	10.33	537.22
Doors, electrical and other fittings	8.40	1.47	17.50	909.87
DIY improvements: double glazing, kitchen units, sheds	1.56	0.40	25.62	1,332.17
Central heating installation	1.74	0.53	30.52	1,587.13
House extensions	15.92	7.19	45.16	2,348.49

Source: CSO (1995)

Figure 9.3: Value of expenditure on building work by tenure, England (1991)[d]

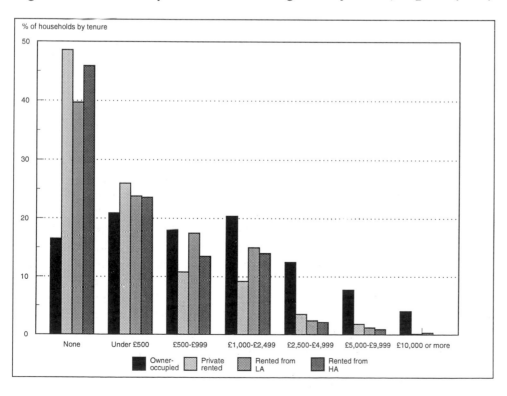

In aggregate, work to the value of some £31.5bn was identified as being completed by residents in 1991, of which the majority (£28bn, or 89%) was carried out by owner-occupiers. This compares with about £7.2bn of expenditure which can be inferred from the FES for 1991. The latter figure excludes DIY work and some work funded by loans, but nevertheless the difference is very difficult to reconcile. The EHCS, as a specialist survey, is likely to provide the most accurate indication of total spending, while the FES may provide an indication of trends over time.

The survey also looked at major work over the 1987-91 period. Some 86% of owners completed major work in this period (Table A9.3). In the rented sector about two thirds of private tenants carried out major works, but the proportions of HA and LA tenants were smaller (51% and 40% respectively). The average value of major work completed by home owners over the period (£5,700) was significantly greater than for tenants. The aggregate value of work over the period was £73.2bn, of which 96% was carried out by home owners. Estimates of work by landlords for the 1987-91 period are not available.

Table 9.5: Value of work carried out by households by tenure, England (1991)

Tenure	% doing any work	Total value (£m)	% of total work done	Average (£)	No of cases (000s)
All work 1991					
Owner-occupied	83.5	27,930	88.7	2,170	12,872
Private rented	51.4	918	2.9	540	1,700
Rented from LA	60.4	2,330	7.4	601	3,877
Rented from HA	54.4	315	1.0	477	662
All households	74.9	31,493	100.0	1,648	19,111
Major work 1987-91					
Owner-occupied	86.0	73,360	96.3	5,699	12,872
Private rented	63.1	1,077	1.4	634	1,700
Rented from LA	39.8	1,579	2.1	407	3,877
Rented from HA	51.0	202	0.3	305	662
All households	73.4	76,218	100.0	3,988	19,111

Source: 1991 EHCS: analysis of data

In addition to work by those resident in dwellings, the 1991 EHCS made estimates of work by landlords and other owners (Table 9.6). Freeholders carried out work to the value of £0.2bn, private developers £0.8bn, private landlords £2.0bn, LAs as landlords £3.9bn, and HAs as landlords £0.4bn. The total value of work by owners and residents was £38.9bn.

Table 9.7 shows the type of work carried out within the overall totals. In 1991, only about a quarter of work by value was related to dwelling repair. A further quarter of work involved internal decoration, and the remaining 50% related to improvements. Not surprisingly, there were substantial variations in this pattern by tenure, with tenants more likely to invest in internal decorations (around two thirds of the value of work by LA or HA tenants and 50% of work by private tenants). Home owners devoted only 17% of investment to internal decorations, but improvements (53%) still predominate over repairs (30%).

Table 9.6: Value of work carried out by landlords and others, England (1991)

All work 1991	Total value (£bn)	Average value (£)
Freeholders	0.2	na
Private developers	0.8	na
Private landlords	2.0	1,240
LAs	3.9	986
HAs	0.4	723

Source: DoE Building Stock Research Division, unpublished tables based on 1991 EHCS

Table 9.7: Type of work by tenure, England (1991)

All work 1991	Owner-occupied	Private rented	LA rented	HA rented	All households
Improvements					
Total value of work (£m)	14,666	293	577	73	15,609
Mean value (£)	1,139	172	149	110	817
% of all work	53	32	25	23	50
Repairs					
Total value of work (£m)	8,463	169	252	36	8,920
Mean value (£)	657	100	65	54	467
% of all work	30	19	11	11	28
Internal decor					
Total value of work (£m)	4,751	451	1,501	206	6,910
Mean value (£)	369	266	387	312	362
% of all work	17	49	64	65	22
Total					
Total value of work (£m)	27,881	914	2,330	315	31,439
Major work 1987-91					
Improvements					
Total value of work (£m)	46,329	630	1,045	113	48,118
Mean value (£)	3,599	371	270	171	2,518
% of all work	68	70	75	72	68
Repairs					
Total value of work (£m)	21,801	271	353	45	22,469
Mean value (£)	1,694	159	91	68	1,176
% of all work	32	30	25	28	32
Total					
Total value of work (£m)	68,130	901	1,399	158	70,587

Source: 1991 EHCS: analysis of data

Figures 9.4-9.10 provide a profile of the average value of work by selected household and dwelling type characteristics. (Table A9.4 provides details of these and additional characteristics.) There are clear links between household characteristics and the average value of work carried out. The average value of work rises from £800 for those with an income of under £4,000 per annum to £3,000 for those with an income of over £24,000 per annum (Figure 9.4). In terms of the age of the head of household the value of work remains fairly level from the ages of 25-54, but falls off for older age groups to less than £350 for those over 85

(Figure 9.5). In terms of household type, families with children carry out the most work (averaging about £2,500). Couples under retirement age and multi-adult households average around £2,000, pensioner couples and lone parent households carry out work averaging around £1,000, and lone adult households (£850) and lone pensioners (£550) carry out least work (Figure 9.6). There is also a relationship between length of residence and the value of work carried out (Figure 9.7), with the amount of work at a peak of around £2,000 for those resident for 1-2 years (the pro rata annual rate for those resident under a year would probably be similar) and declining steadily thereafter.

Figure 9.4: Average value of work carried out by household income, England (1991)[d]

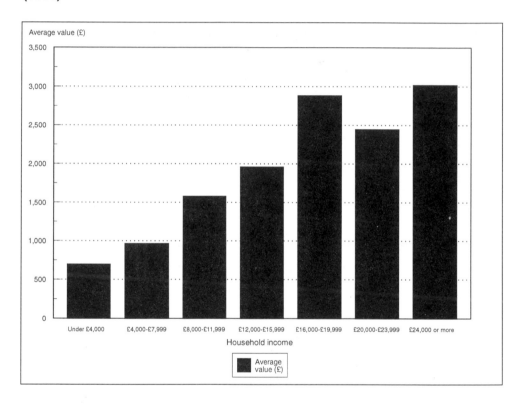

Figure 9.5: Average value of work carried out by age of head of household, England (1991)[d]

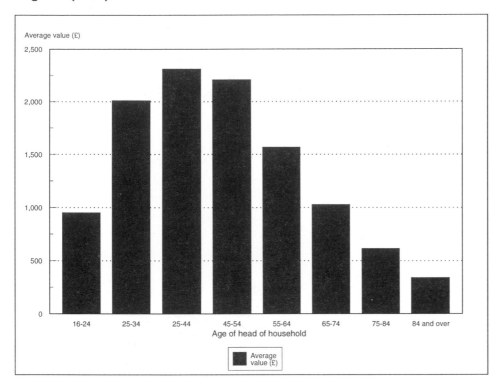

Figure 9.6: Average value of work carried out by household type, England (1991)[d]

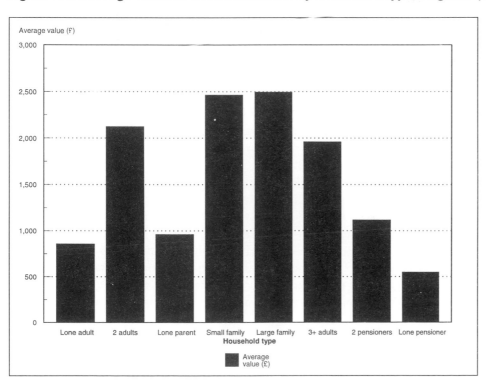

Figure 9.7: Average value of work carried out by length of residence, England (1991)[d]

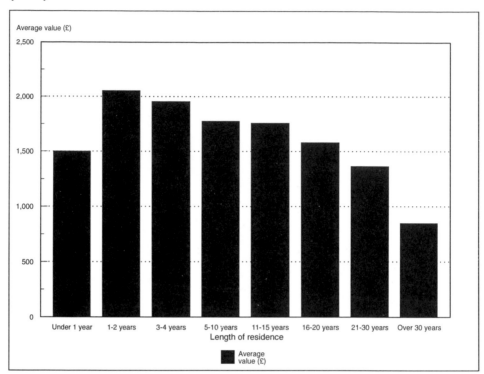

Figures 9.8-9.10 show variations in the value of work carried out by occupants in relation to selected dwelling characteristics. Here the links are less easy to demonstrate. Although occupant characteristics such as incomes would be expected to have a significant impact on investment, the need to spend would also be expected to be important. In terms of dwelling age, which earlier chapters have shown to be an important influence on dwelling condition, the oldest dwellings (pre-1850) generated the highest average value of work (£2,700) (Figure 9.8). A second peak occurs for dwellings in the 1919-44 age group (£1,950). Otherwise, the value of work is somewhat, but not substantially, higher for dwellings built in the 1850-1918 period (£1,600) than for post-war dwellings (£1,500). In general, therefore, the extent of variation in expenditure by age is not substantial.

Figure 9.9 shows variations in the value of work in 1991, and for the period 1987-91 for major work, in terms of general repair cost in 1991. The pattern is complex, but spending is highest on dwellings considered to have no general repair costs in 1991 and lowest on those with the highest costs. In between these extremes there is a peak in spending for dwellings with costs in the £5,000-£9,999 band, but otherwise little variation. The pattern is the same for work carried out in 1991 and for work carried out over the 1987-91 period. Finally, Figure 9.10 shows the relationship between the value of work carried out and dwelling value. There is a clear increase in the value of work carried out as dwelling value increases, from less than £1,000 for dwellings valued at under £40,000 to over £4,000 for dwellings worth more than £160,000. Higher levels of investment in higher value dwellings arise because high value dwellings are generally bigger and other things being equal require more to be spent on them, because those living in these dwellings have higher incomes, and perhaps because higher dwelling values make it more likely that an investment will be recovered.

Figure 9.8: Average value of work carried out by age of dwelling, England (1991)[d]

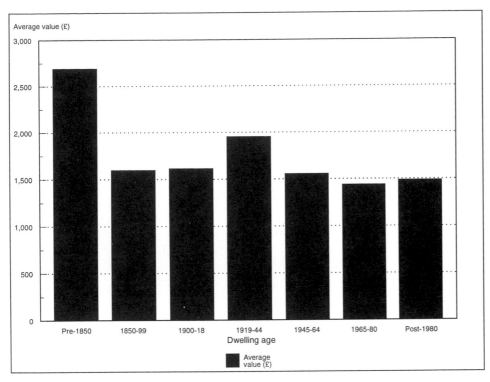

Figure 9.9: Average value of work carried out by general repair cost, England (1991)[d]

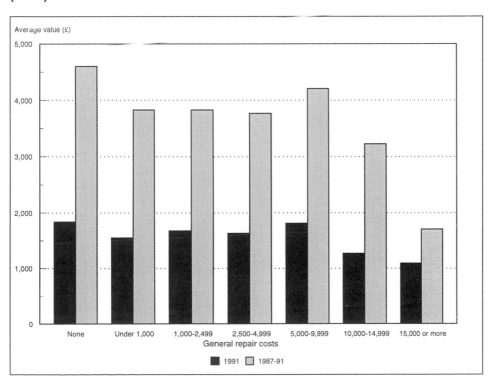

Figure 9.10: Average value of work carried out by value of dwelling, England (1991)[d]

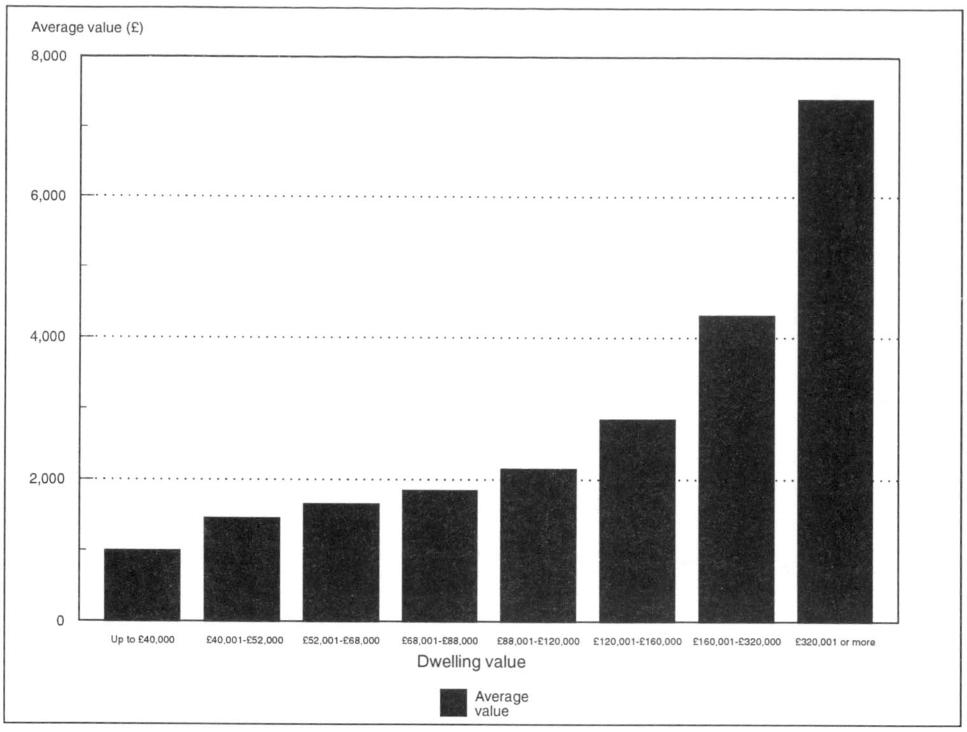

Table 9.8 shows work done in 1991 by households in Scotland. The proportion of households carrying out any work was apparently much lower in Scotland (53%) than in England (75%). Owner-occupiers reported average expenditure of about half the amount undertaken in England and tenants reported very small levels of spending.

Table 9.8: Value of work carried out by households by tenure, Scotland (1991)

Tenure	% doing any work	Total value (£m)	% of total work done	Average (£)	Number of cases (000s)
All work 1991					
Owner-occupied	53.3	1,087	93.2	1,077	1,009
Private rented	19.2	12	1.0	98	127
Rented from LA	21.5	64	5.5	50	804
Rented from HA	16.8	3	0.3	81	49
All households	37.5	1,166	100.0	586	1,988

Source: 1991 SHCS: analysis of data

Building society lending

Information on the amount of lending by building societies for renovation work (rather than house purchase) is not available. Figure 9.11 shows the extent of lending on pre-1919 dwellings and more specifically on pre-1919 terraced houses and converted flats (see also Table A9.5). This showed a significant increase in the late 1970s, levelled off during the 1980s, and fell slightly in the 1990s.

Figure 9.11: Building society lending by type of property, Britain (1973-94)[m]

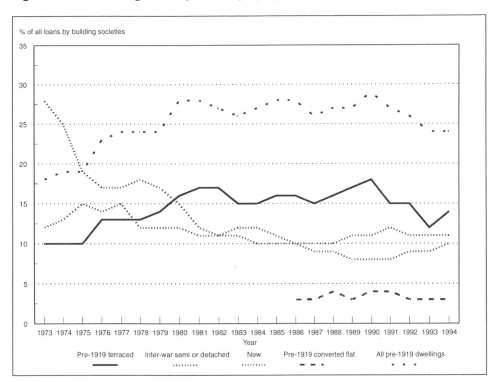

% of all loans by building societies

| Pre-1919 terraced | Inter-war semi or detached | New | Pre-1919 converted flat | All pre-1919 dwellings |

Figure 9.12 shows variations in the propensity of first-time buyers to purchase dwellings of a particular age over time (see also Tables A9.6 and A9.7). First-time buyers remain more likely to buy pre-1919 dwellings than existing owners, and less likely to buy newer dwellings. However, in recent years, the differences have become significantly less marked.

Building industry output

Evidence on the volume of renovation activity is also provided by official statistics on building industry output. Figure 9.13 shows output on housing repair and maintenance work by sector over the period 1985-94 at cash prices (see also Table A9.8). For the private sector the total output is broadly consistent with the FES but investment as a whole is less than the EHCS recorded for 1991, even allowing

for DIY work. Figure 9.13 clearly shows the importance of private investment which significantly exceeded public investment throughout the 1985-91 period. The impact of the period of boom in the economy (1987-90), followed by the subsequent recession in 1991 and later years is also apparent. In real terms output in the public sector has only increased by 10% over the 1985-94 period (5% in the public sector). However, there was an increase between 1985 and the peak years of 1989 and 1990 of 40% (private sector) and 20% (public sector).

Figure 9.14 shows output by size of firm (see also Table A9.9). It can be seen that the repair and maintenance sector is heavily dominated by small firms with seven or less employees, which in 1994 accounted for two thirds of the aggregate value of repair and maintenance work done, including jobs in the public sector. For private sector jobs alone the proportion would be higher.

123

Figure 9.12: Ratio of first-time buyers to existing owners by age of dwelling, Britain (1994/95)[m]

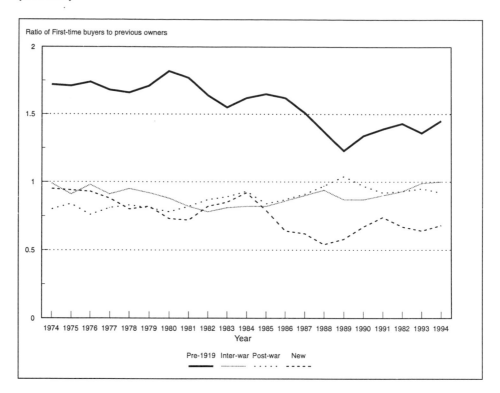

Figure 9.13: Output on housing repair and maintenance, Britain (1985-94)[c]

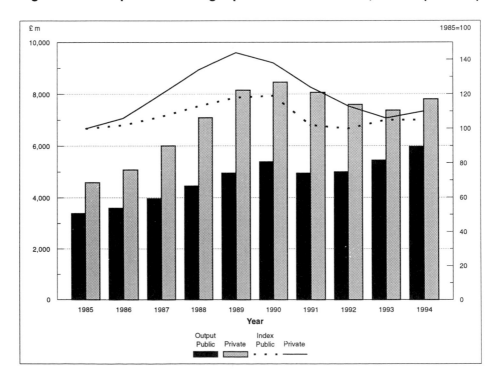

Figure 9.14: Output on housing repair and maintenance by size of firm, Britain (1990, 1992, 1994)[c]

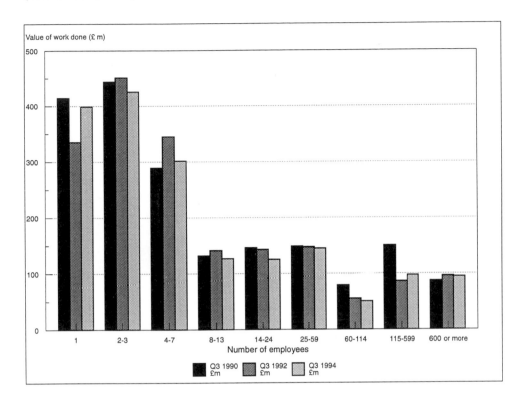

Chapter 10

European comparisons

Comparison of housing conditions within the UK is difficult because of differences in the indicators used in national surveys and differences in definitions. These problems also make it difficult to produce comparisons of housing conditions between the UK and Europe. Figures 10.1-10.5, drawing on data assembled by the European Commission (1993), provide some limited information.

Figure 10.1 shows that the proportion of dwellings which are in owner-occupation is lower in the UK than in Eire, Greece and Spain, but higher than in the countries of northern Europe, such as France, Denmark, The Netherlands and Germany. In terms of the age of the stock, the UK has the highest proportion of pre-1919 housing, followed by Eire, Belgium and France (Figure 10.2). Combining evidence on home ownership and age of the stock suggests that the UK has a more substantial proportion of privately owned older houses than other European countries except Eire and Belgium.

Figure 10.1: Proportion of owner-occupied dwellings in the European Community[n]

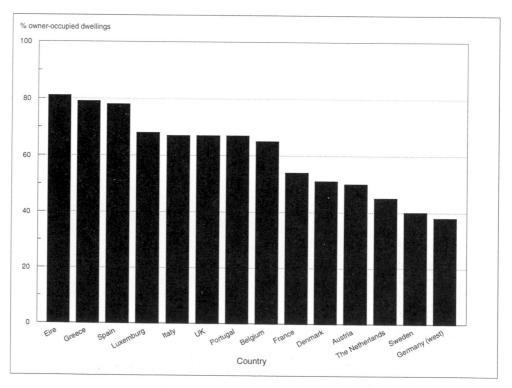

Figure 10.2: Proportion of pre-1919 dwellings in the European Community[n]

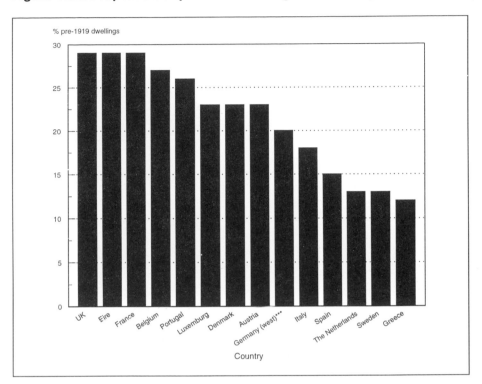

Figure 10.3 shows that the UK has one of the lowest rates of demolition in the European Community. Other countries with an ageing housing stock (Eire, Belgium and Portugal) have much higher levels of clearance.

Figure 10.3: Decreases in dwelling stock per 1,000 dwellings in the European Community[n]

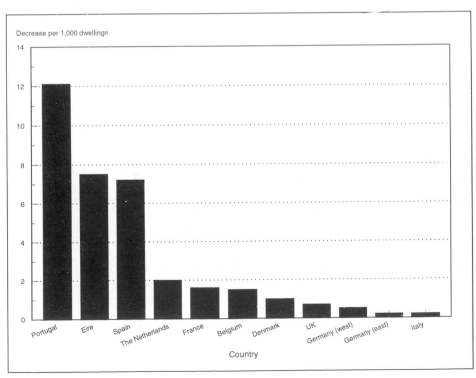

Figure 10.4 shows the proportion of dwellings with a bath/shower in each EC country. The UK ranks highly on this indicator, with 98% of dwellings, in comparison with countries such as Denmark, Italy, Portugal, Belgium and Greece where the proportion is less than 90%.

Figure 10.4: Proportion of dwellings with a bath/shower in the European Community[n]

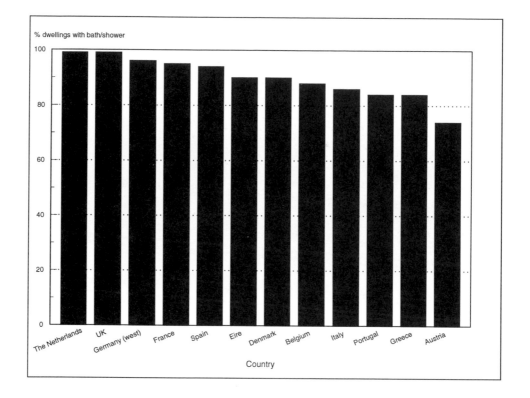

Finally, Figure 10.5 shows the proportion of dwellings with central heating in each EC country. The UK performs less well on this indicator in comparison with other countries with a similar climate. Of the northern European countries, only Belgium and Eire have fewer dwellings with central heating.

Figure 10.5: Proportion of dwellings with central heating in the European Community[n]

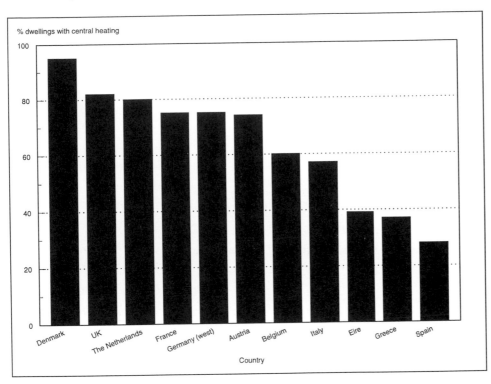

References

Building Societies Association (various years) *Building Society Bulletin*, London: BSA.

Care and Repair England (1995) *Report on agency performance 1994/95*, Nottingham: Care and Repair.

Central Statistical Office (various years) (Reports of the annual FES under various titles, eg (1995) *Family spending: a report on the 1994-95 FES*), London: HMSO.

Council of Mortgage Lenders (various years) *Housing finance*, London: CML.

Department of Finance and Personnel Northern Ireland (various years) *Northern Ireland Annual Abstract of Statistics*, Belfast: Department of Finance and Personnel.

Department of the Environment (1988) *English House Condition Survey 1986*, London: HMSO.

Department of the Environment (1993) *English House Condition Survey 1991*, London: HMSO.

Department of the Environment (1995) *Energy efficiency in council housing: strategic guide: condition of the stock*, London: DoE.

Department of the Environment (1996) *Private sector renewal: a strategic approach*, Circular 17/96, London: HMSO.

Department of the Environment (unpublished) Data on age of stock and poor housing conditions by local authority district, mimeo.

Department of the Environment and Welsh Office (various years) *Local Housing Statistics England and Wales*, London: HMSO.

Department of the Environment, Scottish Development Department, and Welsh Office (various years) *Housing and Construction Statistics Great Britain* (see, especially, the annual publication covering the previous decade), London: HMSO.

Diacon, D. (1991) *Deterioration of the public sector housing stock*, Aldershot: Avebury.

Dunster J. et al (1994) *Domestic energy fact file: owner occupied homes, local authority homes, private rented homes*, Watford: Building Research Institute.

European Commission (1993) *Statistics on housing in the European Community*, Brussels: European Commission.

Laing and Buisson Ltd (1993) *Care of elderly people: market survey 1992/93*, London: Laing and Buisson Publications Ltd.

Leather, P. (1995) Performance of Welsh Care and Repair projects, 1994/95, mimeo.

Leather, P. and Mackintosh, S. (1992) *Maintaining home ownership: the agency approach*, London: Longman/Institute of Housing.

Northern Ireland Housing Executive (1993) *1991 Northern Ireland House Condition Survey*, Belfast: Northern Ireland Housing Executive.

Office of Population Censuses and Surveys (1992) *1991 Census County Monitors*, London: OPCS.

Office of Population Censuses and Surveys (1994) *1993 General Household Survey*, London: HMSO.

Robertson, D. and Bailey, N. (1996) *Review of the impact of housing action areas*, Edinburgh: Scottish Homes.

Scottish Homes (1993) *Scottish House Condition Survey 1991*, Edinburgh: Scottish Homes.

Scottish Office (various years) *Scottish Abstract of Statistics*, Edinburgh: Scottish Office.

Scottish Office (various years) *Statistical Bulletin*, Housing Series, Edinburgh: HMSO.

Welsh Office (1994) *1993 Welsh House Condition Survey*, Cardiff: Welsh Office.

Welsh Office (various years) *Welsh Housing Statistics*, Cardiff: Welsh Office.

Wilcox, S. (1995) *Housing Finance Review 1995/96*, York: Joseph Rowntree Foundation.

Appendix A

Detailed tables

Table A3.1: Mean repair costs, UK

	Urgent repairs (£)		General repairs (£)		Comprehensive repairs (£)		Repair costs for unfit/BTS dwellings (£)	
	Occ	Vac	Occ	Vac	Occ	Vac	Occ	Vac
England 1991	689	2,404	1,178	2,978	2,217	4,156	3,970 (1)	8,838
Northern Ireland 1991	748	3,609	1,025	4,698	4,354	12,992	7,684 (3)	10,457
Wales 1993	na	na	na	na	720	na	3,740 (4)	na
Scotland 1991	213	na	1,168	na	na	na	4,724 (2)	na

Notes: Occ: Occupied; Vac: Vacant. Definitional and other problems preclude most comparisons between countries (see notes to Table 3.1). (1) Mean general repair cost for unfit dwellings. (2) Mean cost of repairs to BTS dwellings. (3) Mean total cost to make fit. (4) Mean repair cost for unfit dwellings.

Table A3.2: Unfitness by urban rural location, UK

			Urban	Rural	Total
England 1991 (1)	Occupied	% unfit	7.4	7.2	
		No unfit (000s)	1,113	301	1,414
	All dwellings	% unfit	7.7	7.2	
		No unfit (000s)	1,192	306	1,498
Northern Ireland 1991 (2)	Occupied	% unfit	4.6	14.5	
		No unfit (000s)	17,570	23,080	40,650
	All dwellings	% unfit	5.2	17.2	23.3
		No unfit (000s)	21,080	29,280	50,360
Wales 1993 (1)		% unfit	13.3	13.1	
		No unfit (000s)	124	27	151
Scotland 1991 (1)		% BTS	4.1	6.8	
		No BTS (000s)	69	24	93

Notes: (1) Occupied dwellings only. (2) Rural includes isolated rural dwellings and dwellings in small settlements.

Sources: 1991 EHCS, 1991 SHCS, 1991 NIHCS: analysis of data; 1993 WHCS: special tabulations

Table A4.1: Age of dwelling stock (1993)

| | Number of dwellings (000s) | | | | |
	Pre-1919	1919-44	1945-64	1965+	Total stock
England	5,196	3,891	4,231	6,407	19,725
Northern Ireland	121	65	130	258	574
Wales	368	157	244	361	1,132
Scotland	463	390	523	766	2,142
Great Britain	6,027	4,438	4,998	7,534	22,999
UK	6,148	4,503	5,128	7,792	23,573
	% of dwellings				
England	26.3	19.7	21.4	32.5	100.0
Northern Ireland	21.1	11.3	22.6	44.9	100.0
Wales	32.5	13.9	21.6	31.9	100.0
Scotland	21.6	18.2	24.4	35.8	100.0
Great Britain	26.2	19.3	21.7	32.8	100.0
UK	26.1	19.1	21.8	33.1	100.0

Sources: OPCS (1994)

Table A4.2: Type of dwelling stock (1993)

| | Number of dwellings (000s) | | | | | |
	Detached house	Semi-detached house	Terraced house	Purpose-built flat	Converted flat	All dwellings
England	4,003	5,954	5,807	2,669	1,096	19,589
Northern Ireland	177	140	210	39	8	574
Wales	267	367	385	83	29	1,131
Scotland	371	419	502	796	54	2,142
Great Britain	4,701	6,740	6,694	3,548	1,179	22,862
UK	4,878	6,880	6,904	3,587	1,187	23,436
	% of dwellings					
England	20.7	30.4	29.6	13.6	5.6	100.0
Northern Ireland	30.8	24.4	36.6	6.8	1.4	100.0
Wales	23.6	32.4	34.1	7.3	2.5	100.0
Scotland	17.3	19.6	23.4	37.2	2.5	100.0
Great Britain	20.6	29.5	29.3	15.5	5.2	100.0
UK	20.8	29.4	29.5	15.3	5.1	100.0

Sources: OPCS (1994)

Table A4.3: Age and type of dwelling stock (1993)

England	Pre-1919	1919-44	% of whole stock 1945-64	Post-1964	All ages
Terraced house	13.0	5.3	4.2	7.1	29.6
Semi-detached house	3.4	10.0	9.7	6.8	29.9
Detached house	3.0	2.9	3.4	9.9	19.2
Converted flat	5.7	0.3	0.2	0.4	6.6
Purpose-built flat	1.1	1.5	4.1	8.0	14.7
All types	26.2	20.0	21.6	32.2	100.0
Northern Ireland					
Terraced house	7.5	4.5	8.7	16.0	36.7
Semi-detached house	1.7	3.8	8.4	10.9	24.8
Detached house	8.9	2.7	4.1	15.0	30.7
Converted flat	1.1	0.1	0.0	0.0	1.2
Purpose-built flat	0.0	0.0	1.9	4.7	6.6
All types	19.2	11.1	23.1	46.6	100.0
Wales					
Terraced house	18.6	2.4	4.5	6.4	31.9
Semi-detached house	4.1	7.6	11.6	9.2	32.5
Detached house	6.5	2.4	3.2	11.5	23.6
Converted flat	1.8	0.4	0.2	0.2	2.6
Purpose-built flat	0.2	0.4	2.1	4.8	7.5
All types	31.2	13.2	21.6	32.1	100.0
Scotland					
Terraced house	10.5	8.0	2.5	2.7	23.7
Semi-detached house	6.8	6.2	4.4	2.3	19.7
Detached house	7.6	1.9	2.5	5.5	17.5
Converted flat	0.1	0.0	0.3	1.8	2.2
Purpose-built flat (tenement)	7.6	5.9	3.1	8.0	24.6
Purpose-built flat (4 in block)	1.1	2.2	5.4	0.7	9.4
Purpose-built flat (tower/deck)	2.4	0.5	0.0	0.0	2.9
All types	36.1	24.7	18.2	21.0	100.0
Great Britain					
Terraced house	13.0	5.4	4.1	6.7	29.2
Semi-detached house	3.8	9.5	9.3	6.5	29.1
Detached house	3.6	2.8	3.3	9.6	19.3
Converted flat	5.0	0.3	0.2	0.5	6.0
Purpose-built flat	2.0	2.1	4.4	7.9	16.4
All types	27.4	20.1	21.3	31.1	100.0
United Kingdom					
Terraced house	12.9	5.4	4.2	6.9	29.3
Semi-detached house	3.7	9.4	9.3	6.6	29.0
Detached house	3.7	2.8	3.3	9.7	19.5
Converted flat	4.9	0.3	0.2	0.5	5.9
Purpose-built flat	1.9	2.1	4.4	7.8	16.2
All types	27.2	19.9	21.3	31.5	100.0

Sources: OPCS (1994)

Table A4.4: Dwellings in poor condition by age

England 1991			Pre-1919	1919-44	1945-64	1964+	All ages
			Number and % of dwellings in each age group				
Unfit	All	No (000s)	804	327	225	142	1,498
		%	15.4	8.4	5.3	2.2	
	Occupied	No (000s)	717	313	206	117	1,353
		%	14.6	8.2	5.0	1.9	
Urgent	All	No (000s)	2,028	952	529	293	3,802
repairs		%	38.9	24.3	12.4	4.6	
over	Occupied	No (000s)	1,879	923	511	261	3,574
£1,000		%	38.3	24.2	12.3	4.2	

Northern Ireland 1991

			Pre-1919	1919-44	1945-64	1964+	All ages
Unfit	All	No (000s)	36	7	5	2	50
		%	29.5	11.3	4.0	0.8	
	Occupied	No (000s)	27	7	4	2	40
		%	26.2	11.5	3.5	0.8	
Urgent	All	No (000s)	56	17	14	6	93
repairs		%	45.7	25.4	10.6	2.3	
over	Occupied	No (000s)	42	14	13	6	75
£1,000		%	40	24	10	2	

Wales 1993 (occupied dwellings only)

			Pre-1919	1919-44	1945-64	1964+	All ages
Unfit	Occupied	No (000s)	75	27	28	22	152
		%	20.3	16.9	11.6	6.0	
Repairs	Occupied	No (000s)	125	37	45	24	231
over		%	33.8	23.4	18.2	6.8	
£1,500							

Scotland 1991 (occupied dwellings only)

			Pre-1919	1919-44	1945-64	1964+	All ages
BTS	Occupied	No (000s)	49	16	17	9	91
		%	11.8	4.5	3.7	1.2	
Urgent	Occupied	No (000s)	59	24	14	9	106
repairs		%	13.7	6.4	2.9	1.3	
over							
£1,000							

Sources: DoE (1993); Scottish Homes (1993); NIHE (1993); Welsh Office (1994)

Table A4.5: Poor condition dwellings by age (1991/93)

Unfit/BTS	Pre-1919	1919-44	% dwellings by age 1945-64	Post-1964	All ages
England	55.5	21.0	15.0	8.5	100.0
Northern Ireland	71.1	14.6	10.2	4.1	100.0
Wales	49.5	17.6	18.7	14.2	100.0
Scotland	51.7	18.4	20.0	10.0	100.0
Disrepair					
England	53.4	25.0	13.9	7.7	100.0
Northern Ireland	60.6	18.0	15.0	6.4	100.0
Scotland	54.2	16.1	19.8	9.9	100.0
Wales	55.2	22.3	13.6	8.9	100.0

Notes: Figures for England, Scotland and Northern Ireland are for 1991, figures for Wales are for 1993. Data available for occupied stock only in Wales and Scotland.

Sources: DoE (1993); Scottish Homes (1993); NIHE (1993); Welsh Office (1994)

Table A4.6: Dwellings in poor condition by type

England 1991		Terraced house	Semi-detached house	Detached house	Converted flat	Purpose-built flat	All types
Unfit	No (000s)	614	387	157	141	180	1,479
	%	10.6	6.5	3.9	12.9	6.7	7.6
Urgent repairs over £1,000	No (000s)	1,527	1,068	654	276	276	3,801
	%	37.6	17.9	11.3	10.3	25.2	19.4

No and % of dwellings in each type category

Northern Ireland 1991

		Terraced house	Semi-detached house	Detached house	Converted flat	Purpose-built flat	All types
Unfit	No (000s)	15	8	25	1	1	50
	%	8.4	5.4	12.1	3.0	15.6	8.8
Urgent repairs over £1,000	No (000s)	31	17	39	3	1	92
	%	17.8	12.2	18.6	7.1	18.2	16.0

Wales 1993 (occupied dwellings only)

		Terraced house	Semi-detached house	Detached house	Converted flat	Purpose-built flat	All types
Unfit	No (000s)	68	45	23		14	150
	%	16.1	13.8	8.6		13.3	13.4
Repairs over £1,500	No (000s)	100	69	50		11	230
	%	37.4	18.8	13.0		9.8	20.3

Scotland 1991 (occupied dwellings only)

		Terraced house	Semi-detached house	Detached house	Converted flat	Purpose-built flat	All types
BTS	No (000s)	16	10	20	6	40	92
	%	3.3	2.5	5.6	14.0	5.3	4.5
Urgent repairs over £1,000	No (000s)	19	16	32	5	34	106
	%	3.9	4.0	9.0	11.6	4.5	5.2

Sources: DoE (1993); Scottish Homes (1993); NIHE (1993); Welsh Office (1994)

Table A4.7: Poor condition dwellings by type (1991/93)

Unfit/BTS	Terraced house	Semi-detached house	Detached house	Converted flat		Purpose-built flat	All types
England	41.5	26.2	10.6	9.5		12.2	100.0
Northern Ireland	29.5	15.1	50.6	2.3		2.5	100.0
Wales	45.3	30.0	15.3		9.3		100.0
Scotland	17.4	10.9	21.7	6.5		43.5	100.0
Disrepair							100.0
England	40.2	28.1	17.2	7.3		7.3	100.0
Northern Ireland	34.3	18.6	42.5	3.0		1.6	100.0
Wales	43.5	30.0	21.7		4.8		100.0
Scotland	17.9	15.1	30.2	4.7		32.1	100.0

(% dwellings by type)

Notes: Figures for England, Scotland and Northern Ireland are for 1991, figures for Wales are for 1993. Data available for occupied stock only in Wales and Scotland.

Sources: DoE (1993); Scottish Homes (1993); NIHE (1993); Welsh Office (1994)

Table A4.8: Unfitness/BTS by age and type of dwelling stock in combination (1991/93)

% of whole stock

England	Pre-1919	1919-44	1945-64	Post-1964	All ages
Terraced house	29.9	6.3	3.0	1.8	41.0
Semi-detached house	7.3	11.0	6.1	1.3	25.7
Detached house	5.9	1.4	1.4	1.8	10.5
Converted flat	9.0	1.2	0.2	0.2	10.6
Purpose-built flat	1.5	1.9	4.3	4.3	12.0
All types	53.6	21.8	15.0	9.4	100.0

Northern Ireland	Pre-1919	1919-44	1945-64	Post-1964	All ages
Terraced house	19.5	6.2	2.4	1.4	29.5
Semi-detached house	6.7	3.7	4.1	0.6	15.1
Detached house	42.4	4.5	2.5	1.2	50.6
Converted flat	1.8	0.0	0.1	0.4	2.3
Purpose-built flat	0.7	0.1	1.1	0.5	2.4
All types	71.1	14.5	10.2	4.1	100.0

Wales	Pre-1919	1919-44	1945-64	Post-1964	All ages
Terraced house	32.9	5.5	3.5	3.4	45.3
Semi-detached house	4.9	8.0	11.4	5.6	29.8
Detached house	8.0	1.9	1.9	3.6	15.3
Flat	3.7	2.2	2.0	1.6	9.5
All types	49.5	17.6	18.7	14.2	100.0

Scotland	Pre-1919	1919-44	% of whole stock 1945-64	Post-1964	All ages
Terraced house	6.0	2.2	5.6	4.1	17.9
Semi-detached house	2.1	5.0	3.8	0.4	11.3
Detached house	18.1	1.9	0.7	1.0	21.7
Converted flat	20.3	4.3	5.1	3.1	32.8
Purpose-built flat (tenement)	1.2	3.8	1.8	0.1	6.9
Purpose-built flat (4 in block)	0.0	0.0	1.9	1.5	3.4
Purpose-built flat (tower/deck)	5.7	0.4	0.0	0.0	6.1
All types	53.4	17.6	18.9	10.2	100.0

Great Britain

	Pre-1919	1919-44	1945-64	Post-1964	All ages
Terraced house	29.5	6.2	3.1	1.9	40.6
Semi-detached house	7.1	10.8	6.2	1.4	25.5
Detached house	6.3	1.4	1.4	1.8	10.9
Flat	10.6	3.2	4.5	4.4	22.7
All types	53.4	21.5	15.2	9.6	100.0

United Kingdom

	Pre-1919	1919-44	1945-64	Post-1964	All ages
Terraced house	29.3	6.2	3.1	1.9	40.5
Semi-detached house	7.1	10.7	6.2	1.4	25.4
Detached house	6.7	1.5	1.4	1.8	11.4
Flat	10.5	3.2	4.5	4.4	22.5
All types	53.7	21.5	15.2	9.5	100.0

Notes: Figures for England, Scotland and Northern Ireland are for 1991, figures for Wales are for 1993. Table includes vacant dwellings in England and Northern Ireland. Converted flats include dwellings with mixed residential/non-residential uses. Data on converted and purpose-built flats not available separately for Wales.

Sources: DoE (1993); Scottish Homes (1993); NIHE (1993): Welsh Office (1994)

Table A4.9: Tenure by country, UK (1994)

	Owner-occupied	Private rented	No of dwellings (000s) Rented from LA	Rented from HA	All dwellings
England	13,670	2,052	3,663	834	20,219
Northern Ireland	412	22	153	13	600
Wales	878	93	211	38	1,220
Scotland	1,259	149	731	72	2,211
Great Britain	15,807	2,294	4,608	944	23,653
UK	16,219	2,316	4,758	957	24,250
			% of dwellings		
England	67.6	10.1	18.1	4.1	100.0
Northern Ireland	68.7	3.7	25.5	2.2	100.0
Wales	72.0	7.6	17.3	3.1	100.0
Scotland	56.9	6.7	33.1	3.3	100.0
Great Britain	66.8	9.7	19.5	4.0	100.0
UK	66.9	9.6	19.6	3.9	100.0

Note: Increase in private owned stock in Northern Ireland from 1993-94 of 13,000 apportioned pro rata between owner-occupation and private renting.

Source: *Housing and Construction Statistics* (various years)

Table A4.10: Age of dwellings by tenure, Great Britain (1993)

	% in each age group by tenure				
	Pre-1919	1919-44	1945-64	Post-1965	All ages
Owned outright	26	24	25	25	100
With mortgage	24	23	18	35	100
LA rented	4	20	39	37	100
HA rented	25	10	10	56	100
Private rented	49	22	18	10	100
All dwellings	22	22	23	32	100
	% in each tenure by age group				
Owned outright	30	28	27	21	26
With mortgage	44	42	31	46	41
LA rented	4	20	35	26	22
HA rented	3	1	1	6	3
Private rented	19	9	6	3	9
All tenures	100	100	100	100	100

Source: OPCS (1994)

Table A4.11: Tenure by dwelling type, Great Britain (1993)

	% in each type category by tenure					
	Detached	Semi-detached	Terraced	Converted flat (1)	Purpose-built flat	All types
Owned outright	31	35	25	3	6	100
With mortgage	25	36	30	3	6	100
LA rented	1	26	33	3	37	100
HA rented	2	11	26	14	46	99
Private rented	13	18	29	26	14	100
All tenures	19	31	29	6	15	100
	% in each tenure by type					
Owned outright	41	29	22	15	11	26
With mortgage	52	47	42	25	17	41
LA rented	1	18	25	11	54	22
HA rented	0	1	3	8	10	3
Private rented	6	5	9	40	9	8
All types	100	100	101	99	101	100

Note: (1) Including with business premises.

Source: OPCS (1994)

Table A4.12: Dwellings in poor condition by tenure

| England 1991 | | % dwellings in each tenure group | | | |
		Owner-occupied	Private rented	LA rented	HA rented
Unfit	No (000s)	715	333	265	41
	%	5.5	20.5	6.9	6.7
Urgent repairs over £1,000	No (000s)	2,247	666	583	77
	%	17.3	41.0	15.1	12.7

Northern Ireland 1991					
Unfit	No (000s)	29	8	3	–
	%	8.5	27.9	2.0	2.1
Urgent repairs over £1,000	No (000s)	54	11	9	–
	%	15.5	38.9	5.6	1.4

Wales 1993					
Unfit	No (000s)	93	18	38	2
	%	11.9	25.6	15.8	6.0
Repairs over £1,500	No (000s)	156	29	42	2
	%	19.9	34.3	18.7	8.4

Scotland 1991					
BTS	No (000s)	36	19	35	18
	%	3.5	15.0	4.3	3.7
Urgent repairs over £1,000	No (000s)	53	21	32	–
	%	5.1	16.6	3.9	0.6

Note: Excludes vacant dwellings.

Sources: DoE (1993); Scottish Homes (1993); NIHE (1993); Welsh Office (1994)

Table A4.13: Poor condition dwellings by tenure (1991/93)

| Unfit/BTS | % dwellings in each country | | | | |
	Owner-occupied	Private rented	LA rented	HA rented	All tenures
England	52.8	24.6	19.6	3.0	100.0
Northern Ireland	72.2	19.6	7.6	0.5	100.0
Wales	61.6	11.8	25.1	1.4	100.0
Scotland	39.4	22.9	36.0	1.7	100.0
Disrepair					
England	62.9	18.6	16.3	2.2	100.0
Northern Ireland	68.0	10.5	20.3	1.2	100.0
Wales	67.9	12.8	18.3	1.0	100.0
Scotland	49.9	20.1	29.8	0.3	100.0

Notes: Figures for England, Scotland and Northern Ireland are for 1991, figures for Wales are for 1993. Excludes vacant dwellings.

Sources: DoE (1993); Scottish Homes (1993); NIHE (1993); Welsh Office (1994)

Table A4.14: Unfitness/BTS by age and tenure of dwelling (1991/93)

England 1991	Owner-occupied	Private rented	LA rented	HA rented	All tenures
		% of total dwelling stock			
Pre-1919	27.4	17.2	1.8	1.4	47.8
1919-44	11.8	3.2	5.4	0.5	20.9
1945+	8.5	1.8	10.5	0.8	21.6
All vacant			9.7		
All	57.4	22.2	17.7	2.7	100.0
Northern Ireland 1991					
Pre-1919	42.0	11.6	0.7	0.0	54.3
1919-44	9.6	3.2	0.8	0.2	13.8
1945+	6.8	1.1	4.6	0.2	12.7
Vacant	16.8		2.4		19.2
All	75.2	18.3	6.1	0.4	100.0
Wales 1993					
Pre-1919	37.6	9.7	1.6	0.6	49.5
1919-44	9.1	1.3	6.7	0.6	17.7
1945+	15.0	0.9	16.8	0.2	32.9
All	61.7	11.9	25.1	1.4	100.0
Scotland 1991					
Pre-1919	32.4	17.1	2.2	1.7	53.4
1919-44	3.6	2.8	11.2	0.1	17.7
1945+	3.1	1.1	24.5	0.2	28.0
All	30.1	21.0	37.9	2.0	100.0

Note: Figures for Scotland and Wales exclude vacant dwellings.

Sources: DoE (1993); Scottish Homes (1993); NIHE (1993); Welsh Office (1994)

Table A4.15: Disrepair by age and tenure of dwelling (1991/93)

England 1991	Owner-occupied	% of total dwelling stock Private rented	LA rented	HA rented	All tenures
Pre-1919	33.9	12.9	1.4	1.2	49.4
1919-44	15.5	3.1	5.4	0.3	24.3
1945+	9.7	1.5	8.5	0.5	20.2
All vacant		6.1			6.1
All	65.2	17.5	15.3	2.0	100.0

Northern Ireland 1991					
Pre-1919	36.8	8.0	0.7	0.1	45.6
1919-44	11.8	2.6	1.3	0.1	15.8
1945+	10.3	1.6	7.8	0.0	19.7
Vacant	15.1		4.0		19.1
All	74.0	16.2	9.8	0.2	100.0

Wales 1993					
Pre-1919	42.1	10.4	1.0	0.5	54.0
1919-44	10.5	1.5	3.5	0.5	16.0
1945 +	15.2	0.9	13.8	0.0	29.9
All	67.8	12.8	18.3	1.0	100.0

Scotland 1991					
Pre-1919	36.5	16.8	1.6	0.3	55.2
1919-44	8.5	2.1	11.6	0.0	22.2
1945 +	4.8	1.1	16.6	0.0	22.5
All	49.8	20.0	29.8	0.3	100.0

Note: Figures for Wales and Scotland exlude vacant dwellings.

Sources: DoE (1993); Scottish Homes (1993); NIHE (1993); Welsh Office (1994)

Table A5.1: Poor condition by income (1991/93)

Number of households in each income band (000s)

England 1991

Income band	In unfit dwellings	With urgent repair costs over £1,000	All households
Under £4,000	415	876	3,606
£4,000-£7,999	437	958	4,651
£8,000-£11,999	229	637	3,049
£12,000-£15,999	137	447	2,745
£16,000-£19,999	98	362	2,170
£20,000-£23,999	49	133	1,128
£24,000 or more	49	295	1,758

Scotland 1991

Income band	In BTS dwellings	With urgent repair costs over £1,000	All households
Under £4,000	19	16	288
£4,000-£7,999	39	36	705
£8,000-£11,999	19	20	362
£12,000-£15,999	8	17	293
£16,000-£19,999	4	5	170
£20,000-£23,999	1	5	96
£24,000 or more	1	7	120

Northern Ireland 1991

Income band	In unfit dwellings	With urgent repair costs over £1,000	All households
Under £4,000	18	27	151
£4,000-£7,999	12	27	176
£8,000-£11,999	5	11	82
£12,000-£15,999	3	5	57
£16,000-£19,999	1	3	34
£20,000-£23,999	1	2	20
£24,000 or more	1	2	25

Wales 1993

Income band	In unfit dwellings	With urgent repair costs over £1,500	All households
Under £4,000	30	42	153
£4,000-£7,999	33	43	219
£8,000-£11,999	11	19	94
£12,000-£19,999	12	21	115
£20,000-£29,999	4	11	54
£30,000 or more	3	6	41

% of households in each income band

England 1991

Income band	In unfit dwellings	With urgent repair costs over £1,000
Under £4,000	11.5	24.3
£4,000-£7,999	9.4	20.6
£8,000-£11,999	7.5	20.9
£12,000-£15,999	5.0	16.3
£16,000-£19,999	4.5	16.7
£20,000-£23,999	4.3	11.8
£24,000 or more	2.8	16.8

Scotland 1991

Income band	In BTS dwellings	With urgent repair costs over £1,000
Under £4,000	6.7	5.7
£4,000-£7,999	5.5	5.1
£8,000-£11,999	5.2	5.5
£12,000-£15,999	2.8	5.9
£16,000-£19,999	2.6	3.2
£20,000-£23,999	1.3	5.0
£24,000 or more	0.9	5.8

Northern Ireland 1991

Income band	In unfit dwellings	With urgent repair costs over £1,000
Under £4,000	12.2	18.1
£4,000-£7,999	6.8	15.1
£8,000-£11,999	5.7	14.0
£12,000-£15,999	5.6	8.7
£16,000-£19,999	2.2	9.1
£20,000-£23,999	4.6	11.5
£24,000 or more	3.4	9.3

Wales 1993

Income band	In unfit dwellings	With repair costs over £1,500
Under £4,000	19.4	27.3
£4,000-£7,999	15.0	19.5
£8,000-£11,999	11.2	20.9
£12,000-£19,999	10.1	18.4
£20,000-£29,999	7.7	20.6
£30,000 or more	6.6	13.9

Sources: DoE (1993); Scottish Homes (1993); NIHE (1993); Welsh Office (1994)

Table A5.2: Incomes of households living in poor conditions (1991/93)

Unfit/BTS

% of households by income	England	Northern Ireland	Wales (1)	Scotland
Under £4,000	29.3	45.3	32.3	21.0
£4,000-£7,999	30.9	29.3	35.5	42.2
£8,000-£11,999	16.2	11.4	11.8	20.5
£12,000-£15,999	9.7	7.9	12.9	8.9
£16,000-£19,999	6.9	1.8	4.3	4.8
£20,000-£23,999	3.4	2.2	3.2	1.4
£24,000 or more	3.5	2.1	0.0	1.2
All incomes	100.0	100.0	100.0	100.0

In disrepair (2)

Under £4,000	23.6	35.1	29.6	15.4
£4,000-£7,999	25.8	34.1	30.3	33.7
£8,000-£11,999	17.2	14.7	13.4	18.6
£12,000-£15,999	12.1	6.4	14.8	16.2
£16,000-£19,999	9.8	4.0	7.7	5.1
£20,000-£23,999	3.6	2.9	4.2	4.5
£24,000 or more	8.0	3.0	0.0	6.5
All incomes	100.0	100.0	100.0	100.0

Notes: Figures for England, Scotland and Northern Ireland are for 1991, figures for Wales are for 1993. (1) Income bands for Wales differ slightly from those for the remainder of the UK (see previous table). (2) For definition of disrepair see previous table.

Sources: DoE (1993); Scottish Homes (1993); NIHE (1993); Welsh Office (1994)

Table A5.3: Poor conditions by employment status (1991/93)

England 1991

Employment status	% in unfit dwellings	% in dwellings with urgent repair costs over £1,000
Working	5.9	18.9
Unemployed	11.6	25.3
Retired	8.2	17.7
Other	10.1	23.6

Northern Ireland 1991

Employment status	% in unfit dwellings	% in dwellings with urgent repair costs over £1,000
Working	5.5	11.9
Unemployed	7.5	14.2
Retired	10.3	17.6
Other	8.5	15.4

Scotland 1991

Employment status	% in BTS dwellings	% in dwellings with urgent repair costs over £1,000
Working	3.6	5.5
Unemployed	7.4	7.2
Retired	4.8	4.1
Other	5.9	5.6

Sources: DoE (1993); Scottish Homes (1993); NIHE (1993); Welsh Office (1994)

Table A5.4: Houesholds living in poor conditions by type (1991/93)

England 1991

Household type	% in unfit dwellings	% in dwellings with urgent repair costs over £1,000
Lone adult under 65/60	12.6	26.4
Two adults	6.2	17.1
Lone parent	5.7	19.2
Small family	4.8	17.7
Large family	7.4	21.8
3+ adults	6.6	22.1
Two pensioners	5.9	16.3
One pensioner	11.6	19.7

Northern Ireland 1991

Household type	% in unfit dwellings	% in dwellings with urgent repair costs over £1,000
Lone adult under 65/60	11.2	21.3
Two adults	6.7	10.5
Lone parent	1.4	11.5
Small family	4.2	9.1
Large family	4.9	10.1
3+ adults	6.5	18.5
Two pensioners	8.9	18.4
One pensioner	13.6	16.0

Wales 1993

Household type	% in unfit dwellings	% in dwellings with repair costs over £1,500
Lone adult under 65/60	14.0	21.0
Two adults	11.3	19.7
Lone parent	14.0	23.2
Small family	12.8	20.4
Large family	14.9	22.8
3+ adults	13.9	19.3
Two pensioners	11.5	16.8
One pensioner	15.9	21.5

Scotland 1991

Household type	% in BTS dwellings	% in dwellings with urgent repair costs over £1,000
Lone adult under 65/60	6.6	6.3
Two adults	3.6	6.2
Lone parent	5.3	6.3
Small family	3.9	4.4
Large family	3.7	6.7
3+ adults	3.9	5.6
Two pensioners	4.4	3.7
One pensioner	5.1	4.2

Sources: DoE (1993); Scottish Homes (1993); NIHE (1993); Welsh Office (1994)

Table A5.5: Households living in poor conditions by age of head of household (1991/93)

England 1991

Age of head of household	% in unfit dwellings	% in dwellings with urgent repair costs over £1,000
16-29	9.2	25.0
30-44	6.5	19.6
45-59/64	6.2	18.1
60/65-74	7.0	16.4
75+	10.9	21.5

Northern Ireland 1991

Age of head of household	% in unfit dwellings	% in dwellings with urgent repair costs over £1,000
16-29	10.2	12.1
30-44	14.6	19.3
45-59/64	28.0	29.6
60/65-74	22.8	20.7
75+	24.4	18.3

Wales 1993

Age of head of household	% in unfit dwellings	% in dwellings with repair costs over £1,500
16-29	15.3	22.3
30-44	12.7	19.5
45-59/64	11.7	18.8
60/65-74	13.4	14.8
75+	16.7	20.8

Scotland 1991

Age of head of household	% in BTS dwellings	% in dwellings with urgent repair costs over £1,000
16-29	5.9	5.3
30-44	3.8	5.7
45-59/64	4.3	5.8
60/65-74	4.6	3.7
75+	5.3	4.9

Sources: DoE (1993); Scottish Homes (1993); NIHE (1993); Welsh Office (1994)

Table A5.6: Households in unfit housing by age and gender, England (1991)

Age of head of houshold	Male headed households (000s)			Female headed households (000s)		
	In fit dwellings	In unfit dwellings	% in unfit dwellings	In fit dwellings	In unfit dwellings	% in unfit dwellings
15-19	14	11	43.8	45	3	5.5
20-24	352	62	14.9	217	15	6.6
25-29	1,051	87	7.7	265	20	7.2
30-34	1,287	119	8.5	275	21	7.0
35-39	1,463	86	5.5	187	16	8.0
40-44	1,635	91	5.3	236	21	8.3
45-49	1,478	68	4.4	176	22	11.0
50-54	1,118	57	4.8	150	25	14.1
55-59	1,070	74	6.5	174	32	15.7
60-64	1,174	78	6.2	324	28	8.0
65-69	1,071	72	6.3	298	36	10.7
70-74	1,013	60	5.6	438	42	8.8
75-79	614	67	9.8	469	60	11.3
80-84	320	34	9.6	312	35	10.2
85+	153	24	13.6	317	48	13.1
All	13,815	989	6.7	3,883	424	9.8
15-29	1,417	160	10.1	527	38	6.7
30-44	4,385	296	6.3	698	58	7.7
45-59	3,666	199	5.1	500	79	13.6
60-74	3,258	210	6.1	1,060	106	9.1
75+	1,087	125	10.3	1,098	143	11.5
All	13,815	989	6.7	3,883	424	9.8

Source: 1991 EHCS

Table A5.7: Households living in poor conditions by length of residence (1991)

England 1991

Length of residence	% in unfit dwellings	% in dwellings with urgent repair costs over £1,000
Up to 2 years	10.3	23.4
2-4 years	5.7	15.1
5-9 years	4.2	16.1
10-19 years	5.7	17.1
20 years +	11.5	28.5

Northern Ireland 1991

Length of residence	% in unfit dwellings	% in dwellings with urgent repair costs over £1,000
Up to 2 years	6.7	14.0
2-4 years	4.5	10.2
5-9 years	2.7	7.5
10-19 years	3.9	10.9
20 years +	14.2	22.7

Scotland 1991

Length of residence	% in unfit dwellings	% in dwellings with urgent repair costs over £1,000
Up to 2 years	4.3	4.9
2-4 years	3.4	5.0
5-9 years	4.7	5.4
10-19 years	4.6	5.5
20 years +	5.5	5.4

Notes: Data not available for Wales.

Sources: DoE (1993); Scottish Homes (1993); NIHE (1993)

Table A5.8: Households in unfit housing by length of residence by tenure, England (1991)

Length of residence	Owner-occupied	% households living in unfit dwellings Private rented	LA rented	HA rented	All tenures
Under 1 year	11.5	20.6	4.2	13.5	12.8
1-2 years	3.1	20.9	4.6	2.7	6.1
3-4 years	5.0	23.0	6.8	5.9	6.2
5-10 years	2.9	19.6	5.0	5.9	4.2
11-15 years	5.3	15.5	8.0	1.4	6.2
16-20 years	3.3	31.0	8.8	8.9	6.0
21-30 years	6.7	31.1	7.4	9.2	8.3
Over 30 years	12.4	41.1	11.0	23.3	15.8
All	5.3	24.8	6.8	7.0	7.4
In unfit dwellings (000s)	684	421	262	46	1,414
All owners (000s)	12,872	1,700	3,877	662	19,111

Source: 1991 EHCS

Table A5.9: Households living in poor conditions by ethnic origin of head of household (1991)

Ethnic origin of head of household	% in unfit dwellings	% in dwellings with urgent repair costs over £1,000
England		
White	7.2	19.0
Black	14.9	28.5
Asian	9.9	32.2
Other	10.3	28.2
Scotland		
White	4.5	5.2
Black	–	–
Asian	10.3	9.7
Other	7.6	4.1

Note: Data on ethnic origin not available for Wales and Northern Ireland.

Sources: DoE (1993); Scottish Homes (1993)

Table A5.10: Households living in unfit/BTS housing by income and tenure (1991/93)

Income	Owner-occupied	% of all households in unfit/BTS dwellings Private rented	LA rented	HA rented	All tenures
England 1991					
Under £8,000	21.9	20.2	15.6	2.7	60.4
£8,000-£15,999	16.3	6.4	2.7	0.3	25.7
£16,000 or more	10.2	3.2	0.2	0.3	13.9
All households	48.4	29.8	18.5	3.3	100.0
Northern Ireland 1991					
Under £8,000	53.1	15.2	5.5	0.6	74.4
£8,000-£15,999	14.8	2.7	1.9	0.0	19.4
£16,000 or more	4.9	1.2	0.2	0.0	6.3
All households	72.8	19.1	7.6	0.6	100.0
Wales 1993					
Under £8,000	33.0	8.8	25.3	1.3	68.4
£8,000-£19,999	17.6	2.8	3.3	0.4	24.1
£20,000 or more	6.0	0.2	1.4	0.0	7.6
All households	56.6	11.8	30.0	1.7	100.0
Scotland 1991					
Under £8,000	19.8	14.5	27.4	1.7	63.4
£8,000-£15,999	13.4	5.8	9.7	0.3	29.2
£16,000 or more	5.9	0.6	0.9	0.0	7.4
All households	39.1	20.9	38.0	2.0	100.0

Note: Income bands differ slightly for Wales.

Sourooo: DoE (1993), Scottish Homes (1993); NIHE (1993); Welsh Office (1994)

Table A5.11: Households living in housing in disrepair by income and tenure (1991/93)

Income	Owner-occupied	Private rented	LA rented	HA rented	All tenures
		% of all households in dwellings in disrepair			
England 1991					
Under £8,000	21.4	12.9	12.7	2.4	49.4
£8,000-£15,999	19.6	6.0	3.3	0.3	29.2
£16,000 or more	18.4	2.5	0.3	0.1	21.3
All households	59.4	21.4	16.3	2.8	100.0
		% of all households in unfit/BTS dwellings			
Northern Ireland 1991					
Under £8,000	47.4	12.1	10.2	0.1	69.8
£8,000-£15,999	17.8	1.3	1.4	0.0	20.5
£16,000 or more	8.0	1.7	0.0	0.0	9.7
All households	73.2	15.1	11.6	0.1	100.0
Wales 1993					
Under £8,000	30.7	8.3	19.3	1.2	59.5
£8,000-£19,999	21.6	3.7	3.0	0.3	28.6
£20,000 or more	10.2	0.8	0.8	0.0	11.8
All households	62.5	12.8	23.1	1.5	100.0
Scotland 1991					
Under £8,000	13.5	13.6	21.8	0.3	49.2
£8,000-£15,999	21.4	5.8	7.5	0.0	34.7
£16,000 or more	15.0	0.7	0.5	0.0	16.2
All households	49.9	20.1	29.8	0.3	100.0

Note: Income bands differ slightly for Wales.

Sources: DoE (1993); Scottish Homes (1993); NIHE (1993); Welsh Office (1994)

Table A7.1: Slum clearance, Great Britain and UK (1969-93)

No of dwellings demolished

Year	England	Wales	Scotland	Great Britain	Northern Ireland	UK
1969	70,296	2,404	17,847	90,547	na	na
1970	68,691	2,427	17,345	88,463	na	na
1971	72,050	2,671	20,554	95,275	na	na
1972	68,205	2,029	18,518	88,752	na	na
1973	62,478	2,442	14,745	79,665	na	na
1974	40,860	1,166	12,024	54,050	na	na
1975	51,162	1,878	10,021	63,061	428	63,489
1976	44,956	1,281	6,370	52,607	1,573	54,180
1977	38,899	1,379	4,977	45,255	715	45,970
1978	32,384	1,581	3,814	37,779	2,363	40,142
1979	28,674	1,345	6,653	36,672	1,776	38,448
1980	28,315	1,232	5,815	35,362	1,403	36,765
1981	22,585	900	4,975	28,460	906	29,366
1982	16,019	1,089	3,703	20,811	2,130	22,941
1983	11,100	522	1,987	13,609	2,276	15,885
1984	9,751	568	1,736	12,055	2,071	14,126
1985	8,604	516	1,615	10,735	2,044	12,779
1986	6,744	282	1,735	8,761	2,016	10,777
1987	6,402	281	1,801	8,484	1,805	10,289
1988	5,237	272	1,175	6,684	1,873	8,557
1989	5,936	221	1,007	7,164	1,540	8,704
1990	5,934	276	2,224	8,434	1,122	9,556
1991	2,222	161	1,816	4,199	1,012	5,211
1992	1,988	84	3,685	5,757	607	6,364
1993	3,856	206	4,311	8,373	877	9,250
1994	–		–	–	617	617
Total 1969-93	713,348	27,213	170,453	911,014	29,154	443,416

Note: Data up to 1972 is for calendar years; after 1972 for financial years.

Source: *Housing and Construction Statistics* (various years)

Table A7.2: Grants by type, England (1969-94)

Year	Improvement	Intermediate	Repair	New system excluding MWA	Total
No of grants					
1969	20,125	48,274	0		68,399
1970	26,097	45,196	0		71,293
1971	44,428	46,439	0		90,867
1972	78,542	45,634	0		124,176
1973	128,381	37,577	0		165,958
1974	164,525	27,823	0		192,348
1975	72,966	12,368	59		85,393
1976	57,784	10,849	85		68,718
1977	47,788	9,037	130		56,955
1978	49,496	7,940	218		57,654
1979	57,222	7,792	345		65,359
1980	65,809	8,143	513		74,465
1981	49,145	14,743	5,053		68,941
1982	54,732	20,600	28,696		104,028
1983	79,531	27,236	113,065		219,832
1984	83,958	29,003	116,146		229,107
1985	52,989	29,012	54,411		136,412
1986	46,994	24,629	41,705		113,328
1987	49,383	19,661	39,864		108,908
1988	48,213	17,107	39,983		105,303
1989	48,711	14,027	35,479		98,217
1990	51,028	12,688	25,361	896	89,973
1991	15,475	4,230	6,509	29,625	55,839
1992	2,464	671	744	51,028	54,907
1993	400	129	131	54,251	54,911
1994	135	40	20	60,521	60,716
Total	1,396,321	520,848	508,517	196,321	2,622,007
% of grants					
1969	29.4	70.6	0.0		100.0
1970	36.6	63.4	0.0		100.0
1971	48.9	51.1	0.0		100.0
1972	63.3	36.7	0.0		100.0
1973	77.4	22.6	0.0		100.0
1974	85.5	14.5	0.0		100.0
1975	85.4	14.5	0.1		100.0
1976	84.1	15.8	0.1		100.0
1977	83.9	15.9	0.2		100.0
1978	85.9	13.8	0.4		100.0
1979	87.6	11.9	0.5		100.0
1980	88.4	10.9	0.7		100.0
1981	71.3	21.4	7.3		100.0
1982	52.6	19.8	27.6		100.0
1983	36.2	12.4	51.4		100.0
1984	36.6	12.7	50.7		100.0
1985	38.8	21.3	39.9		100.0
1986	41.5	21.7	36.8		100.0
1987	45.3	18.1	36.6		100.0
1988	45.8	16.2	38.0		100.0
1989	49.6	14.3	36.1		100.0
1990	56.7	14.1	28.2	1.0	100.0
1991	27.7	7.6	11.7	53.1	100.0
1992	4.5	1.2	1.4	92.9	100.0
1993	0.7	0.2	0.2	98.8	100.0
1994	0.2	0.1	0.0	99.7	100.0
Total	53.3	19.9	19.4	7.5	100.0

Table A7.3: Grants by type, Wales (1969-94)

Year	Improvement	Intermediate	Repair	New system excluding MWA	Total
			No of grants		
1969	3,173	2,037	0		5,210
1970	3,698	2,179	0		5,877
1971	4,509	2,285	0		6,794
1972	10,082	2,850	0		12,932
1973	15,828	2,412	0		18,240
1974	22,363	2,365	0		24,728
1975	6,694	632	30		7,356
1976	5,954	528	75		6,557
1977	6,515	388	114		7,017
1978	5,373	414	144		5,931
1979	5,569	399	148		6,116
1980	6,789	412	147		7,348
1981	5,511	780	809		7,100
1982	5,050	1,236	4,703		10,989
1983	7,231	1,689	18,403		27,323
1984	8,337	2,640	19,001		29,978
1985	4,809	3,512	8,831		17,152
1986	3,984	3,584	11,003		18,571
1987	4,477	3,485	11,135		19,097
1988	5,144	3,100	11,943		20,187
1989	5,722	2,776	11,708		20,206
1990	6,498	2,385	16,229	58	25,170
1991	3,061	1,017	6,006	4,269	14,353
1992	416	287	516	10,453	11,672
1993	64	12	33	11,190	11,299
1994	101	10	38	9,846	10,001
Total	156,952	43,420	121,016	35,816	357,204
			% of grants		
1969	60.9	39.1	0.0		100.0
1970	62.9	37.1	0.0		100.0
1971	66.4	33.6	0.0		100.0
1972	78.0	22.0	0.0		100.0
1973	86.8	13.2	0.0		100.0
1974	90.4	9.6	0.0		100.0
1975	91.0	8.6	0.4		100.0
1976	90.8	8.1	1.1		100.0
1977	92.8	5.5	1.6		100.0
1978	90.6	7.0	2.4		100.0
1979	91.1	6.5	2.4		100.0
1980	92.4	5.6	2.0		100.0
1981	77.6	11.0	11.4		100.0
1982	46.0	11.2	42.8		100.0
1983	26.5	6.2	67.4		100.0
1984	27.8	8.8	63.4		100.0
1985	28.0	20.5	51.5		100.0
1986	21.5	19.3	59.2		100.0
1987	23.4	18.2	58.3		100.0
1988	25.5	15.4	59.2		100.0
1989	28.3	13.7	57.9		100.0
1990	25.8	9.5	64.5	0.2	100.0
1991	21.3	7.1	41.8	29.7	100.0
1992	3.6	2.5	4.4	89.6	100.0
1993	0.6	0.1	0.3	99.0	100.0
1994	1.0	0.2	0.4	98.5	100.0
Total	43.9	12.2	33.9	10.0	100.0

Table A7.4: Grants by type, Scotland (1969-94) (1969-73 all types combined)

Year	Improvement	Intermediate	Repair	Total
	No of grants			
1969	–	1,078	0	1,078
1970	48	1,272	0	1,320
1971	3,640	5,145	0	8,785
1972	6,964	9,183	0	16,147
1973	13,694	15,437	0	29,131
1974	26,736	1,977	0	28,713
1975	8,875	549	0	9,424
1976	6,694	511	1	7,206
1977	6,809	239	3	7,051
1978	6,625	206	9	6,840
1979	7,831	170	718	8,719
1980	10,353	173	2,894	13,420
1981	12,804	152	5,080	18,036
1982	15,376	313	8,268	23,957
1983	15,780	423	29,295	45,498
1984	18,179	1,185	41,297	60,661
1985	17,004	1,242	28,040	46,286
1986	11,289	738	19,426	31,453
1987	11,345	560	18,763	30,668
1988	10,999	363	20,150	31,512
1989	9,902	294	16,719	26,915
1990	9,054	358	14,174	23,586
1991	9,826	323	13,329	23,478
1992	9,812	308	14,778	24,898
1993	8,904	292	11,998	21,194
1994	9,176	244	11,757	21,177
1969-94	243,373	10,620	256,699	567,153
	% of grants			
1969	0.0	100.0	0.0	100.0
1970	3.6	96.4	0.0	100.0
1971	41.4	58.6	0.0	100.0
1972	43.1	56.9	0.0	100.0
1973	47.0	53.0	0.0	100.0
1974	93.1	6.9	0.0	100.0
1975	94.2	5.8	0.0	100.0
1976	92.9	7.1	0.0	100.0
1977	96.6	3.4	0.0	100.0
1978	96.9	3.0	0.1	100.0
1979	89.8	1.9	8.2	100.0
1980	77.1	1.3	21.6	100.0
1981	71.0	0.8	28.2	100.0
1982	64.2	1.3	34.5	100.0
1983	34.7	0.9	64.4	100.0
1984	30.0	2.0	68.1	100.0
1985	36.7	2.7	60.6	100.0
1986	35.9	2.3	61.8	100.0
1987	37.0	1.8	61.2	100.0
1988	34.9	1.2	63.9	100.0
1989	36.8	1.1	62.1	100.0
1990	38.4	1.5	60.1	100.0
1991	41.7	1.4	56.8	100.0
1992	39.4	1.2	59.4	100.0
1993	42.0	1.4	56.6	100.0
1994	43.3	1.2	55.5	100.0
1969-94	47.8	2.1	50.3	100.0

Table A7.5: Grants by type, Northern Ireland (1969-94)

Year	Improvement	Intermediate	Repair	New system excluding MWA	Total
			No of grants		
1973	1,293	1,053	0		2,346
1974	1,153	500	0		1,653
1975	1,106	434	0		1,540
1976	1,908	597	0		2,505
1977	1,853	334	12,943		15,130
1978	3,351	320	18,800		22,471
1979	4,219	288	22,700		27,207
1980	5,788	305	18,132		24,225
1981	4,999	322	18,290		23,611
1982	4,538	274	19,774		24,586
1983	4,308	247	19,828		24,383
1984	4,849	279	21,993		27,121
1985	4,936	248	18,690		23,874
1986	5,017	197	13,984		19,198
1987	4,415	174	7,296		11,885
1988	3,731	162	7,025		10,918
1989	3,111	139	4,594		7,844
1990	2,717	122	4,007		6,846
1991	2,672	92	3,780		6,544
1992	2,520	98	2,663		5,281
1993	2,454	96	2,271	632	5,453
1994	1,209	19	763	4,922	6,913
Total	72,147	6,300	217,533	5,554	301,534
			% of grants		
1973	55.1	44.9	0.0		100.0
1974	69.8	30.2	0.0		100.0
1975	71.8	28.2	0.0		100.0
1976	76.2	23.8	0.0		100.0
1977	12.2	2.2	85.5		100.0
1978	14.9	1.4	83.7		100.0
1979	15.5	1.1	83.4		100.0
1980	23.9	1.3	74.8		100.0
1981	21.2	1.4	77.5		100.0
1982	18.5	1.1	80.4		100.0
1983	17.7	1.0	81.3		100.0
1984	17.9	1.0	81.1		100.0
1985	20.7	1.0	78.3		100.0
1986	26.1	1.0	72.8		100.0
1987	37.1	1.5	61.4		100.0
1988	34.2	1.5	64.3		100.0
1989	39.7	1.8	58.6		100.0
1990	39.7	1.8	58.5		100.0
1991	40.8	1.4	57.8		100.0
1992	47.7	1.9	50.4		100.0
1993	45.0	1.8	41.6	11.6	100.0
1994	17.5	0.3	11.0	71.2	100.0
Total	23.9	2.1	72.1	1.8	100.0

Note: Data for 1973-76 is for approvals, supplied by NIHE.

Source: *Housing and Construction Statistics* (various years)

Table A7.6: Grants per 1,000 privately owned dwellings, UK (1969-94)

Year	England	Wales	Scotland	Northern Ireland
1969	6.0	7.6	1.2	–
1970	6.2	8.6	1.5	–
1971	7.8	9.8	5.9	–
1972	10.5	18.4	10.6	–
1973	13.9	25.5	17.9	7.7
1974	16.0	34.2	33.2	5.4
1975	7.1	10.1	10.9	5.0
1976	5.6	8.9	8.2	8.2
1977	4.6	9.5	8.0	49.6
1978	4.6	7.9	7.6	73.7
1979	5.2	8.1	9.6	89.2
1980	5.8	9.7	14.5	79.4
1981	5.3	8.9	19.9	77.4
1982	7.8	13.4	25.8	79.3
1983	16.1	32.8	47.5	76.0
1984	17.1	36.2	61.7	82.2
1985	10.0	20.4	45.8	68.6
1986	8.2	21.8	30.3	53.3
1987	7.7	22.1	28.7	32.1
1988	7.3	22.9	28.4	28.8
1989	6.6	22.3	23.1	20.0
1990	6.0	27.5	19.4	16.9
1991	3.7	15.2	18.3	15.9
1992	3.6	12.3	18.7	12.5
1993	3.6	11.8	15.5	12.6
1994	3.9	10.3	15.0	15.5

Note: Includes improvement and conversion grants, repair grants, intermediate and standard grants, renovation grants, disabled facilities grants, common parts grants and HMO grants.

Source: *Housing and Construction Statistics* (various years)

Table A7.7: Grants under the old system by type

	% of all grants			
	Improvement	Intermediate	Repair	All types
England	57.6	21.5	21.0	100.0
Northern Ireland	23.2	1.3	75.5	100.0
Wales	48.8	13.5	37.7	100.0
Scotland	47.7	2.1	50.3	100.0

Source: *Housing and Construction Statistics* (various years)

Table A7.8: Grants under the new system by type (1994)

	% of all grants						
	Renovation		Disabled facilities		HMO	Common parts	All except MWA	MWA as % of all
	Mand	Dis	Mand	Dis	All	All		
England	54.3	7.8	33.7	0.8	2.6	0.7	100.0	34.0
Wales	66.0	3.7	24.0	2.7	3.2	0.4	100.0	31.0

Note: Mand: Mandatory; Dis: Discretionary. Northern Ireland has been omitted from the table as the information available does not cover disabled facilities grants.

Source: *Housing and Construction Statistics* (various years)

Table A7.9: Renovation grants under the new system, England

Number of grants

	Renovation		Disabled facilities		MWA	HMO	Common parts	All except MWA	All including MWA
	Mandatory	Discretionary	Mandatory	Discretionary					
1990	259	255	360	13	6,667	5	4	896	7,563
1991	14,995	3,207	10,792	180	29,325	383	68	29,625	58,950
1992	29,166	5,123	15,453	285	28,153	839	162	51,028	79,181
1993	30,705	4,937	16,724	434	25,846	1,195	256	54,251	80,097
1994	32,866	4,739	20,409	501	30,522	1,584	422	60,251	91,043

Value of grants (£000s)

	Renovation		Disabled facilities		MWA	HMO	Common parts	All except MWA	All including MWA
	Mandatory	Discretionary	Mandatory	Discretionary					
1990	1,144	309	656	37	3,541	29	16	2,191	5,732
1991	124,771	12,538	31,905	624	17,119	2,216	511	172,565	189,684
1992	289,640	21,027	57,723	1,321	18,014	7,022	983	377,716	395,730
1993	316,564	23,121	68,633	1,190	17,323	12,237	2,711	424,456	441,779
1994	340,094	22,706	85,507	1,104	21,306	14,592	2,805	466,808	488,114

Value of grants (£000s 1993/93 prices)

	Renovation		Disabled facilities		MWA	HMO	Common parts	All except MWA	All including MWA
	Mandatory	Discretionary	Mandatory	Discretionary					
1990	1,303	352	747	42	4,034	33	18	2,496	6,530
1991	133,728	13,438	34,195	669	18,348	2,375	548	184,953	203,301
1992	298,671	21,683	59,523	1,362	18,576	7,241	1,014	389,494	408,069
1993	316,564	23,121	68,633	1,190	17,323	12,237	2,711	424,456	441,779
1994	333,378	22,258	83,818	1,082	20,885	14,304	2,750	457,590	478,475

Average grant (£)

	Renovation		Disabled facilities		MWA	HMO	Common parts
	Mandatory	Discretionary	Mandatory	Discretionary			
1990	4,417	1,212	1,822	2,846	531	5,800	4,000
1991	8,321	3,910	2,956	3,467	584	5,786	7,515
1992	9,931	4,104	3,735	4,635	640	8,369	6,068
1993	10,310	4,683	4,104	2,742	670	10,240	10,590
1994	10,348	4,791	4,190	2,204	698	9,212	6,647

Average grant (£ 1993/94 prices)

	Renovation		Disabled facilities		MWA	HMO	Common parts
	Mandatory	Discretionary	Mandatory	Discretionary			
1990	5,032	1,380	2,076	3,242	605	6,607	4,557
1991	8,918	4,190	3,169	3,716	626	6,201	8,054
1992	10,240	4,232	3,852	4,780	660	8,630	6,257
1993	10,310	4,683	4,104	2,742	670	10,240	10,590
1994	10,144	4,697	4,107	2,160	684	9,030	6,516

Source: *Housing and Construction Statistics* (various years)

Table A7.10: Renovation grants under the new system, Wales

Number of grants

	Renovation		Disabled facilities		MWA	HMO	Common parts	All except MWA	All including MWA
	Mandatory	Discretionary	Mandatory	Discretionary					
1990	30	1	26	1	1,352	0	0	58	1,410
1991	2,609	419	1,124	42	6,744	69	6	4,269	11,013
1992	7,524	539	2,042	123	4,957	216	9	10,453	15,410
1993	7,892	380	2,331	310	4,768	249	28	11,190	15,958
1994	6,503	364	2,365	266	4,332	311	37	9,846	14,178

Value of grants (£000s)

	Renovation		Disabled facilities		MWA	HMO	Common parts	All except MWA	All including MWA
	Mandatory	Discretionary	Mandatory	Discretionary					
1990	290	5	45	8	828	0	0	348	1,176
1991	36,654	3,203	4,322	154	4,874	827	38	45,198	50,072
1992	124,726	6,328	9,068	449	3,643	2,886	85	143,542	147,185
1993	140,258	7,704	11,052	1,210	4,015	3,390	133	163,747	167,762
1994	121,303	6,488	10,699	1,069	3,789	4,731	278	144,568	148,357

Value of grants (£000s 1993/94 prices)

	Renovation		Disabled facilities		MWA	HMO	Common parts	All except MWA	All including MWA
	Mandatory	Discretionary	Mandatory	Discretionary					
1990	330	6	51	9	943	0	0	396	1,340
1991	39,285	3,433	4,632	165	5,224	886	41	48,443	53,667
1992	128,615	6,525	9,351	463	3,757	2,976	88	148,018	151,774
1993	140,258	7,704	11,052	1,210	4,015	3,390	133	163,747	167,762
1994	118,908	6,360	10,488	1,048	3,714	4,638	273	141,713	145,427

Average grant (£)

	Renovation		Disabled facilities		MWA	HMO	Common parts
	Mandatory	Discretionary	Mandatory	Discretionary			
1990	9,667	5,000	1,731	8,000	612	0	0
1991	14,049	7,644	3,845	3,667	723	11,986	6,333
1992	16,577	11,740	4,441	3,650	735	13,361	9,444
1993	17,772	20,274	4,741	3,903	842	13,614	4,750
1994	18,653	17,824	4,524	4,019	875	15,212	7,514

Average grant (£ 1993/94 prices)

	Renovation		Disabled facilities		MWA	HMO	Common parts
	Mandatory	Discretionary	Mandatory	Discretionary			
1990	11,012	5,696	1,972	9,114	698	0	0
1991	15,058	8,193	4,121	3,930	775	12,846	6,788
1992	17,094	12,106	4,579	3,764	758	13,778	9,739
1993	17,772	20,274	4,741	3,903	842	13,614	4,750
1994	18,285	17,472	4,435	3,939	857	14,912	7,365

Source: *Housing and Construction Statistics* (various years)

Table A7.11: Renovation grants under the new system, Northern Ireland

Number of grants

	Renovation		Replacement	Repairs	MWA	HMO	Common parts	All except MWA	All including MWA
	Mandatory	Discretionary							
1993	30	19	3	580	324	0	0	632	956
1994	898	296	37	3,677	1,453	14	0	4,922	6,375

Source: *Housing and Construction Statistics* (various years)

Table A7.12: Minor works assistance by type, England (1990-94)

Year	Thermal insulation		Patch and mend (1)		Staying put (2)		Elderly adaptation (3)		Lead pipes (4)		All minor works	
	No	%	No	%	No	%	No	%	No	%	No	%
1990/91	5,512	35.9	1	0.0	9,454	61.5	407	2.6			15,374	100.0
1991/92	5,823	20.7	118	0.4	21,934	78.1	208	0.7			28,083	100.0
1992/93	5,309	19.3	21	0.1	21,749	79.2	384	1.4			27,463	100.0
1993/94	4,080	14.2	125	0.4	24,121	83.7	210	0.7	284	1.0	28,820	100.0

Notes: (1) Grant for a temporary improvement to a property which is in a clearance area or will be within 12 months. (2) Repairs, improvements or adaptations to properties owned or tenanted by a person aged 60 or more. (3) Adaptations to property to enable an older person, not the owner or tenant, who is or who proposes to be resident in the property to be cared for by a friend or relative. (4) Replacement of lead water service pipes (introduced from September 1992).

Table A7.13: Average value of improvement and mandatory renovation grants (1979-94)

| | Average grant values (constant 1993/94 prices) | | | | | |
| | Old system | | | | New system | |
	England	Wales	Scotland	Northern Ireland	England	Wales
1979	4,074	4,423	3,575	–	–	–
1980	3,810	4,078	3,398	–	–	–
1981	4,587	4,291	3,231	–	–	–
1982	6,001	5,525	4,050	8,925	–	–
1983	6,769	6,538	5,848	10,446	–	–
1984	7,923	7,975	4,803	11,049	–	–
1985	7,823	6,980	4,429	10,886	–	–
1986	6,571	6,181	6,668	10,771	–	–
1987	5,687	5,938	6,886	9,847	–	–
1988	5,211	5,568	7,568	8,881	–	–
1989	4,749	5,034	7,779	9,553	–	–
1990	4,524	5,037	7,687	9,569	5,032	11,012
1991	6,308	6,840	7,776	9,819	8,918	15,058
1992	6,708	6,581	6,860	9,694	10,240	17,094
1993	–	–	7,353	–	10,310	17,772
1994	–	–	6,742	–	10,144	18,285

Notes: Average grant amounts for Northern Ireland under new system not available. Average amounts for 1985 Act grants not shown after 1992 for England, Wales and Northern Ireland due to small numbers.

Source: *Housing and Construction Statistics* (various years); NIHE; Scottish Homes

Table A7.14: Declared renewal areas in England at end of March 1995

Area	LA	Declaration date	Dwellings in area
Castleton	Rochdale	14-Aug-90	1,575
Whitworth Road	Rochdale	14-Aug-90	1,366
Hyde	Tameside	11-Sep-90	3,102
Shelton	Stoke-on-Trent	22-Oct-90	2,229
Smawthorne	Wakefield	21-Nov-90	2,015
Daneshill	Leicester	29-Nov-90	534
Westcotes	Leicester	29-Nov-90	720
Monega	Newham	06-Dec-90	2,350
Sutton Village	St Helens	18-Dec-90	750
Easton	Bristol	01-Jan-91	2,630
North Saltley	Birmingham	14-Jan-91	1,920
South Saltley	Birmingham	14-Jan-91	1,673
Sparkbrook	Birmingham	14-Jan-91	1,166
Handsworth	Birmingham	14-Jan-91	2,800
Cape Hill	Sandwell	18-Jan-91	2,671
Rumworth	Bolton	30-Jan-91	2,654
Darnall	Sheffield	06-Feb-91	1,259
Trees	Rossendale	06-Feb-91	379
New Brighton South	Wirral	28-Feb-91	1,086
Rock Ferry West	Wirral	28-Feb-91	440
North Reddish	Stockport	13-Mar-91	4,535
Forest Town	Mansfield	01-Apr-91	340
Willow Green	Leicester	22-Apr-91	764
Seacombe	Wirral	21-May-91	1,388
East Accrington	Hyndburn	23-May-91	1,582
New Brighton North	Wirral	17-Jun-91	940
Rock Ferry East	Wirral	22-Jun-91	860
Brookhouse/Bastwell	Blackburn	01-Jul-91	3,250
Rugby	Rugby	30-Jul-91	1,360
Central	Burnley	18-Sep-91	1,652
Radcliffe	Bury	25-Sep-91	2,373
Haslingden No 1	Rossendale	13-Oct-91	1,282
Whitehaven	Copeland	22-Oct-91	1,050
Burngreave	Sheffield	30-Oct-91	1,656
Halliwell	Bolton	05-Nov-91	3,438
Hirst	Wansbeck	01-Dec-91	2,747
Sharrow	Sheffield	05-Feb-92	2,700
Southfield, Nelson	Pendle	04-Mar-92	1,388
Chesterton/Helena	Newham	17-Mar-92	620
Linacre	Sefton	24-Mar-92	1,200
Whitchurch	North Shropshire	30-Mar-92	1,162
Gorton	Manchester	15-Apr-92	2,177
Ermine Road	Chester	22-Apr-92	335
West Accrington/ Scatcliffe	Hyndburn	24-Apr-92	1,558
The Measham	North West Leicester	28-Apr-92	492
All Saints	Wolverhampton	29-Apr-92	533
Poulton	Wirral	21-May-92	1,506
The Pear Tree	Derby	09-Jun-92	2,598
Central	Middlesbrough	01-Jul-92	440
Charterhouse	Coventry	08-Sep-92	1,395
Smawthorne Central/ Glasshoughton	Wakefield	17-Sep-92	1,399
Western Road	Leicester	29-Oct-92	590
Alexandra	Chester	18-Nov-92	480
Stonebridge	Chester	18-Nov-92	358

Grasslot	Allerdale	27-Jan-93	336
Mossbay	Allerdale	27-Jan-93	361
Barton/Treadworth	Gloucester	01-Mar-93	2,876
Plashet	Newham	19-Apr-93	2,084
Ribblebank	Preston	21-Apr-93	733
Gorse Hill	Trafford	27-Apr-93	1,790
Murray Street	Hartlepool	01-May-93	835
Willow Brook	Leicester	01-May-93	1,048
Whitmore Reans	Wolverhampton	05-May-93	1,866
Caldmore/Palfrey	Walsall	12-May-93	2,228
Eccles	Salford	14-Jun-93	2,805
East Wigan and Ince	Wigan	30-Jun-93	1,193
Lye	Dudley	29-Jul-93	1,047
Central	Barrow	07-Sep-93	1,401
North Belgrave Phase 1	Leicester	30-Sep-93	920
Cobridge	Stoke-on-Trent	30-Sep-93	2,723
Westwood & Colhurst	Oldham	01-Oct-93	2,282
Morecambe West End	Lancaster	13-Oct-93	2,676
East Chorley	Chorley	02-Nov-93	827
Manningham	Bradford	16-Nov-93	2,000
Scotswood	Newcastle	01-Dec-93	791
Newgate Lane	Mansfield	15-Dec-93	821
Newtown/Nichols' Town/Radcliffe	Southampton	19-Jan-94	1,567
Clerk Green	Kirklees	18-Mar-94	886
St Agnes/Werburghs	Bristol	01-Apr-94	na
Boundary	Sefton	23-Jun-94	1,250
Lawkholm	Bradford	01-Jul-94	1,300
Shirebrook	Bolsover	04-Jul-94	817
Bengeworth	Wychavon	01-Nov-94	841
Total dwellings			**125,563**
Average number of dwellings			**1,495**

Note: Where only the month of declaration is known, declaration is assumed to have taken place on the 1st of the month.

Table A7.15: Declared renewal areas in Wales at end of March 1995

Area	LA	Declaration date	Dwellings in area
Renewal areas			
Holyhead	Ynys Mon	Jul-91	1,685
South Riverside	Cardiff	Oct-91	2,314
West Rhyl	Rhuddlan	Mar-92	1,671
Coronation Road	Newport	Sep-92	857
Rhosllanerchrugog	Wrexham	Nov-92	1,371
Bethesda	Arfon	Mar-93	1,156
Colwyn Bay	Colwyn	Nov-93	1,380
Blaenau Ffestiniog	Meirionnydd	Sep-94	1,343
Penmaenmawr	Aberconwy	Nov-94	561
Smithfield	Wrexham	Dec-94	1,118
South Barry	Vale of Glamorgan	Mar-95	310
Ammanford	Dinefwr	Mar-95	1,000
South Llanelli	Llanelli	Mar-95	1,256
Valleys Action Programme Areas			
Trehafod	Rhonnda & Taff Ely	Dec-91	520
Oakdale	Islwn	Jan-92	620
Abertysswg	Rhymney Valley	Apr-92	556
Llanhileth	Blaenau Gwent	Jun-92	718
Tiryberth	Rhymney Valley	Nov-94	258
Rural Renewal Areas			
Llanfyllin	Montgomery	Nov-92	225
Amlwch	Ynys Mon	Nov-92	353
	Total dwellings		**19,272**
	Average number of dwellings		**964**

Source: Welsh Office

Table A7.16: Size distribution of declared renewal areas, England and Wales

	Number of renewal areas	
No dwellings	**England**	**Wales**
Up to 499	11	4
500-999	18	6
1,000-1,499	20	7
1,500-1,999	11	2
2,000-2,499	9	1
2,500-2,999	11	0
3,000-3,499	3	0
3,500 or more	1	0
Average	**1,495**	**964**

Table A7.17: Changing proportion of spending in renewal areas by programme

				% of spending			
Year	Demolition	Grants	Group repair	Acquisition land/ buildings	Environment	HA/ private rehab	Total
1990/91	39.0	4.0	27.0	2.0	8.0	20.0	100.0
1991/92	11.0	23.0	10.0	42.0	6.0	7.0	100.0
1992/93	8.0	28.0	5.0	46.0	5.0	8.0	100.0
1993/94	13.0	29.0	10.0	38.0	5.0	4.0	100.0

Table A7.18: Housing action area improvements by source, Scotland (1979-95)

Period	LA	HA	% of grant Owner-occupier	Private landlord	Other	All improved
1979-92	9.5	47.8	24.9	14.7	3.2	34,200
1992-95	0.9	25.9	52.7	20.0	0.6	3,637
Total	8.7	45.7	27.5	15.2	2.9	37,837

Table A7.19: Renovations to local authority stock (1969-94)

Year	England	Wales	Scotland	Northern Ireland
1969	26,560	2,809	11,067	na
1970	40,357	1,603	17,508	na
1971	59,144	1,994	27,756	na
1972	97,482	6,516	32,681	na
1973	110,053	7,874	70,147	237
1974	73,494	3,820	43,814	1,025
1975	36,163	943	24,734	835
1976	38,983	18	35,760	1,615
1977	37,551	2,000	56,402	1,363
1978	60,871	2,000	44,770	842
1979	75,967	2,000	34,805	1,064
1980	77,275	2,000	22,282	7,892
1981	52,931	2,000	26,065	59,609
1982	57,722	2,000	51,214	43,581
1983	85,461	2,000	41,583	14,008
1984	86,612	2,390	33,774	50,382
1985	96,482	1,728	58,993	17,496
1986	133,661	2,788	71,397	23,262
1987	148,362	5,886	86,912	40,282
1988	169,001	8,333	72,373	28,458
1989	194,928	8,444	53,699	14,163
1990	231,828	10,843	83,931	9,072
1991	184,762	10,513	69,673	9,542
1992	177,233	9,491	80,155	8,912
1993	248,722	23,264	93,038	6,346
1994	297,737	20,397	95,967	8,309

Notes: England: data for 1969-77 is for approvals; Wales: data not available 1977-83; Scotland: all data is for approvals; Northern Ireland: data not available 1969-81.

Sources: *Housing and Construction Statistics* (various years); Northern Ireland Annual Abstract of Statistics (various years)

Table A7.20: Average value of local authority renovation, housing association renovation and private sector grants, 1993/94 prices, England (1979-94)

Year	LA	£ HA	Private grants
1979	10,667	26,568	4,074
1980	–	26,254	3,810
1981	–	30,612	4,587
1982	–	28,291	6,001
1983	5,712	28,552	6,769
1984	7,702	25,944	7,923
1985	6,688	23,291	7,823
1986	5,937	23,111	6,571
1987	4,756	23,179	5,687
1988	4,498	24,882	5,211
1989	4,154	21,601	4,749
1990	3,749	23,747	5,032
1991	3,550	32,506	8,918
1992	3,021	32,368	10,240
1993	2,270	38,597	10,310
1994	2,168	30,820	10,144

Note: Private sector grants are all improvement, repair and intermediate grants 1979-89; and renovation grants 1990-94.
Source: *Housing and Construction Statistics* (various years)

Table A7.21: Renovations to housing association stock (1969-94)

Year	England	Wales	Scotland	Northern Ireland
1969	1,457	0	5	–
1970	2,684	17	46	–
1971	5,029	0	97	–
1972	4,198	2	165	–
1973	3,201	18	132	–
1974	3,952	21	159	–
1975	4,603	14	461	–
1976	13,388	0	156	6
1977	18,789	511	330	11
1978	13,056	237	1,447	36
1979	17,173	218	2,703	125
1980	14,832	252	2,787	155
1981	11,243	694	1,833	202
1982	17,362	1,009	3,422	276
1983	14,511	993	2,530	279
1984	18,453	760	1,424	329
1985	11,350	945	1,124	337
1986	12,712	907	1,414	442
1987	10,934	948	1,262	338
1988	11,235	867	1,225	191
1989	13,026	812	1,122	215
1990	10,657	399	816	366
1991	6,421	305	1,680	175
1992	7,531	322	1,785	269
1993	6,011	300	1,524	127
1994	5,741	287	–	172

Note: England: data shows completions except 1969-77; Scotland: data shows approvals only; Northern Ireland: data not available 1969-75.
Source: *Housing and Construction Statistics* (various years); Northern Ireland Annual Abstract of Statistics (various years)

Table A7.22: Grants for people with disabilities, England

Year	No disabled grants	All grants excl MWA	Disabled grants as % of all grants	Disabled grants (£000s)	All grants (£000s)	£ disabled grants as % of all grants	Disabled grants (£000 1993/94 prices)
1969	0	68,399	0.0	0	12,794	0.0	–
1970	0	71,293	0.0	0	17,968	0.0	–
1971	0	90,867	0.0	0	29,683	0.0	–
1972	0	124,176	0.0	0	56,551	0.0	–
1973	0	165,958	0.0	0	101,966	0.0	–
1974	0	192,348	0.0	0	148,560	0.0	–
1975	125	85,393	0.1	0	63,858	0.0	–
1976	562	68,718	0.8	229	64,125	0.4	–
1977	751	56,955	1.3	359	60,117	0.6	–
1978	1,139	57,654	2.0	732	76,219	1.0	–
1979	1,704	65,359	2.6	1,257	100,198	1.3	3,088
1980	2,515	74,465	3.4	2,273	127,303	1.8	4,717
1981	3,403	68,941	4.9	3,667	148,152	2.5	6,931
1982	6,216	104,028	6.0	9,917	282,159	3.5	17,526
1983	11,935	219,832	5.4	24,179	655,490	3.7	40,840
1984	15,226	229,107	6.6	35,717	839,383	4.3	57,411
1985	15,675	136,412	11.5	36,125	525,099	6.9	55,055
1986	19,176	113,328	16.9	38,924	394,922	9.9	57,576
1987	23,793	108,908	21.8	41,849	362,013	11.6	58,774
1988	26,836	105,303	25.5	50,473	347,074	14.5	66,420
1989	29,919	98,217	30.5	54,839	328,356	16.7	67,439
1990	32,588	89,973	36.2	68,265	314,019	21.7	77,769
1991	16,719	55,839	29.9	52,282	299,353	17.5	56,035
1992	16,452	54,907	30.0	61,788	398,895	15.5	63,715
1993	17,288	54,911	31.5	70,426	428,720	16.4	70,426
1994	20,926	60,716	34.5	86,712	468,358	18.5	85,000

Source: *Housing and Construction Statistics* (various years)

Table A7.23: Grants for people with disabilities, Wales

Year	No disabled grants	All grants excl MWA	Disabled grants as % of all grants	Disabled grants (£000s)	All grants (£000s)	£ disabled grants as % of all grants	Disabled grants (£000 1993/94 prices)
1969	0	5,210	0.0	0	1,307	0.0	–
1970	0	5,877	0.0	0	1,784	0.0	–
1971	0	6,794	0.0	0	2,849	0.0	–
1972	0	12,932	0.0	0	7,879	0.0	–
1973	0	18,240	0.0	0	14,312	0.0	–
1974	0	24,728	0.0	0	22,784	0.0	–
1975	6	7,356	0.1	0	7,666	0.0	–
1976	16	6,557	0.2	14	7,635	0.2	–
1977	68	7,017	1.0	30	8,089	0.4	–
1978	92	5,931	1.6	57	8,331	0.7	–
1979	168	6,116	2.7	119	10,398	1.1	292
1980	205	7,348	2.8	201	13,798	1.5	417
1981	267	7,100	3.8	291	14,514	2.0	550
1982	497	10,989	4.5	837	26,265	3.2	1,479
1983	887	27,323	3.2	1,784	74,373	2.4	3,013
1984	1,539	29,978	5.1	3,834	101,663	3.8	6,163
1985	1,755	17,152	10.2	4,003	57,221	7.0	6,101
1986	2,207	18,571	11.9	4,322	58,171	7.4	6,393
1987	2,325	19,097	12.2	4,763	59,491	8.0	6,689
1988	2,687	20,187	13.3	5,488	64,050	8.6	7,222
1989	2,993	20,206	14.8	6,879	65,844	10.4	8,460
1000	3,385	25,170	13.4	7,799	84,266	9.3	8,885
1991	1,724	14,353	12.0	6,626	93,931	7.1	7,102
1992	2,223	11,672	19.0	9,745	148,731	6.6	10,049
1993	2,643	11,299	23.4	12,263	164,298	7.5	12,263
1994	2,634	10,001	26.3	11,789	145,077	8.1	11,556

Source: *Housing and Construction Statistics* (various years)

Table A8.1: Percentage shares of public spending on housing, England (1979-95)

Year	LA new build	LA renovation	LA grants to HAs	Private sector renovation	LA mortgage	Housing Corporation
1979/80	33	21	5	6	18	11
1980/81	30	20	5	8	18	15
1981/82	23	19	4	10	24	16
1982/83	18	24	3	14	20	19
1983/84	17	26	3	24	11	17
1984/85	18	30	3	20	9	16
1985/86	19	35	3	15	7	19
1986/87	16	40	4	14	5	19
1987/88	15	43	4	13	5	18
1988/89	18	43	3	10	7	18
1989/90	15	48	5	8	7	15
1990/91	12	39	4	11	4	24
1991/92	9	32	4	12	3	37
1992/93	4	30	6	10	3	46
1993/94	5	34	8	12	2	37
1994/95	3	40	7	12	2	32

Source: Wilcox (1995)

Table A8.2: Percentage shares of public spending on housing, Wales (1981-95)

Year	LA new build	LA renovation	LA grants to HAs	Private sector renovation	LA mortgage	Housing Corporation
1981/82	35	19	0	14	4	25
1982/83	22	26	0	23	4	24
1983/84	18	19	0	43	3	16
1984/85	17	21	0	38	2	19
1985/86	15	28	0	31	1	23
1986/87	12	33	0	27	2	22
1987/88	14	33	0	24	1	22
1988/89	11	34	0	23	1	25
1989/90	8	39	3	19	1	24
1990/91	5	29	0	25	1	31
1991/92	3	23	0	35	0	36
1992/93	3	17	0	40	0	38
1993/94	2	20	0	41	0	33

Source: Wilcox (1995)

Table A8.3: Percentage shares of public spending on housing, Northern Ireland (1985-98)

Year	NIHE new build	NIHE renovation	Private sector renovation	Voluntary housing
1985/86	33	29	22	15
1986/87	32	27	23	17
1987/88	28	33	19	18
1988/89	27	35	18	19
1989/90	27	35	17	18
1990/91	24	37	17	19
1991/92	26	34	17	21
1992/93	21	33	16	27
1993/94	23	37	16	24
1994/95	25	36	16	22
1995/96	26	32	17	23
1996/97	26	35	17	20
1997/98	28	36	17	19

Source: Wilcox (1995)

Table A8.4: Public expenditure on housing renovation, England, 1993/94 prices (1979-95)

Year	LA renovation	Private sector renovation	HA renovation	Total renovation spending
		£m		
1979/80	1,776	558	456	2,790
1980/81	1,390	546	389	2,325
1981/82	1,172	607	344	2,123
1982/83	1,700	972	491	3,163
1983/84	1,939	1,757	414	4,110
1984/85	2,057	1,397	479	3,933
1985/86	2,004	885	264	3,154
1986/87	2,250	768	294	3,311
1987/88	2,447	751	253	3,451
1988/89	2,506	603	280	3,388
1989/90	3,631	601	281	4,514
1990/91	1,961	556	253	2,770
1991/92	1,589	584	209	2,382
1992/93	1,610	543	244	2,397
1993/94	1,684	587	232	2,503
1994/95	1,891	578	232	2,701
		% renovation spending		
1979/80	64	20	16	100
1980/81	60	23	17	100
1981/82	55	29	16	100
1982/83	54	31	16	100
1983/84	47	43	10	100
1984/85	52	36	12	100
1985/86	64	28	8	100
1986/87	68	23	9	100
1987/88	71	22	7	100
1988/89	74	18	8	100
1989/90	80	13	6	100
1990/91	71	20	9	100
1991/92	67	25	9	100
1992/93	67	23	10	100
1993/94	67	23	9	100
1994/95	70	21	9	100

Sources: Wilcox (1995); *Housing and Construction Statistics* (various years)

Table A8.5: Public expenditure on housing renovation, Wales, 1993/94 prices (1981-95)

Year	LA renovation	Private sector renovation	HA renovation	Total renovation spending
		£m		
1981/82	46	39	21	106
1982/83	84	77	29	190
1983/84	81	189	28	299
1984/85	71	138	20	229
1985/86	76	93	22	190
1986/87	116	111	21	248
1987/88	138	119	22	279
1988/89	131	112	22	264
1989/90	181	115	18	314
1990/91	121	137	9	267
1991/92	91	147	10	248
1992/93	81	197	10	288
1993/94	87	192	12	291
		% renovation spending		
1981/82	43	37	20	100
1982/83	44	41	15	100
1983/84	27	63	9	100
1984/85	31	60	9	100
1985/86	40	49	12	100
1986/87	47	45	8	100
1987/88	49	43	8	100
1988/89	50	42	8	100
1989/90	58	37	6	100
1990/91	45	51	4	100
1991/92	37	59	4	100
1992/93	28	68	4	100
1993/94	30	66	4	100

Sources: Wilcox (1995); *Housing and Construction Statistics* (various years)

Table A8.6: Public expenditure on housing renovation, Northern Ireland, 1993/94 prices (1985-95)

Year	NIHE renovation	Private sector renovation	HA renovation	Total renovation spending
		£m		
1985/86	120	91	8	220
1986/87	101	83	10	194
1987/88	112	63	8	183
1988/89	109	55	5	169
1989/90	93	44	5	142
1990/91	81	36	9	126
1991/92	71	34	6	111
1992/93	73	35	9	117
1993/94	75	32	5	112
1994/95	73	31	5	109

	LA renovation	Private sector renovation	HA renovation	Total renovation spending
	% renovation spending			
1984/85	55	42	4	100
1985/86	52	43	5	100
1986/87	61	34	4	100
1987/88	65	33	3	100
1988/89	66	31	3	100
1989/90	64	29	7	100
1990/91	64	31	5	100
1991/92	63	30	7	100
1992/93	67	29	4	100
1993/94	66	29	5	100

Sources: Wilcox (1995); *Housing and Construction Statistics* (various years)

Table A9.1: Average weekly spending on repairs, maintenance and decoration by tenure (1990-95)

Tenure	1986	1987	1988	1989	1990	1991	1992	1993	1994-95
£ per week									
All households	4.87	4.91	5.00	5.64	6.19	7.25	7.32	7.42	6.60
Owner-occupied owned outright	5.60	6.11	5.85	5.51	6.95	9.50	9.21	9.90	7.73
Owner-occupied with mortgage	8.12	8.03	7.92	8.36	9.38	10.45	10.9	10.25	9.74
Rented from LA	1.25	1.02	1.11	1.07	1.57	1.40	1.29	1.44	1.47
Rented from HA	–	0.89	1.05	0.67	1.52	1.90	2.01	1.19	0.78
Private rented unfurnished	1.21	0.99	1.19	–	2.12	1.78	1.56	2.53	2.12
Private rented furnished	0.73	0.74	1.07	0.91	1.33	0.39	0.74	1.41	0.60
Rent free	2.21	2.07	1.77	2.19	3.33	2.60	4.20	11.18	–
£ per annum									
All households	253	255	260	293	322	377	381	386	343
Owner-occupied owned outright	291	318	304	287	361	494	479	515	402
Owner-occupied with mortgage	422	418	412	435	488	543	567	533	506
Rented from LA	65	53	58	56	82	73	67	75	76
Rented from HA	–	46	55	35	79	99	105	62	41
Private rented unfurnished	63	51	62	–	110	93	81	132	110
Private rented furnished	38	38	56	47	69	20	38	73	31
Rent free	115	108	92	114	173	135	218	581	–
£ per annum (1993/94 prices)									
All households	375	359	342	361	367	404	393	386	336
Owner-occupied owned outright	431	446	400	352	412	529	494	515	394
Owner-occupied with mortgage	625	586	542	535	556	582	585	533	496
Rented from LA	96	74	76	68	93	78	69	75	75
Rented from HA	0	65	72	43	90	106	108	62	40
Private rented unfurnished	93	72	81	0	126	99	84	132	108
Private rented furnished	56	54	73	58	79	22	40	73	31
Rent free	170	151	121	140	197	145	225	581	0
Price factor	1.48	1.40	1.32	1.23	1.14	1.07	1.03	1.00	0.98

Source: CSO (various years)

Table A9.2: Average weekly spending on repairs, maintenance and decoration by age group (1994-95)

Age group, all tenures	£ per week	£ per annum
Under 30	3.99	207
30-49	8.22	427
50-64	8.39	436
65-74	4.81	250
75+	3.03	158

Source: CSO (1995)

Table A9.3: Value of occupant work by tenure, England (1991)

Value of work	Owner-occupied	Private rented	Rented from LA	Rented from HA	All tenures
No of households (000s)					
None	2,130	826	1,541	304	4,800
Under £500	2,686	443	922	156	4,207
£500-£999	2,314	184	679	89	3,266
£1,000-£2,499	2,630	156	583	93	3,461
£2,500-£4,999	1,610	60	93	14	1,776
£5,000-£9,999	992	30	48	6	1,076
£10,000-£19,999	398	2	12	0	411
£20,000 or more	113	0	0	0	113
% of households by tenure					
None	16.5	48.6	39.7	45.9	25.1
Under £500	20.9	26.0	23.8	23.6	22.0
£500-£999	18.0	10.8	17.5	13.5	17.1
£1,000-£2,499	20.4	9.2	15.0	14.0	18.1
£2,500-£4,999	12.5	3.5	2.4	2.1	9.3
£5,000-£9,999	7.7	1.8	1.2	0.9	5.6
£10,000-£19,999	3.1	0.1	0.3	0.0	2.2
£20,000 or more	0.9	0.0	0.0	0.0	0.6

Source: 1991 EHCS: analysis of data

Table A9.4: Average value of work carried out by selected household/dwelling characteristics, England (1991)

Characteristic Household income	Average (£)	No of cases (000s)
Under£4,000	695	3,606
£4,000-£7,999	964	4,651
£8,000-£11,999	1,577	3,049
£12,000-£15,999	1,959	2,745
£16,000-£19,999	2,883	2,170
£20,000-£23,999	2,445	1,128
£24,000 or more	3,016	1,758
Age of head of household		
16-24	949	718
25-34	2,007	3,126
35-44	2,309	3,736
45-54	2,206	3,093
55-64	1,565	2,954
65-74	1,026	3,031
75-84	612	1,911
85 and over	338	541

Household type

Lone adult	855	1,613
2 adults	2,122	3,223
Lone parent	957	782
Small family	2,462	3,260
Large family	2,492	2,025
3+ adults	1,958	2,270
2 pensioners	1,116	3,096
1 pensioner	547	2,842

Ethnic group of head of household

White	1,665	18,281
Black	1,016	263
Asian	1,597	353
Other	1,007	148

Length of residence

Under 1 year	1,498	1,420
1-2 years	2,052	2,355
3-4 years	1,953	2,514
5-10 years	1,773	4,811
11-15 years	1,756	2,227
16-20 years	1,578	1,579
21-30 years	1,363	2,200
Over 30 years	847	2,006

General repair costs

None	1,841	4,005
Under £1,000	1,550	8,801
£1,000-£2,499	1,676	3,682
£2,500-£4,999	1,633	1,748
£5,000-£9,999	1,812	655
£10,000-£14,999	1,269	162
£15,000 or more	1,094	57

Dwelling age

Pre-1850	2,688	604
1850-99	1,595	2,701
1900-18	1,613	1,759
1919-44	1,952	3,821
1945-64	1,554	4,206
1965-80	1,438	4,491
Post-1980	1,485	1,527

Dwelling type

Terraced	1,547	5,613
Semi-detached	1,660	5,948
Detached	2,679	4,020
Converted flat	719	1,120
Purpose-built flat	544	2,353

Dwelling fitness

Fit	1,673	17,698
Unfit	1,334	1,414

Dwelling value	Average (£)	No of cases (000s)
Up to £40,000	990	5,257
£40,001-£52,000	1,451	3,716
£52,001-£68,000	1,652	4,237
£68,001-£88,000	1,840	2,694
£88,001-£120,000	2,148	1,720
£120,001-£160,000	2,844	878
£160,001-£320,000	4,312	569
£320,000 or more	7,391	40

Source: 1991 EHCS

Table A9.5: Building society lending by dwelling age/type, Great Britain (1973-94)

	All purchasers				
Year	Pre-1919 terraced	Inter-war semi or detached	New	Pre-1919 converted flat	All pre-1919 stock
1973	10	12	28	–	18
1974	10	13	25	–	19
1975	10	15	19	–	19
1976	13	14	17	–	23
1977	13	15	17	–	24
1978	13	12	18	–	24
1979	14	12	17	–	24
1980	16	12	15	–	28
1981	17	11	12	–	28
1982	17	11	11	–	27
1983	15	11	12	–	26
1984	15	10	12	–	27
1985	16	10	11	–	28
1986	16	10	10	3	28
1987	15	9	10	3	26
1988	16	9	10	4	27
1989	17	8	11	3	27
1990	18	8	11	4	29
1991	15	8	12	4	27
1992	15	9	11	3	26
1993	12	9	11	3	24
1994	14	10	11	3	24

Source: BSA/CML (various years)

Table A9.6: Building society lending by age of stock and type of purchaser, Great Britain (1974-94)

	% first-time buyers buying				% previous owners			
Year	Pre-1919	Inter-war	Post-war	New	Pre-1919	Inter-war	Post-war	New
1974	24	19	33	24	14	19	41	26
1975	25	18	39	19	14	20	46	20
1976	29	19	34	18	17	20	44	19
1977	30	19	36	16	18	21	44	18
1978	30	18	36	15	18	19	43	19
1979	31	18	35	15	18	20	43	19
1980	36	17	34	12	20	20	44	17
1981	36	16	38	10	21	20	46	14
1982	33	16	41	10	20	20	48	12
1983	31	16	43	11	20	20	48	13
1984	33	15	40	12	21	19	48	13
1985	35	15	40	10	21	19	48	13
1986	35	15	42	8	21	18	48	12
1987	32	15	45	8	21	17	49	13
1988	32	16	46	7	23	17	47	13
1989	31	14	47	8	25	16	45	14
1990	32	13	45	9	24	16	46	14
1991	32	14	45	10	23	15	49	13
1992	30	15	46	9	21	16	49	14
1993	28	15	48	9	21	15	50	14
1994	28	16	47	9	19	16	51	14

Source: BSA/CML (various years)

Table A9.7: Ratio of first-time buyers to existing owner purchasers by age of dwelling, Great Britain (1974-94)

	Ratio of first-time buyers: previous owners			
Year	Pre-1919	Inter-war	Post-war	New
1974	1.72	0.99	0.80	0.95
1975	1.71	0.91	0.84	0.94
1976	1.74	0.98	0.76	0.93
1977	1.68	0.91	0.81	0.88
1978	1.66	0.95	0.83	0.80
1979	1.71	0.92	0.81	0.82
1980	1.82	0.88	0.78	0.73
1981	1.77	0.82	0.82	0.72
1982	1.64	0.78	0.87	0.82
1983	1.55	0.81	0.89	0.85
1984	1.62	0.82	0.83	0.92
1985	1.65	0.82	0.84	0.79
1986	1.62	0.86	0.87	0.64
1987	1.51	0.90	0.91	0.62
1988	1.37	0.94	0.97	0.54
1989	1.23	0.87	1.04	0.58
1990	1.34	0.87	0.97	0.67
1991	1.39	0.90	0.92	0.74
1992	1.43	0.93	0.93	0.67
1993	1.36	0.99	0.95	0.64
1994	1.45	1.00	0.92	0.68

Source: BSA/CML (various years)

Table A9.8: Output on housing repair and maintenance, Great Britain (1985-94)

Year	Cash prices Public	Private	Total	Index Public	Private
1985	3,382	4,584	7,966	100	100
1986	3,585	5,077	8,662	102	106
1987	3,956	6,011	9,967	107	120
1988	4,446	7,084	11,530	113	134
1989	4,943	8,149	13,092	118	144
1990	5,384	8,455	13,839	119	138
1991	4,938	8,063	13,001	102	124
1992	4,991	7,595	12,586	100	113
1993	5,439	7,370	12,809	105	106
1994	5,963	7,804	13,767	105	110

Source: *Housing and Construction Statistics* (various)

Table A9.9: Share of housing repair and maintenance output by size of firm, Great Britain (1990, 1992, 1994)

No of employees	Value of work done and % by no of employees Q3 1990 £m	%	Q3 1992 £m	%	Q3 1994 £m	%
1	414.2	21.9	334.8	18.6	398.9	22.6
2-3	443.7	23.5	451.1	25.1	425.6	24.1
4-7	288.9	15.3	344.7	19.1	301.3	17.1
8-13	132.0	7.0	141.3	7.8	126.9	7.2
14-24	146.3	7.7	143.1	7.9	125.4	7.1
25-59	149.0	7.9	147.8	8.2	145.2	8.2
60-114	79.3	4.2	55.3	3.1	50.6	2.9
115-599	150.4	8.0	86.2	4.8	97.3	5.5
600+	87.2	4.6	96.2	5.3	94.6	5.4
Total	1,891.0	100.0	1,800.5	100.0	1,765.8	100.0

Source: *Housing and Construction Statistics* (various years)

Appendix B

Key data on housing conditions and renovation activity by local authority

LA	Density (pph) 1991	% owner-occupier 1991	% private rented 1991	% private dwgs pre-1919 1986	Unfit per 1,000 private dwgs 1986	Demol per 1,000 private dwgs 1978-94	Old grants per 1,000 private dwgs 1978-94	Ren grants per 1,000 private dwgs 1990-94	DFGs per 1,000 private dwgs 1990-94	MWA per 1,000 private dwgs 1990-94	Renovs per 1,000 LA dwgs 1978-94	HA rens per 1,000 private dwgs 1978-94	Ave mand renov grant 1994/95	Ave mand DF grant 1994/95
Aberconwy	0.9	74.7	14.1	24.9	7.2	3.27	110.65	15.26	9.27	22.71	260.61	0.75	17,575	4,511
Adur	13.9	79.9	6.3	8.5	26.3	0.29	41.64	3.26	3.65	12.78	668.18	0.05	4,614	4,514
Allerdale	0.8	66.2	16.1	61.2	101.9	25.56	245.98	13.63	2.93	17.08	551.38	38.49	12,578	3,987
Alnwick	0.3	56.9	22.5	53.0	93.3	6.40	184.78	9.53	2.41	2.17	360.17	8.73	12,295	4,174
Alyn & Deeside	4.8	76.6	6.9	20.0	43.7	2.54	104.34	20.84	4.05	7.48	199.43	0.85	29,779	11,278
Amber Valley	4.2	77.0	7.9	45.8	93.1	6.26	197.05	6.36	5.70	11.50	279.65	1.23	6,000	2,492
Arfon	1.3	65.6	12.5	48.4	48.4	3.33	340.74	34.11	6.09	8.33	109.34	3.27	15,139	7,077
Arun	5.9	81.7	10.4	14.8	28.2	0.62	64.91	5.08	8.72	0.00	236.31	3.65	11,325	2,940
Ashfield	9.9	71.5	6.8	36.7	79.1	1.18	116.04	12.98	1.56	8.97	378.55	0.99	7,652	8,209
Ashford	1.6	70.6	9.8	30.7	40.1	1.65	79.64	3.87	2.54	21.13	440.98	0.58	12,436	5,962
Aylesbury Vale	1.6	72.5	10.2	20.1	28.3	2.25	83.40	3.58	9.62	2.23	841.19	0.77	12,437	3,200
Babergh	1.3	74.2	11.0	31.6	40.3	1.15	103.41	6.00	10.05	7.66	137.93	0.00	11,068	2,803
Barking & Dagenham	42.1	51.8	5.0	11.1	20.4	1.26	139.29	16.00	7.59	5.41	449.66	0.67	8,845	6,105
Barnet	32.8	68.9	18.3	27.4	32.0	0.26	52.92	3.83	2.04	7.33	876.88	5.90	8,042	9,237
Barnsley	6.7	61.8	8.0	43.5	79.4	15.16	146.76	13.19	11.81	17.31	832.92	9.22	4,395	2,470
Barrow-in-Furness	9.4	78.4	8.6	59.2	103.2	0.56	117.68	28.76	2.79	4.30	495.72	2.78	2,763	5,868
Basildon	14.6	68.0	4.5	2.2	9.1	0.87	18.79	1.05	4.17	0.96	824.55	0.00	6,182	5,919
Basingstoke	2.3	71.1	10.9	16.2	23.9	0.90	74.83	2.67	9.07	9.43	829.48	1.58	6,845	3,169
Bassetlaw	1.6	69.1	9.2	29.0	68.3	3.39	128.36	12.25	7.08	14.95	411.58	1.51	5,806	5,379
Bath	27.4	64.7	17.1	52.8	103.0	9.44	104.78	6.01	3.23	13.43	1,239.89	8.68	18,467	1,646
Berwick-upon-Tweed	0.3	49.8	22.2	54.4	95.4	4.9	97.22	8.23	3.75	5.63	845.21	1.73	33,019	2,416
Beverley	2.8	80.6	7.7	18.7	43.1	1.42	43.60	1.68	1.82	6.32	418.18	1.16	15,724	4,376
Bexley	35.6	78.8	9.0	14.7	31.2	1.17	105.87	7.48	7.55	7.23	202.44	2.09	4,516	4,811
Birmingham	36.2	60.1	13.5	37.8	95.1	12.42	149.41	12.24	4.86	13.93	466.55	40.34	15,028	8,870
Blaby	6.3	85.7	5.7	13.1	16.1	1.61	51.00	14.42	3.22	13.82	1,056.62	0.86	7,780	5,443
Blackburn	10.0	69.6	8.7	63.8	111.1	170.90	269.85	24.36	5.82	35.29	403.79	13.63	12,417	1,830
Blackpool	41.8	75.9	13.8	21.5	57.2	2.89	52.60	4.22	4.07	11.95	536.34	3.15	8,447	3,148
Blaenau Gwent	6.0	62.1	6.7	43.4	117.7	44.82	383.80	54.34	8.29	45.54	928.87	6.74	25,710	5,776
Blyth Valley	11.3	63.0	9.4	19.4	29.5	7.52	69.66	10.27	3.03	2.59	734.21	11.47	8,877	3,518
Bolsover	4.4	67.1	9.1	49.7	98.6	32.11	268.09	10.74	5.54	1.65	1,428.78	2.32	7,788	2,623
Bolton	18.5	69.8	8.3	42.8	76.4	67.88	148.62	10.43	5.12	8.63	1,368.71	13.06	15,696	5,005
Boothferry	1.0	75.5	8.8	44.0	77.0	5.12	94.03	7.78	2.76	6.20	197.58	2.00	12,549	3,198
Boston	1.5	66.9	9.0	36.1	57.3	12.31	120.10	9.22	3.55	24.30	161.19	0.58	9,602	1,934
Bournemouth	32.8	72.5	18.7	28.6	50.1	0.73	37.36	1.87	2.43	39.21	1,314.51	0.58	10,904	3,191

LA	Density (pph) 1991	% owner-occupier 1991	% private rented 1991	% private dwgs pre-1919 1986	Unfit per 1,000 private dwgs 1986	Demol per 1,000 private dwgs 1978-94	Old grants per 1,000 private dwgs 1978-94	Ren grants per 1,000 private dwgs 1990-94	DFGs per 1,000 private dwgs 1990-94	MWA per 1,000 private dwgs 1990-94	Renovs per 1,000 LA dwgs 1978-94	HA rens per 1,000 private dwgs 1978-94	Ave mand renov grant 1994/95	Ave mand DF grant 1994/95
Bracknell	8.8	67.4	10.5	10.1	17.9	0.43	33.11	0.89	2.36	0.85	545.06	10.38	16,838	5,834
Bradford	12.5	71.2	12.2	39.4	73.5	20.56	127.05	13.26	4.16	4.81	65.09	8.55	12,450	4,403
Braintree	1.9	69.2	8.5	22.5	31.7	0.81	89.75	5.52	11.37	9.10	331.28	0.99	13,920	4,902
Breckland	0.8	71.4	13.0	28.9	39.2	2.38	110.83	8.60	4.89	2.55	122.34	4.15	9,499	4,275
Brecknock	0.2	70.2	14.2	42.8	53.9	7.83	261.32	22.30	3.72	19.85	1,887.92	1.34	20,556	7,318
Brent	55.0	57.7	24.7	35.6	62.1	2.09	66.57	4.51	1.22	1.15	199.43	64.30	—	—
Brentwood	4.7	78.8	8.5	16.5	19.0	1.02	41.37	4.39	3.15	8.44	1,126.36	0.51	8,740	2,288
Bridgnorth	0.8	68.6	15.3	36.4	56.5	3.12	113.71	8.62	2.78	18.12	160.22	0.20	21,819	3,397
Brighton	25.1	64.7	19.5	55.4	55.1	3.67	96.46	13.96	1.22	17.71	773.47	0.92	6,228	5,191
Bristol	34.3	63.6	14.2	49.0	99.7	6.19	81.34	4.66	2.89	8.00	1,967.70	18.07	15,065	5,821
Broadland	1.9	82.4	14.9	13.6	22.8	1.57	100.41	14.33	4.80	8.55	1,385.16	0.00	7,069	2,639
Bromley	19.1	77.9	11.7	19.3	23.2	1.41	94.92	5.12	2.47	12.48	117.18	22.62	7,223	6,717
Bromsgrove	4.2	77.1	6.0	14.5	17.7	1.43	54.28	0.89	9.09	0.00	304.10	1.04	25,671	2,349
Broxbourne	15.6	78.1	6.1	11.5	19.9	0.65	89.72	5.94	5.54	10.19	227.32	3.76	7,582	3,841
Broxtowe	13.2	77.7	9.4	18.5	51.1	1.32	99.14	4.88	1.27	2.18	504.74	1.52	8,144	2,344
Burnley	8.2	74.2	9.8	65.2	113.1	52.85	247.01	21.07	13.97	22.73	320.39	21.29	8,490	1,926
Bury	17.8	76.6	7.4	33.8	54.5	29.61	95.78	8.71	4.85	5.13	795.24	11.69	9,314	3,929
Calderdale	5.3	72.9	10.0	55.2	98.5	15.32	199.67	15.96	13.91	0.00	188.10	9.47	13,735	3,499
Cambridge	22.6	54.2	22.4	40.3	41.4	1.28	105.63	6.82	4.26	5.83	1,044.93	8.42	7,074	5,100
Camden	78.5	33.8	32.3	77.2	89.4	1.18	102.53	0.63	0.36	0.90	215.94	69.60	14,828	8,333
Cannock Chase	11.3	70.6	6.8	15.9	45.7	9.72	30.46	5.47	8.34	0.00	699.35	14.15	5,339	4,014
Canterbury	4.0	74.9	13.3	22.9	39.3	0.40	64.53	3.88	2.89	4.89	434.70	1.94	10,410	6,154
Caradon	1.2	76.0	10.5	35.0	54.5	3.18	111.13	7.92	22.64	12.97	1,000.40	0.08	15,904	1,677
Cardiff	23.2	69.6	14.6	33.0	62.9	9.10	293.06	29.01	20.83	27.01	727.97	13.85	18,281	6,661
Carlisle	1.0	67.2	10.6	45.6	82.5	16.48	86.69	10.52	1.63	12.12	571.72	6.79	14,233	11,056
Carmarthen	0.5	73.6	11.3	47.9	52.1	3.52	384.51	27.68	3.92	11.82	531.32	3.23	28,252	4,591
Carrick	1.8	74.5	12.1	35.0	55.3	3.85	96.37	9.18	3.85	8.35	64.21	3.07	11,154	3,468
Castle Morpeth	0.8	70.2	11.9	22.0	43.2	0.41	198.47	10.03	1.24	0.55	297.34	0.46	8,410	1,676
Castle Point	19.3	89.4	4.6	2.9	11.2	0.72	36.61	0.00	0.00	0.00	163.43	0.13	—	—
Ceredigion	0.4	72.2	16.0	48.7	130.2	0.51	190.39	28.01	4.93	4.70	25.26	1.98	18,743	8,079
Charnwood	5.1	78.5	8.4	21.4	25.8	8.70	95.79	19.94	3.54	3.50	1,742.97	4.91	3,595	3,468
Chelmsford	4.5	78.0	7.6	12.6	21.5	1.38	39.47	2.26	2.35	7.72	184.40	1.21	6,247	4,012
Cheltenham	22.1	72.8	13.4	36.2	76.4	4.13	226.14	10.67	5.49	8.15	750.98	9.70	13,456	5,902
Cherwell	2.0	69.3	14.6	20.2	28.4	5.42	74.53	2.27	2.26	8.79	1,162.89	0.77	16,114	3,920

LA	Density (pph) 1991	% owner-occupier 1991	% private rented 1991	% private dwgs pre-1919 1986	Unfit per 1,000 private dwgs 1986	Demol per 1,000 private dwgs 1978-94	Old grants per 1,000 private dwgs 1978-94	Ren grants per 1,000 private dwgs 1990-94	DFGs per 1,000 private dwgs 1990-94	MWA per 1,000 private dwgs 1990-94	Renovs per 1,000 LA dwgs 1978-94	HA rens per 1,000 private dwgs 1978-94	Ave mand renov grant 1994/95	Ave mand DF grant 1994/95
Chester	2.6	71.4	13.0	29.0	58.3	4.18	75.30	10.76	2.08	4.51	541.56	6.29	14,492	6,510
Chesterfield	15.1	63.6	8.3	34.4	76.1	19.39	138.45	18.52	3.89	19.50	460.50	8.98	11,078	4,780
Chester-le-Street	7.8	66.4	4.6	30.6	45.1	5.82	88.47	3.46	2.98	7.97	1,260.06	1.45	7,844	2,213
Chichester	1.3	69.5	14.8	29.0	44.8	0.74	61.92	6.85	9.22	3.58	65.39	0.65	8,890	2,917
Chiltern	4.6	79.4	16.5	18.3	21.0	0.52	50.10	2.50	2.33	3.64	301.59	0.21	6,528	2,383
Chorley	4.8	79.3	10.2	33.5	48.8	20.54	93.33	11.59	5.33	15.44	609.09	14.88	8,724	3,942
Christchurch	8.1	81.3	15.9	9.4	23.0	0.57	33.96	2.28	5.39	8.46	367.85	0.00	5,863	4,210
City of London	15.1	47.1	27.2	3.0	19.0	0.00	1.45	0.00	0.00	0.00	–	9.44	–	6,079
Cleethorpes	4.2	81.1	8.0	29.2	57.9	0.26	112.86	11.39	4.44	16.52	876.46	1.04	6,877	2,720
Colchester	4.3	73.6	11.7	25.7	35.0	0.36	81.86	18.08	2.30	11.42	866.00	0.74	9,312	3,546
Colwyn	1.0	75.5	14.1	26.2	8.0	3.91	127.19	24.62	6.12	38.13	546.33	5.45	16,710	3,185
Congleton	4.0	81.1	5.8	22.5	34.8	4.75	68.25	4.00	2.45	3.64	171.29	1.62	11,689	7,502
Copeland	1.0	65.4	14.1	47.0	82.9	9.62	136.16	12.00	2.22	11.33	377.82	39.41	12,056	6,434
Corby	6.6	57.0	4.4	7.8	25.5	0.08	43.08	0.55	3.99	1.60	468.32	0.00	9,342	4,370
Cotswold	0.6	65.1	19.4	40.6	61.7	5.68	86.21	3.30	4.32	8.11	391.95	6.55	20,205	4,921
Coventry	30.5	71.0	11.7	19.0	57.0	1.49	118.76	19.76	1.72	2.94	463.36	25.35	6,537	14,414
Craven	0.4	76.5	14.1	58.1	100.1	1.5⁻	96.27	3.94	1.70	0.17	268.81	0.81	3,617	2,755
Crawley	19.9	60.6	8.8	6.5	13.4	0.00	14.98	0.96	3.60	0.68	1,395.40	0.23	14,189	5,355
Crewe & Nantwich	2.4	74.2	8.5	42.0	76.0	20.93	100.59	8.77	2.32	16.13	311.46	6.94	4,317	4,395
Croydon	36.2	72.8	13.8	37.6	40.9	0.63	93.15	9.58	1.42	7.52	253.16	8.41	5,416	7,911
Cynon Valley	3.7	72.8	9.3	60.2	139.6	28.83	436.16	75.27	6.94	75.73	226.63	15.05	18,213	3,257
Dacorum	6.2	65.9	8.2	20.5	22.6	1.02	57.07	5.65	2.56	12.89	50.92	1.98	10,268	5,162
Darlington	5.0	70.9	10.8	34.0	67.0	1.54	85.86	11.53	1.35	9.76	449.86	9.03	7,947	3,080
Dartford	10.9	73.4	8.5	26.6	39.0	1.06	82.81	0.00	0.00	0.37	965.68	3.56	–	–
Daventry	0.9	75.0	8.2	28.7	33.8	1.21	117.54	4.80	5.33	10.71	483.91	1.37	13,689	3,424
Delyn	2.4	76.1	7.1	23.1	14.6	4.96	111.71	14.06	15.81	10.70	126.75	0.44	18,127	4,421
Derby	28.0	68.9	12.0	29.8	74.9	53.28	138.39	21.32	7.57	16.01	480.45	17.90	12,400	3,217
Derbyshire Dales	0.8	73.2	13.3	53.7	80.3	23.04	129.28	4.85	2.85	5.01	1,123.12	1.45	4,138	3,653
Derwentside	3.2	63.3	6.6	55.2	97.7	37.79	187.52	25.39	7.32	33.01	731.60	6.51	10,244	3,527
Dinefwr	0.4	75.5	9.6	53.5	121.6	15.16	201.33	25.49	8.47	23.31	468.07	3.23	26,224	3,522
Doncaster	5.0	66.9	7.8	22.0	50.5	2.63	127.40	8.31	5.02	1.40	148.99	2.95	6,463	2,889
Dover	3.3	71.1	14.2	42.8	62.4	1.95	106.97	10.63	2.86	7.41	1,248.41	10.23	7,530	4,413
Dudley	31.1	68.6	5.8	10.5	38.2	6.59	29.53	7.47	3.14	2.13	499.94	7.81	17,413	7,542
Durham	4.3	61.9	9.0	30.3	56.8	6.75	71.89	4.67	2.41	0.99	461.15	8.37	5,363	3,578

LA	Density (pph) 1991	% owner-occupier 1991	% private rented 1991	% private dwgs pre-1919 1986	Unfit per 1,000 private dwgs 1986	Demol per 1,000 private dwgs 1978-94	Old grants per 1,000 private dwgs 1978-94	Ren grants per 1,000 private dwgs 1990-94	DFGs per 1,000 private dwgs 1990-94	MWA per 1,000 private dwgs 1990-94	Renovs per 1,000 LA dwgs 1978-94	HA rens per 1,000 private dwgs 1978-94	Ave mand renov grant 1994/95	Ave mand DF grant 1994/95
Dwyfor	0.4	70.4	16.9	49.6	120.1	6.18	303.62	52.89	6.96	13.03	84.28	3.48	25,464	5,080
Ealing	49.7	63.8	20.4	43.3	66.6	0.87	30.51	7.55	2.05	1.45	582.77	22.48	13,382	16,172
Easington	6.8	53.8	7.6	36.9	75.4	26.66	102.78	17.41	5.65	2.64	848.14	15.40	10,891	2,369
East Cambridgeshire	0.9	68.9	13.7	31.0	43.7	10.79	113.76	7.50	7.82	11.33	144.85	0.76	11,398	6,370
East Devon	1.4	78.2	11.7	31.4	50.6	0.33	45.38	4.82	2.48	7.01	153.23	4.89	7,450	2,797
East Dorset	2.2	85.2	11.6	11.7	14.0	0.28	22.49	4.65	2.99	4.98	336.04	0.00	10,094	3,418
East Hampshire	2.0	77.9	11.0	22.1	31.1	1.92	62.51	11.42	2.50	4.15	678.85	0.34	8,749	6,350
East Herts	2.4	73.6	10.0	24.9	26.6	1.22	111.52	5.20	1.82	0.70	435.34	0.08	8,216	2,875
East Lindsey	0.7	73.5	15.4	32.7	53.1	8.80	107.22	9.38	3.63	5.56	227.35	0.45	6,069	2,779
East Northants	1.3	73.1	9.3	35.0	75.0	7.54	66.57	3.84	4.61	17.91	162.69	1.34	8,094	2,883
East Staffs	2.5	74.4	9.6	42.9	87.5	13.80	221.34	11.06	7.49	27.30	220.17	5.12	13,785	3,566
East Yorkshire	0.8	73.8	14.3	32.5	61.9	5.95	53.01	4.97	2.66	1.57	1,245.96	0.48	8,997	2,936
Eastbourne	18.4	71.0	15.5	32.6	47.7	0.60	64.64	8.42	2.56	14.52	745.45	1.74	7,695	3,399
Eastleigh	13.3	81.4	7.1	9.5	18.4	0.65	97.24	5.57	4.24	8.73	666.43	2.94	11,044	3,827
Eden	0.2	70.1	18.8	65.7	108.7	7.90	134.69	10.59	4.47	7.97	261.49	1.99	19,953	1,127
Ellesmere Port	9.3	70.5	5.6	16.4	38.0	1.45	57.48	9.62	27.09	0.31	830.25	0.75	9,140	2,226
Elmbridge	11.8	77.1	12.1	21.4	24.7	1.19	44.58	4.19	2.06	4.80	3,082.36	0.25	9,568	8,483
Enfield	31.7	73.6	10.9	30.6	46.7	0.13	130.71	11.11	5.29	0.00	2,061.27	11.40	9,595	8,681
Epping Forest	3.4	74.9	8.0	17.5	20.6	1.49	67.43	1.98	1.82	8.83	42.06	0.82	15,897	5,485
Epsom and Ewell	19.7	83.9	9.0	11.9	16.9	0.35	17.17	1.69	1.38	2.68	182.50	1.27	9,535	3,316
Erewash	9.7	76.0	7.6	33.1	73.2	17.39	106.24	11.54	3.53	14.81	480.36	2.84	9,665	4,545
Exeter	20.9	68.0	16.1	34.1	75.2	0.60	107.49	12.32	11.58	32.93	44.43	1.79	3,231	2,063
Fareham	13.4	86.0	6.0	6.7	16.2	0.70	56.18	3.50	3.73	6.11	642.66	0.45	9,427	4,175
Fenland	1.4	74.5	10.3	29.1	44.4	18.68	126.46	6.58	7.40	8.42	980.97	1.02	14,164	4,813
Forest Heath	1.5	56.8	25.9	25.1	33.2	2.71	44.64	3.52	6.64	3.72	774.53	0.14	10,883	1,751
Forest of Dean	1.4	75.0	8.8	41.9	63.6	6.60	163.21	14.10	4.05	16.38	488.81	0.91	10,378	3,966
Fylde	4.3	80.9	12.2	25.0	50.2	3.22	75.94	6.44	4.32	13.81	386.54	1.05	12,422	3,008
Gateshead	13.9	52.7	11.4	44.3	81.4	36.85	211.61	12.69	2.92	8.12	1,228.02	17.95	10,396	3,459
Gedling	9.2	81.0	8.0	16.2	19.9	5.44	72.55	12.96	2.28	9.11	382.46	2.95	4,431	4,026
Gillingham	29.4	80.4	9.2	32.4	43.2	0.58	137.01	3.94	2.82	11.93	233.28	1.58	12,418	9,274
Glanford	1.2	78.3	9.1	28.5	43.5	3.71	117.66	6.76	7.02	9.22	801.18	0.30	11,811	2,866
Gloucester	25.1	76.0	9.6	35.0	82.8	7.89	98.67	17.14	4.07	5.51	171.78	4.08	8,878	4,841
Glyndwr	0.4	70.2	13.6	38.6	34.3	3.94	185.45	19.17	3.32	16.31	116.44	1.86	13,936	5,636
Gosport	34.1	70.1	12.5	22.3	34.3	1.48	95.68	7.96	3.28	2.56	54.79	1.35	7,061	2,532

LA	Density (pph) 1991	% owner-occupier 1991	% private rented 1991	% private dwgs pre-1919 1986	Unfit per 1,000 private dwgs 1986	Demol per 1,000 private dwgs 1978-94	Old grants per 1,000 private dwgs 1978-94	Ren grants per 1,000 private dwgs 1990-94	DFGs per 1,000 private dwgs 1990-94	MWA per 1,000 private dwgs 1990-94	Renovs per 1,000 LA dwgs 1978-94	HA rens per 1,000 private dwgs 1978-94	Ave mand renov grant 1994/95	Ave mand DF grant 1994/95
Gravesham	9.3	70.9	9.1	28.7	39.3	1.20	84.94	6.71	1.35	6.90	528.25	3.32	6,598	8,595
Great Grimsby	32.2	70.9	9.4	37.5	74.2	23.32	193.82	18.35	9.17	50.65	2,726.27	10.78	4,836	2,982
Great Yarmouth	5.0	69.1	11.0	35.7	51.3	5.02	139.25	14.06	4.22	27.73	203.83	1.50	10,928	3,106
Greenwich	43.6	47.1	14.6	51.2	53.2	0.88	111.58	13.33	2.97	18.06	154.21	24.49	12,084	11,561
Guildford	4.5	73.9	12.3	26.5	29.3	0.79	77.85	4.94	2.57	4.58	156.19	2.00	7,713	4,433
Hackney	92.9	26.9	25.2	88.5	99.4	18.43	146.60	7.53	1.35	9.38	207.46	99.21	18,534	12,015
Halton	16.8	63.0	12.1	21.5	38.1	19.09	137.97	0.00	0.00	0.00	197.44	5.15	–	–
Hambleton	0.6	70.9	15.3	38.9	68.3	0.87	98.46	2.24	1.37	1.99	466.31	2.03	12,380	3,266
Hammersmith	91.9	41.9	34.2	88.3	98.1	1.76	198.51	8.44	2.76	7.59	100.63	83.49	17,175	7,057
Harborough	1.1	80.6	8.4	30.3	35.8	1.66	114.50	7.96	3.51	3.42	798.48	0.99	9,655	4,891
Haringey	66.8	49.8	25.4	66.1	80.2	1.96	173.93	4.26	1.18	6.92	434.18	53.70	16,594	11,414
Harlow	24.8	48.4	5.5	3.5	8.9	0.00	15.72	0.27	1.69	0.00	432.10	0.00	7,759	2,956
Harrogate	1.1	75.4	15.5	35.8	66.6	1.61	48.08	4.25	1.77	7.09	755.57	2.11	8,557	3,173
Harrow	39.4	77.9	12.8	13.7	19.3	0.15	62.87	7.56	0.82	0.89	221.56	9.32	6,477	14,788
Hart	3.8	81.0	11.0	13.1	20.7	1.39	48.05	1.31	2.06	0.71	529.33	0.64	15,452	5,145
Hartlepool	9.6	63.1	10.8	35.0	68.3	57.16	164.29	22.28	9.14	13.26	508.69	15.34	9,246	1,531
Hastings	27.2	68.1	18.5	49.6	69.4	2.62	256.31	23.58	2.51	23.40	276.02	3.67	9,381	6,794
Havant	21.7	72.6	6.1	7.0	14.4	1.92	26.88	4.32	9.57	3.28	128.91	0.85	4,680	3,091
Havering	19.5	78.8	6.2	6.7	21.3	0.38	53.44	3.53	1.06	0.57	562.70	1.51	3,807	8,533
Hereford	24.7	63.7	12.9	25.1	59.9	2.74	88.46	4.04	3.08	0.89	239.99	9.04	5,550	2,610
Hertsmere	9.0	72.1	8.8	11.1	14.9	0.00	38.29	0.90	1.35	1.40	329.61	0.00	10,796	9,081
High Peak	1.6	74.4	10.1	51.9	102.3	3.85	166.61	12.07	5.10	6.38	221.13	1.31	8,511	1,364
Hillingdon	21.0	73.2	11.2	6.9	23.0	0.10	5.25	5.76	3.46	0.77	13.75	0.10	5,413	4,044
Hinckley & Bosworth	3.2	81.9	6.5	17.7	49.0	4.41	49.68	5.69	1.15	11.53	237.23	1.46	8,156	3,371
Holderness	0.9	80.1	8.9	25.1	39.2	7.31	73.91	2.04	1.02	6.23	189.24	12.23	20,192	6,111
Horsham	2.1	76.5	10.9	20.7	29.7	0.42	58.03	1.39	3.79	6.74	671.83	6.99	8,679	1,930
Hounslow	35.5	61.2	16.2	26.1	49.1	0.54	79.01	2.82	2.23	0.42	137.79	6.46	9,690	9,389
Hove	35.7	68.9	21.7	45.2	68.4	1.37	75.89	10.34	2.61	14.82	524.03	4.24	4,209	4,818
Hull	35.6	49.4	13.4	40.6	81.1	107.12	101.52	29.62	2.77	1.41	212.33	15.54	7,515	2,976
Huntingdon	1.6	72.1	14.0	18.6	26.5	2.37	82.81	1.24	1.13	0.92	600.25	2.26	15,591	10,307
Hyndburn	10.7	79.0	8.3	70.2	121.1	53.18	132.24	12.66	5.75	3.65	261.27	21.55	17,854	3,889
Ipswich	29.7	64.9	14.2	31.6	33.9	9.57	165.58	9.19	5.26	2.60	200.52	10.91	7,272	7,794
Islington	110.7	26.7	25.1	96.1	104.9	8.43	148.35	1.80	0.80	3.89	431.24	100.53	16,217	20,040
Islwyn	6.5	71.6	6.9	43.8	28.9	9.17	571.00	89.62	64.16	29.52	675.98	2.37	16,015	1,942

LA	Density (pph) 1991	% owner-occupier 1991	% private rented 1991	% private dwgs pre-1919 1986	Unfit per 1,000 private dwgs 1986	Demol per 1,000 private dwgs 1978-94	Old grants per 1,000 private dwgs 1978-94	Ren grants per 1,000 private dwgs 1990-94	DFGs per 1,000 private dwgs 1990-94	MWA per 1,000 private dwgs 1990-94	Renovs per 1,000 LA dwgs 1978-94	HA rens per 1,000 private dwgs 1978-94	Ave mand renov grant 1994/95	Ave mand DF grant 1994/95
Kennet	0.7	59.9	20.4	39.5	60.8	0.38	86.75	4.55	6.88	1.57	625.08	6.99	10,882	6,746
Kensington	115.9	39.9	46.3	76.9	89.8	2.49	85.16	2.13	0.48	2.35	617.95	106.86	23,140	6,586
Kerrier	1.9	76.5	12.4	46.7	69.5	10.90	87.94	13.33	5.39	11.08	722.26	0.51	11,646	3,105
Kettering	3.3	75.7	8.3	34.3	74.6	4.15	157.99	0.00	0.00	6.00	358.24	10.55	–	–
Kings Lynn	0.9	69.6	14.3	31.4	45.3	8.54	114.56	7.10	4.92	2.60	406.12	0.17	9,852	5,023
Kingston	35.4	74.7	15.0	27.2	31.2	0.74	88.99	5.76	1.51	5.20	2,090.37	13.01	9,919	7,815
Kingswood	24.3	81.5	5.5	16.2	19.5	4.16	84.18	7.78	5.46	11.40	320.90	0.61	13,905	1,261
Kirklees	9.1	70.5	9.9	44.6	80.8	11.12	120.63	8.99	4.49	0.00	697.30	5.76	12,824	3,095
Knowsley	15.6	53.3	7.5	8.2	30.3	1.68	158.59	10.66	11.99	12.77	288.11	1.18	7,021	2,222
Lambeth	89.8	36.2	26.9	69.0	82.7	11.37	85.29	1.60	0.45	0.00	65.02	55.08	11,153	4,599
Lancaster	2.1	76.7	14.4	35.3	70.1	1.92	88.63	8.72	8.08	9.75	479.54	4.49	6,241	2,383
Langbaurgh	5.9	68.3	8.1	27.6	55.2	34.43	141.84	6.53	3.99	4.57	167.13	9.01	7,615	2,950
Leeds	12.1	61.4	11.4	21.7	45.7	35.49	69.23	9.42	10.90	5.57	67.20	18.57	7,079	3,120
Leicester	36.9	57.5	15.3	41.6	103.2	8.72	263.40	28.12	4.91	2.93	295.44	47.36	10,623	4,556
Leominster	0.4	72.4	16.0	54.4	79.6	20.20	169.21	18.89	3.93	14.27	183.35	2.47	10,099	3,554
Lewes	3.0	78.8	10.2	19.8	32.4	1.26	63.16	11.76	1.72	9.37	694.18	5.30	11,932	3,500
Lewisham	66.5	47.8	18.9	68.4	68.3	1.79	32.57	5.62	0.85	6.59	97.85	23.10	11,079	10,778
Lichfield	2.8	77.8	7.4	17.2	20.5	1.67	51.77	2.24	5.52	3.99	243.49	1.19	14,130	4,334
Lincoln	23.0	62.3	11.0	47.4	94.5	6.33	62.86	10.41	3.14	4.95	306.94	1.87	9,248	2,493
Liverpool	40.1	51.1	20.3	48.8	94.0	20.28	130.42	19.61	4.88	0.57	174.58	115.76	11,833	7,489
Llanelli	3.2	72.5	6.3	38.7	74.8	2.20	349.66	40.94	7.53	28.04	63.22	3.43	20,774	3,239
Lliw Valley	2.9	75.6	5.8	41.8	72.9	9.99	330.50	28.69	15.04	6.08	257.18	1.08	14,857	5,146
Luton	39.6	74.1	10.3	15.8	30.9	7.70	87.13	10.08	1.73	7.64	25.18	3.65	8,923	3,817
Macclesfield	2.9	76.9	8.5	23.2	47.5	4.00	70.45	6.64	2.68	2.02	712.93	5.64	8,333	2,745
Maidstone	3.5	74.5	10.5	27.6	37.2	1.36	71.44	8.78	1.08	31.00	1,176.09	1.94	4,667	6,549
Maldon	1.5	80.6	8.6	27.3	36.3	1.15	56.07	2.94	5.08	2.60	167.10	0.46	6,605	2,605
Malvern Hills	1.0	74.1	12.2	44.3	52.2	12.58	119.97	9.69	1.93	10.99	667.72	6.58	13,896	7,744
Manchester	34.9	41.2	20.3	56.8	104.0	17.81	147.53	12.21	11.55	16.95	202.34	89.20	12,273	5,364
Mansfield	13.1	69.2	8.9	32.1	72.3	4.51	140.66	10.13	10.20	14.44	1,291.82	12.36	7,926	2,651
Medina	6.1	78.3	17.6	44.5	62.1	0.94	76.08	8.42	6.25	22.89	613.28	0.63	17,808	5,637
Meirionnydd	0.2	72.2	13.3	54.8	20.3	6.33	307.39	11.40	3.44	16.47	22.11	1.90	23,116	7,000
Melton	0.9	74.1	13.3	29.0	47.0	20.94	147.09	8.15	7.67	10.44	347.44	0.00	7,228	1,297
Mendip	1.3	73.0	12.7	40.5	61.7	4.40	110.52	10.01	4.56	16.07	676.95	4.64	10,680	3,666
Merthyr Tydfil	5.4	64.5	9.7	48.6	88.2	53.55	422.59	23.92	2.44	40.60	303.44	10.39	31,303	6,938

LA	Density (pph) 1991	% owner-occupier 1991	% private rented 1991	% private dwgs pre-1919 1986	Unfit per 1,000 private dwgs 1986	Demol per 1,000 private dwgs 1978-94	Old grants per 1,000 private dwgs 1978-94	Ren grants per 1,000 private dwgs 1990-94	DFGs per 1,000 private dwgs 1990-94	MWA per 1,000 private dwgs 1990-94	Renovs per 1,000 LA dwgs 1978-94	HA rens per 1,000 private dwgs 1978-94	Ave mand renov grant 1994/95	Ave mand DF grant 1994/95
Merton	44.4	70.5	15.8	35.0	39.1	5.93	73.33	9.86	1.50	3.26	1,097.41	8.80	6,532	8,783
Mid Bedfordshire	2.2	72.2	11.3	23.1	31.9	3.10	62.72	2.06	1.52	1.85	755.66	0.58	4,947	4,645
Mid Devon	0.7	69.4	14.4	46.4	69.2	2.31	118.20	7.22	7.97	29.98	144.69	5.41	21,006	4,926
Mid Suffolk	0.9	74.0	11.8	35.9	44.8	7.72	75.01	4.97	3.50	6.86	341.72	0.47	12,541	3,553
Mid Sussex	3.6	79.8	16.4	17.4	19.6	0.17	40.20	1.45	1.91	3.68	1,021.60	5.22	8,940	3,917
Middlesbrough	26.1	61.0	11.1	31.2	62.8	132.07	163.86	29.27	6.87	19.49	194.39	16.21	–	–
Milton Keynes	5.7	69.2	8.7	10.6	18.3	0.91	69.32	6.10	4.76	10.01	509.75	2.76	7,128	3,375
Mole Valley	3.1	76.0	11.0	22.4	25.6	3.64	80.15	1.68	3.65	4.12	564.69	7.62	11,473	6,487
Monmouth	0.9	74.5	10.2	29.3	68.1	1.19	146.42	9.19	4.15	15.50	135.09	0.51	18,046	3,500
Montgomery	0.3	66.1	15.3	47.4	76.9	11.13	183.20	26.92	4.73	19.12	202.11	1.28	24,135	4,464
Neath	3.2	73.7	6.8	33.6	59.3	6.07	369.16	52.90	22.98	9.21	211.37	2.48	12,892	5,880
New Forest	2.1	81.0	9.5	15.1	26.6	1.81	64.01	6.46	5.67	1.39	278.97	0.25	14,071	5,142
Newark	1.6	72.4	10.4	23.5	42.1	2.16	128.78	8.62	14.73	12.09	133.70	3.82	11,717	3,775
Newbury	1.9	74.1	20.7	19.8	28.4	1.56	62.06	2.95	2.79	4.92	578.09	7.53	12,105	5,420
Newcastle-on-Tyne	23.2	49.9	15.5	37.1	75.0	36.78	88.42	3.22	1.92	5.05	296.62	38.94	10,363	6,988
Newcastle-under-Lyne	5.6	71.0	7.8	28.6	67.6	15.05	66.70	2.44	2.30	6.12	176.93	4.16	12,788	4,721
Newham	58.4	49.8	19.4	68.3	80.6	16.14	49.58	5.19	0.41	0.85	29.05	27.56	–	–
Newport	7.0	67.5	9.4	28.4	16.7	26.08	177.23	19.24	3.92	33.46	179.51	11.35	17,817	5,179
North Bedfordshire	2.8	73.2	21.8	27.9	37.6	3.06	40.53	7.17	1.87	5.73	660.11	5.62	6,699	5,896
North Cornwall	0.6	71.8	14.6	41.7	67.9	1.86	126.57	12.12	1.99	9.13	107.59	1.56	13,874	8,563
North Devon	0.8	73.8	15.3	43.2	65.7	1.80	109.12	15.98	7.60	10.58	88.27	5.97	4,231	2,311
North Dorset	0.9	70.8	14.9	40.7	61.5	3.49	64.30	2.59	1.32	0.72	456.68	8.00	11,060	3,608
North East Derbyshire	3.5	69.0	5.4	23.0	55.8	9.24	95.71	4.06	4.42	10.36	906.70	0.50	7,314	2,159
North Herts	3.0	65.2	11.0	25.6	35.8	1.62	43.16	6.13	4.90	8.26	553.35	1.40	8,339	7,878
North Kesteven	0.9	72.9	12.2	21.3	37.1	1.62	71.93	6.51	3.28	12.78	1,927.13	0.28	18,549	4,897
North Norfolk	0.9	69.2	15.6	39.3	57.8	6.08	130.38	7.97	3.75	18.53	131.68	2.38	10,961	5,155
North Shropshire	0.8	70.1	15.0	48.8	72.7	5.66	147.98	11.63	3.65	14.02	201.87	0.38	13,348	4,967
North Tyneside	23.0	60.0	11.3	32.8	68.8	10.50	204.05	6.54	5.35	19.85	481.28	18.79	8,334	3,550
North Warwickshire	2.1	73.0	9.1	24.1	58.3	1.70	62.32	5.38	5.05	13.17	779.58	0.44	9,091	3,322
North West Leicester	2.9	73.5	9.3	35.7	76.1	3.12	180.44	18.87	5.62	19.36	406.15	8.59	6,115	2,073
North Wiltshire	1.5	72.0	13.2	31.7	37.4	2.80	108.57	5.60	2.12	5.81	237.01	0.09	14,389	8,305
Northampton	22.4	70.4	7.9	26.8	32.3	6.25	41.21	7.39	8.18	15.2	359.34	13.38	7,951	2,455
Northavon	2.8	83.3	6.7	12.3	14.9	1.13	36.66	2.68	2.10	5.62	252.99	1.18	7,107	1,575
Norwich	31.0	46.9	15.8	52.8	52.3	3.14	141.87	20.78	11.48	6.89	229.38	12.01	6,959	4,218

LA	Density (pph) 1991	% owner-occupier 1991	% private rented 1991	% private dwgs pre-1919 1986	Unfit per 1,000 private dwgs 1986	Demol per 1,000 private dwgs 1978-94	Old grants per 1,000 private dwgs 1978-94	Ren grants per 1,000 private dwgs 1990-94	DFGs per 1,000 private dwgs 1990-94	MWA per 1,000 private dwgs 1990-94	Renovs per 1,000 LA dwgs 1978-94	HA rens per 1,000 private dwgs 1978-94	Ave mand renov grant 1994/95	Ave mand DF grant 1994/95
Nottingham	35.3	51.9	15.5	40.8	97.3	40.20	178.84	10.40	4.79	0.24	155.39	48.31	10,553	5,789
Nuneaton	14.8	76.4	6.7	21.8	55.5	0.97	51.51	8.66	6.77	5.71	312.53	9.61	7,927	2,441
Oadby & Wigston	21.9	85.8	6.3	8.5	10.5	0.45	78.03	5.59	4.90	3.32	993.24	1.63	5,240	6,097
Ogwr	4.6	76.3	6.9	30.2	56.5	7.21	248.84	26.30	6.62	24.19	34.59	0.51	15,625	4,711
Oldham	15.4	67.3	8.3	42.1	76.2	64.63	174.12	11.31	2.53	8.95	653.50	22.91	24,204	3,597
Oswestry	1.3	69.3	12.6	48.2	72.3	7.59	78.30	6.44	3.25	0.00	107.94	2.60	7,752	2,697
Oxford	24.1	55.6	22.2	37.2	40.2	3.66	96.93	8.30	9.40	52.27	581.32	9.58	10,707	3,811
Pendle	5.0	79.1	8.1	75.9	131.0	24.29	202.31	20.40	6.80	1.11	578.32	5.26	5,374	2,570
Penwith	2.1	72.0	14.2	55.6	81.9	6.98	108.79	13.96	6.39	17.94	232.17	0.29	8,034	2,686
Peterborough	4.6	65.3	13.9	24.6	34.2	2.59	150.57	8.78	1.87	17.61	33.48	5.86	14,259	4,430
Plymouth	32.8	63.9	16.4	35.4	77.4	1.71	101.11	4.83	3.63	21.88	870.00	15.23	17,421	5,885
Poole	20.5	79.8	10.0	16.0	32.4	1.58	57.46	4.21	1.43	3.12	1,194.66	0.60	5,140	3,473
Port Talbot	3.4	69.5	5.3	32.1	39.3	8.79	279.32	58.86	13.18	6.56	1,751.45	3.42	9,940	4,268
Portsmouth	41.6	67.1	16.2	51.0	51.7	3.09	136.93	11.43	4.55	13.22	1,094.34	21.43	11,580	3,682
Preseli	0.6	69.1	12.1	32.3	103.9	3.79	244.22	30.55	17.53	27.62	121.07	0.77	33,183	4,273
Preston	8.9	67.7	13.4	36.4	68.7	20.75	156.74	7.86	3.94	1.61	228.95	8.91	15,641	4,970
Purbeck	1.0	72.6	16.1	25.3	42.8	0.29	37.04	2.99	3.92	11.37	999.93	0.65	4,883	2,287
Radnor	0.2	69.8	18.2	49.4	51.0	2.94	211.23	24.90	14.81	21.07	62.79	4.47	17,574	3,811
Reading	31.9	67.5	16.7	38.4	39.1	5.09	112.32	12.18	3.69	2.40	277.19	1.75	9,187	6,882
Redbridge	40.1	78.2	11.4	19.3	24.0	1.00	218.94	5.01	1.47	0.98	495.13	2.23	13,941	8,995
Redditch	14.4	65.4	5.9	10.5	12.6	0.80	43.96	5.45	2.61	7.79	586.35	0.05	7,167	4,459
Reigate & Banstead	9.1	76.8	9.4	22.9	26.2	0.39	44.78	2.29	1.51	3.33	384.16	0.52	6,565	5,818
Restormel	1.9	74.8	13.5	36.6	57.7	3.90	113.42	9.51	5.86	19.82	429.67	0.79	7,824	3,896
Rhondda	0.0	78.0	7.9	78.8	129.1	19.36	772.80	71.29	11.75	47.95	1,021.16	7.33	16,218	3,094
Rhuddlan	5.0	75.8	12.9	17.0	24.0	0.20	28.39	13.13	4.82	14.45	131.04	3.65	12,069	6,375
Rhymney Valley	5.8	69.3	7.2	38.5	46.3	19.24	297.03	36.10	11.56	55.59	879.17	4.88	16,591	4,537
Ribble Valley	0.9	81.7	10.5	46.4	64.8	1.11	109.84	3.44	3.26	28.01	1,635.59	1.63	23,714	2,088
Richmond	29.1	70.0	19.2	48.6	51.7	0.34	83.48	8.01	3.34	3.88	657.38	12.77	6,052	3,859
Richmondshire	0.3	61.2	24.2	49.9	86.2	5.54	86.38	2.30	6.74	1.71	363.41	0.68	22,466	3,757
Rochdale	12.7	64.1	8.1	41.0	73.5	49.11	161.45	10.89	6.27	6.14	493.69	16.47	5,136	3,696
Rochester	9.1	76.6	16.3	26.1	36.2	2.10	108.01	8.93	6.75	10.31	483.45	1.19	7,265	4,778
Rochford	4.6	86.4	6.1	7.0	14.8	0.82	37.32	1.66	2.34	0.04	460.88	0.00	7,652	1,552
Rossendale	4.8	73.8	7.3	61.4	106.5	38.41	208.21	12.80	7.77	14.48	601.07	22.34	16,470	2,700
Rother	1.6	79.4	11.1	31.9	39.5	0.58	59.23	17.56	2.63	2.89	1,640.91	1.10	6,546	5,617

LA	Density (pph) 1991	% owner-occupier 1991	% private rented 1991	% private dwgs pre-1919 1986	Unfit per 1,000 private dwgs 1986	Demol per 1,000 private dwgs 1978-94	Old grants per 1,000 private dwgs 1978-94	Ren grants per 1,000 private dwgs 1990-94	DFGs per 1,000 private dwgs 1990-94	MWA per 1,000 private dwgs 1990-94	Renovs per 1,000 LA dwgs 1978-94	HA rens per 1,000 private dwgs 1978-94	Ave mand renov grant 1994/95	Ave mand DF grant 1994/95
Rotherham	8.9	61.9	8.0	22.3	48.0	42.05	188.36	8.81	43.14	13.07	224.49	9.13	6,424	2,736
Rugby	2.4	75.5	10.2	30.0	35.9	8.90	81.29	28.75	5.06	17.74	210.20	14.60	5,236	3,474
Runnymede	9.2	76.9	10.0	20.3	23.3	4.07	111.23	4.82	3.90	12.45	420.03	0.29	8,374	4,062
Rushcliffe	2.4	79.3	10.6	21.1	38.4	0.18	125.37	3.07	5.85	6.78	998.65	1.04	4,693	2,447
Rushmoor	21.1	67.0	16.6	21.3	30.8	7.79	87.62	1.63	7.48	3.43	1,225.64	0.31	9,314	7,173
Rutland	0.8	66.5	19.8	38.6	45.3	0.55	85.88	5.34	4.56	5.63	489.22	0.44	6,146	1,560
Rydale	0.6	76.6	20.1	31.1	56.9	0.89	68.05	3.93	5.05	7.36	232.62	12.61	19,754	3,121
Salford	22.8	52.7	12.1	41.7	81.8	96.36	133.87	17.44	3.19	0.85	565.89	39.65	10,314	7,866
Salisbury	1.0	62.8	19.4	39.0	61.3	2.61	63.37	1.17	9.88	8.78	83.12	0.27	9,882	3,400
Sandwell	33.9	54.4	7.4	31.8	80.8	65.69	113.40	14.68	4.33	4.37	202.96	18.97	23,574	6,860
Scarborough	1.3	70.9	14.4	40.0	74.1	3.60	68.99	6.57	4.21	5.10	413.13	2.56	12,791	4,375
Scunthorpe	18.2	62.1	7.6	17.5	48.7	3.41	107.94	6.07	8.80	5.52	540.39	15.39	5,295	2,439
Sedgefield	4.2	58.2	6.9	37.8	69.8	7.95	97.66	5.02	3.14	10.97	353.07	11.62	6,980	7,273
Sedgemoor	1.7	76.4	9.1	34.4	54.0	2.68	81.69	0.86	3.14	4.40	247.85	0.47	14,598	2,568
Sefton	18.9	72.9	13.6	35.1	69.7	-.24	111.40	5.54	2.43	1.18	99.18	32.38	8,138	4,740
Selby	1.2	76.9	9.4	27.7	39.5	-.57	84.43	6.82	2.54	4.93	727.01	0.79	7,321	3,753
Sevenoaks	3.0	75.2	20.1	26.0	28.3	0.82	58.04	6.68	3.24	2.07	338.33	2.88	8,984	5,265
Sheffield	13.6	56.8	9.8	38.2	74.4	101.07	119.56	6.92	9.62	6.68	144.32	9.84	11,890	4,159
Shepway	2.6	73.2	15.9	36.8	55.0	2.69	89.57	5.51	2.26	8.17	1,523.01	6.21	9,441	6,592
Shrewsbury	1.5	71.8	11.2	29.3	48.3	3.07	70.47	12.05	3.82	4.71	115.95	2.45	9,003	4,310
Slough	36.8	66.5	11.1	10.6	26.9	0.39	34.13	8.76	6.49	3.62	345.26	0.84	13,848	6,460
Solihull	11.2	76.7	6.2	5.5	7.5	0.74	31.18	7.00	3.70	3.21	3,051.40	0.54	2,363	2,772
South Bedfordshire	5.1	76.9	7.3	14.4	22.4	1.45	64.67	2.43	1.87	5.52	230.46	0.65	4,552	2,558
South Bucks	4.3	76.2	18.3	11.0	14.2	1.80	41.56	3.96	2.90	1.50	836.75	0.05	14,442	4,897
South Cambridgeshire	1.3	72.4	11.8	21.6	30.5	1.46	27.91	2.60	2.60	2.49	312.58	7.08	12,954	2,923
South Derbyshire	2.1	76.9	8.4	35.4	75.7	9.40	142.61	7.48	3.03	7.47	669.36	1.17	6,777	3,350
South Hams	0.9	75.9	13.2	37.7	58.6	1.50	76.50	8.67	7.58	6.75	138.17	2.29	10,921	2,826
South Hereford	0.6	74.7	14.5	53.5	78.6	20.23	113.29	5.35	1.52	3.34	47.41	0.79	19,683	2,072
South Holland	0.9	73.4	8.9	29.3	48.0	7.64	79.03	6.57	3.54	14.68	370.20	0.79	10,125	4,426
South Kesteven	1.2	69.6	11.9	32.7	51.1	10.55	75.28	4.10	2.32	12.60	409.21	0.87	10,291	5,675
South Lakeland	0.6	73.7	14.6	45.4	79.4	2.65	60.87	3.78	1.79	2.56	220.44	1.63	20,598	2,699
South Norfolk	1.1	77.3	10.5	22.6	30.9	2.94	66.15	7.23	2.83	17.26	855.33	0.00	19,188	4,641
South Northants	1.1	74.6	11.2	28.0	32.9	1.48	118.85	9.26	8.59	10.25	548.47	0.51	11,611	1,988
South Oxfordshire	1.8	74.3	12.7	25.6	34.2	1.09	56.63	4.53	3.28	6.65	36.21	4.99	14,204	2,245

LA	Density (pph) 1991	% owner-occupier 1991	% private rented 1991	% private dwgs pre-1919 1986	Unfit per 1,000 private dwgs 1986	Demol per 1,000 private dwgs 1978-94	Old grants per 1,000 private dwgs 1978-94	Ren grants per 1,000 private dwgs 1990-94	DFGs per 1,000 private dwgs 1990-94	MWA per 1,000 private dwgs 1990-94	Renovs per 1,000 LA dwgs 1978-94	HA rens per 1,000 private dwgs 1978-94	Ave mand renov grant 1994/95	Ave mand DF grant 1994/95
South Pembs	1.0	69.8	14.2	42.5	48.7	6.32	345.22	41.67	9.22	43.04	1,802.90	1.14	32,000	9,548
South Ribble	9.0	84.8	5.9	16.7	31.6	1.74	109.76	4.23	6.00	21.45	705.65	1.24	22,572	5,603
South Shropshire	0.4	72.3	16.7	58.5	85.2	7.12	90.15	5.46	3.56	36.00	326.71	0.55	23,806	4,322
South Somerset	1.5	71.7	10.4	36.6	56.8	1.77	48.69	4.80	10.39	5.57	441.08	0.49	13,842	2,478
South Staffs	2.6	78.8	6.8	12.0	14.4	5.62	26.38	1.73	1.08	12.50	857.76	0.77	13,014	3,281
South Tyneside	24.6	50.2	10.2	47.6	86.7	57.82	126.84	9.37	3.97	16.67	547.28	35.74	12,617	4,692
South Wight	2.0	79.8	17.3	40.5	56.6	1.08	120.02	13.04	9.40	8.73	813.40	0.31	8,610	3,549
Southampton	39.5	60.9	15.4	24.2	26.9	11.90	121.82	11.55	2.85	17.68	261.02	14.29	11,587	5,413
Southend	38.0	75.6	13.6	36.6	59.5	0.41	129.53	6.58	3.29	2.13	321.90	11.09	4,785	2,694
Southwark	76.0	27.2	21.7	44.6	55.1	58.53	120.89	7.12	1.35	0.48	57.54	31.66	21,961	5,597
Spelthorne	15.9	80.0	9.9	11.2	21.5	0.73	77.74	2.82	8.50	6.56	102.68	11.10	4,517	4,732
St Albans	7.8	76.0	10.3	18.8	21.6	0.62	52.42	4.57	2.34	8.82	1,567.44	0.50	7,898	6,701
St Edmundsbury	1.4	65.3	13.6	29.4	38.2	5.14	98.58	3.74	3.74	3.15	212.58	1.91	10,658	3,778
St Helens	13.4	67.5	7.8	29.3	58.8	62.08	142.49	17.34	5.75	40.79	778.42	38.68	15,149	4,731
Staff Moorlands	1.7	83.5	6.9	31.2	69.8	3.94	77.75	4.38	4.19	0.00	455.68	1.32	15,417	3,656
Stafford	2.0	74.5	9.6	23.2	27.8	3.69	45.50	4.21	3.69	0.00	1,071.56	1.63	4,029	3,144
Stevenage	28.9	55.2	5.9	11.9	19.4	0.00	25.66	1.87	3.02	3.77	501.69	5.24	3,610	3,569
Stockport	22.6	77.8	8.7	26.4	48.1	10.70	89.06	6.16	3.80	4.20	653.62	8.80	14,889	2,627
Stockton	8.5	68.4	8.3	15.8	37.6	6.82	93.82	20.71	16.23	7.65	525.36	11.62	2,888	1,520
Stoke-on-Trent	26.4	66.4	9.0	40.9	86.4	45.36	141.67	20.06	7.17	2.45	227.37	16.29	13,026	3,334
Stratford	1.1	73.1	11.8	31.0	36.7	11.45	54.87	1.96	1.36	6.29	1,312.83	0.15	11,187	6,749
Stroud	2.2	75.5	8.7	37.3	44.0	10.94	125.15	12.70	5.13	23.39	531.17	1.61	13,413	5,325
Suffolk Coastal	1.2	71.0	17.9	37.2	53.6	2.65	132.62	5.08	4.74	7.33	479.46	1.97	9,217	2,234
Sunderland	21.3	53.3	8.1	43.1	78.7	4.23	63.54	7.64	3.64	10.03	1,554.34	10.48	16,697	4,426
Surrey Heath	8.3	81.1	9.3	12.9	21.3	1.82	39.93	3.01	1.86	1.98	847.49	0.04	9,167	3,635
Sutton	38.9	75.2	10.3	32.6	37.2	0.62	71.64	4.91	1.86	13.50	328.60	24.82	6,203	8,527
Swale	3.1	74.3	20.4	34.6	45.3	3.94	200.30	21.77	8.80	22.64	325.42	0.28	6,521	5,528
Swansea	7.4	68.0	10.9	33.8	63.5	3.27	279.95	27.78	25.51	7.35	594.38	8.92	16,228	3,171
Taff-Ely	5.7	76.3	6.3	36.0	64.9	3.33	327.71	21.87	6.48	8.60	163.22	2.43	28,019	3,776
Tameside	21.0	66.9	8.0	38.4	72.7	39.93	163.67	8.83	2.53	5.70	197.27	22.13	17,065	4,796
Tamworth	22.7	69.8	6.7	15.8	18.8	1.19	46.95	2.55	4.75	9.62	196.43	0.65	5,747	4,306
Tandridge	3.1	78.6	9.4	24.1	27.5	0.16	90.17	0.41	2.05	0.00	934.15	0.00	1,670	4,586
Taunton Deane	2.0	69.2	11.6	39.0	60.0	3.30	85.74	13.11	6.30	10.76	881.16	2.59	8,466	3,128
Teesdale	0.3	67.5	19.9	68.0	112.2	8.81	156.12	3.16	2.89	9.08	570.92	12.41	8,034	2,307

LA	Density (pph) 1991	% owner-occupier 1991	% private rented 1991	% private dwgs pre-1919 1986	Unfit per 1,000 private dwgs 1986	Demol per 1,000 private dwgs 1973-94	Old grants per 1,000 private dwgs 1978-94	Ren grants per 1,000 private dwgs 1990-94	DFGs per 1,000 private dwgs 1990-94	MWA per 1,000 private dwgs 1990-94	Renovs per 1,000 LA dwgs 1978-94	HA rens per 1,000 private dwgs 1978-94	Ave mand renov grant 1994/95	Ave mand DF grant 1994/95
Teignbridge	1.6	78.6	11.7	33.2	53.0	3.00	67.95	10.33	7.04	9.63	137.65	0.31	8,741	3,858
Tendring	3.8	83.1	9.7	18.7	33.0	2.82	76.45	9.90	4.61	0.00	816.61	0.68	7,319	3,142
Test Valley	1.6	70.4	13.2	20.1	29.3	3.33	70.57	6.73	2.48	7.07	984.94	4.11	12,593	4,800
Tewkesbury	1.7	76.3	11.4	16.8	19.9	4.00	100.63	7.48	9.24	3.39	94.90	7.16	9,914	2,946
Thamesdown	7.4	73.0	9.1	24.8	29.6	3.89	98.85	9.91	3.26	8.03	316.38	6.18	8,430	4,277
Thanet	12.0	73.2	14.5	36.9	57.9	1.57	90.05	4.51	1.78	8.52	917.46	3.15	18,071	5,012
The Wrekin	4.8	66.3	6.9	20.6	24.3	7.41	66.94	3.79	9.10	6.55	147.80	2.30	12,407	2,777
Three Rivers	8.8	73.2	8.3	12.7	16.5	0.51	39.39	4.68	4.59	6.51	365.04	2.14	4,678	3,606
Thurrock	7.8	69.2	5.6	14.5	16.7	0.53	54.29	2.21	5.06	1.03	248.17	1.02	7,921	3,443
Tonbridge	4.2	73.9	19.3	28.7	37.5	2.92	81.68	4.72	5.32	8.78	780.11	0.84	14,853	4,287
Torbay	19.0	78.0	15.6	27.9	47.7	1.23	126.35	12.17	7.77	0.02	215.96	1.90	8,702	3,838
Torfaen	7.2	61.6	5.4	26.3	25.8	13.77	164.71	16.06	16.06	34.58	426.11	2.64	22,057	5,513
Torridge	0.5	75.4	14.6	50.5	75.3	0.45	152.31	7.53	3.57	10.99	33.78	4.02	15,587	5,357
Tower Hamlets	81.6	23.2	18.5	45.5	53.7	25.13	50.11	0.00	0.00	0.42	581.92	100.59	—	—
Trafford	20.2	72.8	10.2	29.6	67.5	12.12	67.12	9.46	5.66	4.59	113.95	7.88	8,482	5,515
Tunbridge Wells	3.0	71.3	15.1	51.1	61.1	1.16	84.63	9.55	1.46	1.25	238.66	1.48	10,853	6,052
Tynedale	0.3	66.5	15.2	52.2	89.9	1.06	104.47	3.01	1.65	2.91	56.02	0.89	11,207	4,360
Uttlesford	1.0	72.6	13.1	31.5	40.3	0.60	51.91	2.34	1.19	1.94	85.47	0.00	13,940	5,050
Vale of Glamorgan	3.8	75.4	11.7	28.0	27.2	1.57	179.10	24.52	21.68	12.12	255.03	2.61	9,418	2,324
Vale of White Horse	1.9	74.2	12.9	15.1	24.2	3.46	34.78	6.66	6.93	12.7	313.07	0.38	12,479	6,897
Vale Royal	3.0	74.8	6.5	31.0	48.5	5.08	87.60	3.73	1.74	1.19	246.83	0.06	6,620	3,250
Wakefield	9.3	61.0	7.4	34.4	65.3	15.88	114.46	13.95	5.16	4.62	418.39	4.15	9,507	4,888
Walsall	24.5	60.7	7.4	25.5	62.5	7.69	151.71	4.65	3.15	12.25	411.76	17.31	13,729	8,427
Waltham Forest	53.5	61.5	17.5	61.6	80.0	7.44	53.72	3.59	0.52	0.77	154.26	12.20	20,875	13,853
Wandsworth	72.4	53.6	25.7	68.7	83.6	1.84	228.37	11.33	1.31	5.65	1,123.42	51.96	12,426	8,018
Wansbeck	9.1	59.6	8.8	44.1	81.0	10.53	184.34	42.01	6.90	3.82	987.56	13.76	7,198	5,740
Wansdyke	2.5	78.8	7.3	31.4	37.1	0.47	78.24	8.75	7.82	12.13	1,723.48	2.41	10,260	1,720
Warrington	10.4	73.5	7.1	22.3	37.9	11.33	91.09	8.89	4.00	22.77	207.05	4.41	9,062	4,729
Warwick	4.1	73.2	12.1	25.9	30.8	0.51	6.45	0.30	0.31	1.90	316.49	1.03	5,830	3,181
Watford	34.8	71.0	11.1	37.1	40.3	0.90	100.79	8.95	1.71	5.31	1,095.22	1.63	6,592	5,277
Waveney	2.9	73.5	13.5	35.7	51.0	11.49	254.66	14.65	13.25	3.11	373.91	4.71	4,305	2,217
Waverley	3.3	75.0	10.9	30.8	33.3	0.25	69.15	1.74	1.33	1.08	120.09	1.08	7,688	3,307
Wealden	1.6	83.0	9.6	26.5	40.9	0.77	67.67	11.84	2.71	27.32	558.93	0.43	12,252	5,452
Wear Valley	1.2	62.6	10.9	63.4	107.4	17.83	230.26	11.92	4.50	20.10	543.43	13.21	9,698	3,155

LA	Density (pph) 1991	% owner-occupier 1991	% private rented 1991	% private dwgs pre-1919 1986	Unfit per 1,000 private dwgs 1986	Demol per 1,000 private dwgs 1978-94	Old grants per 1,000 private dwgs 1978-94	Ren grants per 1,000 private dwgs 1990-94	DFGs per 1,000 private dwgs 1990-94	MWA per 1,000 private dwgs 1990-94	Renovs per 1,000 LA dwgs 1978-94	HA rens per 1,000 private dwgs 1978-94	Ave mand renov grant 1994/95	Ave mand DF grant 1994/95
Wellingborough	4.2	70.5	7.5	29.6	35.1	10.04	123.15	13.33	6.64	2.94	654.14	2.69	4,632	2,124
Welwyn Hatfield	7.2	60.8	7.9	6.7	9.8	0.83	25.03	0.21	2.17	0.62	1,019.18	0.00	6,988	3,046
West Devon	0.4	76.3	14.9	50.8	75.9	1.67	133.00	2.96	2.41	3.60	56.57	1.61	8,613	2,343
West Dorset	0.8	70.4	14.6	37.8	58.6	3.63	86.18	9.11	3.48	17.88	229.23	5.22	8,753	3,750
West Lancashire	3.2	71.7	6.1	23.5	38.5	3.75	91.95	7.72	4.71	18.69	647.12	1.99	19,609	2,634
West Lindsey	0.7	72.6	13.1	40.6	62.3	2.63	141.69	7.59	3.52	30.33	499.35	1.74	6,513	3,242
West Oxfordshire	1.3	70.3	17.0	29.4	37.7	1.85	59.02	2.92	18.77	1.66	516.57	3.20	5,311	2,411
West Somerset	0.4	69.3	16.4	48.1	80.9	5.74	140.20	10.35	10.76	4.42	231.68	19.39	10,014	1,589
West Wiltshire	2.1	75.8	10.5	27.6	32.6	3.52	82.80	7.67	3.26	4.27	40.83	2.90	7,578	2,339
Westminster	81.1	35.1	44.5	69.6	84.2	13.02	83.12	2.00	0.88	9.73	381.14	99.41	11,085	1,373
Weymouth	14.7	72.7	13.3	33.0	53.7	1.44	126.08	7.80	2.98	8.85	460.13	9.25	7,373	4,114
Wigan	15.4	70.0	5.9	33.4	62.9	38.49	100.15	12.94	3.35	9.88	567.62	8.34	5,387	2,329
Winchester	1.5	69.5	14.6	23.7	25.6	0.98	95.58	5.01	2.36	19.21	134.07	57.84	18,075	3,795
Windsor	6.7	73.7	13.7	26.7	28.7	0.40	63.86	3.08	1.33	2.03	328.50	10.24	5,238	7,420
Wirral	20.8	73.2	12.0	36.6	72.0	23.54	132.47	14.01	5.17	4.10	293.53	27.14	16,689	3,609
Woking	13.6	77.0	10.1	17.0	19.2	0.82	53.67	1.79	2.40	2.58	2,100.34	30.17	7,526	5,893
Wokingham	7.8	85.2	7.8	10.5	18.7	0.37	28.29	0.68	2.70	2.10	300.19	1.34	12,902	5,475
Wolverhampton	35.2	57.7	8.6	26.1	70.0	29.91	106.47	13.60	3.46	17.38	566.82	15.38	8,870	3,443
Woodspring	4.7	79.5	9.7	23.0	24.7	1.70	35.31	2.90	2.08	5.19	1,007.07	1.19	4,795	3,688
Worcester	24.6	71.9	10.4	30.8	69.0	2.71	105.75	5.35	3.10	19.65	442.90	6.47	11,407	2,831
Worthing	29.6	80.2	12.9	18.2	37.4	0.34	57.70	6.74	3.40	16.07	853.02	4.18	10,043	5,293
Wrexham Maelor	3.1	60.4	8.4	22.8	18.3	14.61	40.03	12.07	5.76	12.49	625.97	0.21	25,515	4,773
Wychavon	1.5	73.4	9.0	29.8	35.2	2.31	110.53	4.68	5.00	16.81	725.27	0.32	9,527	3,865
Wycombe	4.9	75.6	10.4	17.5	26.9	2.44	62.93	2.31	1.14	9.29	479.92	1.47	12,083	4,049
Wyre	3.6	85.0	7.6	19.3	42.1	2.17	30.67	8.48	7.53	5.60	351.70	2.54	7,004	2,698
Wyre Forest	4.9	74.9	6.7	22.9	27.4	11.72	86.95	5.64	4.64	23.55	1,352.92	1.68	27,779	4,358
Ynys Mon	1.0	68.9	12.3	38.9	30.2	2.54	160.27	27.25	2.63	9.05	542.20	1.05	19,807	6,800
York	33.5	64.7	13.2	32.9	66.1	8.98	134.97	6.81	2.20	21.94	1,057.64	10.59	19,675	5,485

Regardless of Frontiers
Children's rights and global learning

Regardless of Frontiers
Children's rights and global learning

Don Harrison

Trentham Books

Stoke on Trent, UK and Sterling, USA

Trentham Books Limited

Westview House   22883 Quicksilver Drive
734 London Road   Sterling
Oakhill   VA 20166-2012
Stoke on Trent   USA
Staffordshire
England ST4 5NP

First published 2008

British Library Cataloguing-in-Publication Data
A catalogue record for this book is available from the British Library

ISBN: 978 1 85856 400 5

Cover image: Panama – Children of different countries learning together.

The Material on pages 16 and 19 is reproduced from *Deadlines: Media bias about the Third World - A simulation for secondary schools (1984)/ TILT NINE* (1985) with the permission of Oxfam GB, Oxfam House, John Smith Drive, Cowley, Oxford OX4 2JY, UK www.oxfam.org.uk/education. Oxfam GB does not necessarily endorse any text or activities that accompany the materials.'

Designed and typeset by Trentham Print Design Ltd, Chester and printed in Great Britain by Hobbs the Printers, Hampshire.

Contents

Acknowledgements • vi

Introduction • vii

Chapter 1: **Children's rights** • 1

Chapter 2: **Global learning** • 13

2.1: Learning rights • 13

2.2: Welfare rights • 21

2.3: Classroom experience • 44

Chapter 3: **Crossing frontiers** • 61

3.1: The movement for rights education • 62

3.2: Models for rights education • 66

Chapter 4: **Practical guidance** • 79

Chapter 5: **Resources** • 89

Bibliography • 99

Index • 101

Acknowledgements

This book is dedicated to the children whose lives I have been privileged to share in Burkina Faso, England, Malawi, Malaysia, Panama, Peru, Scotland and Somalia. Some of their words and pictures are presented here, acknowledging a trusted copyright put in my hands to further their rights to expression. Most will now be adults and will be pleased to know that their visions may be helping teachers and other school pupils to learn about their worlds of childhood.

Fieldwork examples from projects with children come mostly from Save the Children's development education unit which has inspired a lot of the thinking and practice in this book. Many thanks are due to Andrew Hutchinson for his vision that Global Child Rights Education is both possible and valuable. Thanks also for project work from the City Academy in Bristol.

Introduction

A s the title suggests, this book is about children sharing ideas across frontiers of any kind, as required by Article 13.1 of the UN *Convention on the Rights of the Child*

> The child shall have the right to freedom of expression; this right shall include freedom to seek, receive and impart information and ideas of all kinds, regardless of frontiers, either orally, in writing or in print, in the form of art, or through any other media of the child's choice.

Chapter 1 introduces the UN *Convention* as an important educational document although not all teachers may be familiar with it. It relates the *Convention* to other visions for improving children's lives, including the UK's *Every Child Matters*.

Chapter 2 separates learning *through* rights and learning *about* rights. Each is shown in fieldwork sections based on my experience as an English teacher and NGO education worker.

I began my career as a pre-university English teacher in Malawi and, after qualifying as an English teacher, in Cameroon and Yorkshire. During the early 1980s I worked for Oxfam as a regional education adviser. From this phase I have chosen examples of *learning rights*: expression, information and respect as groundwork for envisioning learning across frontiers.

After teaching English in Malaysia during the later 1980s, I worked for Save the Children's Education unit, creating materials and training teachers. Recently I have worked for Citizenship NGOs and as an English teacher for refugees in Bristol. From this phase I have chosen examples and children's drawings of *welfare rights*, to give a global rights dimension to the five outcomes of *Every Child Matters*.

Chapter 3 offers practical advice for teachers, based on my previous practice and my later career. Returning to Save the Children's education unit from 2004 to 2005 and then as a lecturer for humans rights education at Bath Spa University, I have had opportunities to clarify my thinking about a coherent model for teaching children's rights.

The last chapters give more practical information about activities and resources that I recommend for teachers who wish to develop their pupils' learning about rights with a global dimension.

My hope is that readers of this book will be inspired to help make children's own realities a more visible and vocal source of learning about children. As T S Eliot wrote in his poem *Burnt Norton*

> Go, said the bird, for the leaves were full of children,
> Hidden excitedly, containing laughter.
> Go, go, go, said the bird: human kind
> Cannot bear very much reality.

1
Children's rights

This section introduces the 1989 UN *Convention on the Rights of the Child* (from here simply called the *Convention*). It stresses the educational dimensions of the *Convention* for rights and responsibilities and relates them to other important documents: *Every Child Matters*, the Millennium Development Goals and the UK Human Rights Act.

The Convention on the Rights of the Child

States Parties undertake to make the principles and provisions of the Convention widely known, by appropriate and active means, to adults and children alike. Article 42

Children's rights are the human rights all children should have. Universally accepted values are still evolving, so as the twenty-first century progresses children's rights will be seen differently. Like all rights, there are reciprocal responsibilities.

All children are entitled to special rights on account of being young. This is a comparatively recent development. The notion of childhood as distinct from adulthood evolved over the twentieth century, inspired by visionary books such as Aries' *Centuries of Childhood* to Cunningham's *The Invention of Childhood* (Cunningham, 2006; Osler and Starkey, 2005).

The history of children's rights can be dated from 1924, when English philanthropist Eglantyne Jebb presented five points to the League of Nations in Geneva. The League adopted them and proclaimed the first ever international *Declaration of the Rights of the Child*, also known as the *Declaration of Geneva*. With her sister Dorothy Buxton, Eglantyne Jebb founded the Save the Children Fund and she devoted her short life to the welfare of the world's children.

The understanding of children's rights has developed over time. This is apparent when we compare the language and concepts of the 1924 *Declaration* with the 1989 *Convention on the Rights of the Child*. The Geneva Declaration stated:

- The child must be given the means for its normal development both materially and spiritually

- The child that is hungry must be fed; the child that is sick must be nursed; the child that is backward must be helped; the delinquent child must be reclaimed; and the orphan and the waif must be sheltered and succoured

- The child must be first to receive relief in times of distress

- The child must be put in a position to earn a livelihood and must be protected against every form of exploitation

- The child must be brought up in the consciousness that its talents must be devoted to the service of its fellow men
(Quoted in Save the Children's *Changing Childhoods* 1996: 66)

This 1924 *Declaration* was an idealistic statement of principles to guide the way adult societies should care for their children. After the collapse of the League of Nations and the descent into a world war that brutalised children's lives, the new United Nations made a renewed attempt to take an idealistic approach to children. It revived and expanded Jebb's original points into a ten point *Declaration of the Rights of the Child* in 1959 and created the *International Year of the Child* in 1979. This led to the setting up of a working group to consider the government of Poland's proposal for a stronger and more official convention for children's rights. After ten more years of consultation, which to a limited extent involved children, the new convention was drafted and presented to the UN General Assembly on 20 November 1989. This date is now International Children's Day.

The 1989 *Convention on the Rights of the Child* is the key document now in place. It is in three parts. The first lays down 42 rights for all children up to the age of eighteen. The second and third parts are about the implementation of these rights. A UN Committee on the Rights of the Child is empowered to review the progress of governments that have ratified the *Convention*. By 2006 every independent nation state in the world, bar the USA and Somalia, had signed up to what has become the most widely accepted international document of all time. The UK Government ratified the *Convention* in 1991 with a few reservations and has to some extent incorporated its provisions into its policies for children as in the values enshrined in the policy document of 2004, *Every Child Matters*.

The 42 new rights for children represent a large expansion on the League's original five points, particularly in regard to children's participation in society. There are many ways of viewing and summarising what the *Convention* offers children. Amnesty International, Plan International, Save the Children, UNICEF and other non-government organisations (NGOs) produce child-friendly posters and leaflets that outline the *Convention*. The newly clarified rights for children cover provision, protection and participation.

Provision rights include: survival and development (Article 6), health care (Article 24), adequate standard of living (Article 27), education (Articles 28 and 29) and play and leisure (Article 30).

Protection rights include: protection from abuse and neglect (Article 19), being without a family (Article 20), being a refugee (Article 22), and against child labour (Article 32), drug abuse (Article 33), sexual exploitation (Article 34), torture, and armed conflicts (Articles 37 and 38).

Participation rights include: holding and expressing opinions (Articles 12 and 13), association (Article 15) and information (Article 17) as well as the social and cultural rights of minorities and indigenous peoples (Article 30).

As this brief summary indicates, there is no particular rational order in the *Convention*. The structure closely follows the arrangement of rights in the 1948 *Universal Declaration of Human Rights*. Underlying the provision, protection and participation rights are the unequivocal statements in the opening Articles of the *Convention* that the rights apply to all children and young people on a basis of equality and non-discrimination (Article 2) and that the 'best interests of the child' should be paramount (Article 3).

All the rights in the *Convention* apply to 'every human being below the age of eighteen years unless, under the law applicable to the child, majority is attained earlier' (from Article One). The rights apply to all children 'without discrimination of any kind' (from Article Two). This has raised philosophical questions about who exactly can be called a child. Priscilla Alderson, among others, has developed understanding of the rights of the youngest children (Alderson, 2000) and more recently of premature babies. The rights of unborn children were an issue of contested debate during the drawing up of the *Convention*.

In a recent book on child rights legislation around the world, Michael Freeman wrote about the need to revise the *Convention* in the light of the rights of special groups of children that were not specifically acknowledged in 1989, including 'children with HIV/AIDS, street children, child soldiers, the gay child, the indigenous child' (Freeman, 2004, II 289). Freeman's view is that these are problems which were not seen as significant then and are 'better grappled with today'. This gives an additional perspective for seeing the value for teaching and learning based on the *Convention*. It is the most universally agreed statement to date of all the entitlement to rights of all the world's children.

The *Convention* relates to educational policy in general as well as to schooling and curriculum provision. Awareness of the *Convention* itself is crucial. Teachers have to know what is provided for in its education rights and the implications for strengthening children's participation in society as young citizens.

Governments that ratify the *Convention* are signing up to Article 42 to make the *Convention* widely known. The UK Government has yet to put this Article to full effect, although there are recent moves in the Ministry of Justice to increase funding and support for awareness of human rights. Many countries have greater public awareness than the UK and a growing culture of children's rights, as evident from posters in public places. The non-government organisation materials and projects featured in this book could certainly be more widely used in the UK and official summary statements and visual support material need to be made available. Article 42 provides for active means of learning and underlines the importance of making adults as well as children aware of the rights all children should have.

Children's responsibilities

The child must be brought up in the consciousness that its talents must be devoted to the service of its fellow men. (*Declaration of Geneva* 1924, point 5)

The language of public service is beginning to re-surface in the UK. There are ideas for national service schemes and Community Service Volunteers advertise regularly for people to help with local community development projects. Citizens in the UK may have lost the sense of social cohesion they once felt they had. People lead more individualised or techno-dominated lives and affluence has increased. A comparison of lifestyles in Scotland and Panama (see section 2.2) highlights the way European children risk losing a community focus, whereas children elsewhere are more likely to relate closely to adults with whom they do things together as they always have.

Eglantyne Jebb's original vision for children's rights included the right to grow up with a spirit of service to others. Philosophies of rights emphasise that the giving of rights implies the recognition of reciprocal duties (Freeman, 2002). Rights imply responsibilities, although some people find the *Convention* very strong on rights but less forceful about telling children about their social responsibilities. The National Curriculum for Citizenship in England focuses on responsibilities more than rights. The way forward must be to reconcile the two concepts so that young people are guided towards a balanced view of how they relate to each other.

Teachers may be concerned that pupils who express strong opinions about their own rights may be less caring about those of others. Emphasising *our* rights rather than *my* rights can foster a global approach. Teachers should give importance to understanding rights but should always link rights to their reciprocal responsibilities. The *Convention* only uses the word responsible in Article 29, in the phrase 'responsible life in a free society', where it competes with many other areas of social, cultural and environmental learning.

The educational literature draws attention to how responsibilities relate to rights (Osler and Starkey, 2005). The problem is that the match may not be obvious enough for young learners to understand and put into practice. It is easy to match the right to free expression with an acknowledgement that this right should go with a responsibility to respect the free expression of others, but more difficult to guide children towards a sense of the responsibility for the right to freedom from torture and unjust imprisonment.

The Citizenship curriculum is the appropriate context for teaching about human rights. Rights do not come free: they need to be understood as a reciprocal deal. This can be likened to a playground swap, where something is given and something else is given back. Classroom discussion might be triggered by an incident in which a child has acted in an anti-social manner: how do the others feel about it and what do they think should be done? Caring for others can be learned through caring for people with visible needs in the local community. The principle is established at local level that if you expect people to respect your wishes, wants or feelings it is right to respect theirs. These principles underpin rights and responsibilities. Charters announcing the principles agreed by the class can be produced and displayed.

On a more abstract and distant level, rights and responsibilities can be linked in a rights framework. This begins with personal rights such as identity, expression, food, shelter, care and education and extends to a wider range as presented in the *Convention* such as survival, protection and justice for everyone. It includes the rights of special groups like disabled children or children who are refugees and asylum seekers. Teachers can build on pupils' understanding of the value of caring for others to develop their thinking about specific situations. The real life situations of this other group will be remote from their own experience.

As pupils become more aware of rights issues they may be able to take on some of the responsibility for helping children who need it to get their rights. Learning about social responsibilities is an essential component of effective citizenship education and is enhanced by being seen through a prism of rights. Learning about the importance of acting to care for people in an African country who are going hungry is given more value if it is not just seen as something that needs to be done because teachers or the global community say so. It is better to put this kind of learning in a universal framework of the rights which are shared by all children. This approach helps to establish a sense of shared humanity.

The right to adequate nutrition for normal healthy development may seem obvious but pupils need to learn that not every child has enough to eat. They should be encouraged to develop a sense of responsibility towards the children elsewhere whose nutrition is threatened by social, environmental, political or economic factors. This is the beginning of sound learning for global rights and responsibilities, exploring and sharing values. This is much more than an add-on of charitable activity in an after-school club. It involves the kind of education in values that the school, its teachers and its learning activities stand for.

The *Convention* and other relevant documents

For children growing up in the UK today there are two key statements of entitlement: the *Convention on the Rights of the Child* and *Every Child Matters*. Here I outline the wide range of rights for children in the UN *Convention* as they relate to the outcomes of the UK Government's policy for *Every Child Matters*, although this is not always seen as a rights-based document. Nonetheless, it relates directly to areas of rights for children.

The *Convention* rights outlined above can be grouped in many ways

- rights to equality
- rights to family care
- rights to survival and development
- rights to identity and expression
- rights for refugee children
- rights for children with disabilities
- rights to health care and economic security
- rights to education and leisure
- rights to protection from harmful work
- rights to protection from abuse and torture
- rights to rehabilitation
- rights to justice

The UN *Convention* provides for the rights of all children in the world. *Every Child Matters*, a Government Green Paper published in 2003, concerns provision for children in the UK and has been further strengthened by the 2004 *Children Act* and the appointment in 2005 of a Commissioner for Children in England. The other three UK countries already had commissioners.

Every Child Matters defines five outcomes for children. They should:

- be healthy
- stay safe
- enjoy and achieve
- make a positive contribution
- achieve economic well-being

Every Child Matters sets out for teachers the immediate aims for education. Where pupils are learning about the lives of children beyond the UK, the same outcomes should be applied, so helping summarise the wider range of rights in the *Convention*. The next chapter provides visual evidence from children in five countries to illustrate the importance of the outcomes for all children everywhere and to relate these to the *Convention*.

Behind these two statements for children lie two statements of entitlement for children and adults. *The Human Rights Act*, which applies to UK citizens, and the *Millennium Development Goals* concerned particularly with people in poorer countries of the world.

The 1998 UK *Human Rights Act* came into law in 2000. It brings the *European Convention on Human Rights* into UK law, providing all citizens with:

- the right to life
- rights to protection from torture and forced labour
- rights to liberty, security and justice

- ▓ rights to privacy and family life
- ▓ rights to freedom of conscience, expression and assembly
- ▓ the right to marry

The *Millennium Development Goals* came out of the UN Millennium Summit in New York in 2000 and are aspirations for the global community. They aim by 2015 to

- ▓ eradicate extreme poverty and hunger
- ▓ achieve universal primary education
- ▓ promote gender equality and empower women
- ▓ reduce child mortality
- ▓ improve maternal health
- ▓ combat HIV/AIDS, malaria and other diseases
- ▓ ensure environmental sustainability
- ▓ secure a global partnership for development

The UK agreements for children's welfare and their rights as citizens are set within a context of agreements for all children's rights and the well-being of the least well off. They provide a context for learning about, from and with children at local, national and global levels.

Summary – the background to children's rights

All children have responsibilities as global citizens. Teachers can help them to understand this through the intersecting fields of education in human rights, citizenship and peace.

The most important of the international statements on children's rights is the 1989 UN *Convention on the Rights of the Child* which the UK Government ratified in 1991. Children's rights provide a universal value base, as codified in the 1989 UN *Convention*.

Awareness of the importance of child rights education is growing in the context of human rights education movements dating from the end of the Second World War or even earlier and the creation of the United Nations. The principles for which I argue, and which inform this book are:

- that children learning their rights should at the same time learn to understand their reciprocal responsibilities

- and that child rights education should be seen in a global context. It is especially important that our pupils learn not from traditional – or adult – constructions, but by listening to what children in various countries themselves say about their experiences of childhood.

2

Global learning

This chapter looks at examples of *learning rights* and *welfare rights* across frontiers. The guidance is drawn from localised examples I have my experienced which will, I hope, be helpful for teachers in a range of subjects and school contexts.

2.1: Learning rights
The right of children to expression
The everyday lives of children can become a visible and aural source for learning across frontiers of nation state, language or culture. Pupils can be helped to explore and express ideas about their world and their values, as shown in the following examples. Exchanging such accounts with pupils in different parts of the world brings authenticity and excitement to the learning process. The rights of children to express their views and ideas are recognised in Articles 12 and 13 of the *Convention*:

> States Parties shall assure to the child who is capable of forming his or her own views the right to express those views freely in all matters affecting the child, the views of the child being given due weight in accordance with the age and maturity of the child. (13.1)

Article 13.1 extends the right to expression to children sharing information and ideas across frontiers. This book shows ways that children's expression can add value to learning about children's rights to achieve in and contribute to society regardless of frontiers. The experiences of children in another country imbue lessons with a global learning dimension.

My first example of the right to expression is drawn from a secondary classroom in the North West Province of Cameroon in the mid 1970s. The school was a purpose built secondary campus on a hillside in the grassland savannah area of the country, formerly the British colony of Southern Cameroons. The pupils were sitting in rows at wooden desks facing a black-painted board. The subject for their writing that day was 'Memories of primary school'.

As a teacher of English I would emphasise to language teachers how important it is to give pupils a positive voice. I found that children's creative work need not just be ticked and returned but can be used for wider communication. During the four years I spent as an Inter-

---

Being a child from the interior villages of Africa, I thought that school was designed for those who hated hardship and had great love for pleasure. I saw that many of my age-mates were not carrying babies but going to school.

The Miss asked me to sit with a boy and of course this was very strange for I had never sat with a boy before. I refused and stood there till long break. After a month school started to bore me because our teacher was a very wild and hatesome somebody. I thought I was going to paradise, but I was beaten terribly!

Figure 1: Pupil writing from Cameroon (reproduced in SC/UNICEF (1990) The Whole Child*).*

national Voluntary Service teacher in Cameroon, West Africa during the 1970s, one of the few girls in my English class wrote a short essay on her early memories of schooling (Figure 1). She showed that primary school had not turned out to be the paradise she had imagined when she saw her peers – mainly boys – going there. She was delighted when I promoted her piece of writing with other English teachers. I used it in an article for the *Human Rights Education Newsletter* in 1998, in which I imagined children's voices from around the world responding to the Crick Report on Citizenship. It has also appeared in the 1990 Save the Children and UNICEF topic book *The Whole Child* under the title 'First experiences of school'. The topic of schooling is rich for pupil expression because everyone has something to recall from these early memories. Save the Children recently instigated an exchange of memory books called *Starting School.*

The right of children to information

All children have a right to accurate and beneficial information. This includes learning to understand the hidden messages in certain sources of information. Article 17 of the *Convention* declares:

> States Parties recognise the important function performed by the mass media and shall ensure that the child has access to information and material from a diversity of national and international sources, especially those aimed at the promotion of his or her social, spiritual and moral well-being and physical and mental health.

Consequently, criteria are needed for evaluating how effectively the resources used in schools present children's lives. Films and class materials can be used to help children understand the limitations and bias of the media. The best of the NGO resources emphasise visual images which show children growing up in developing countries in ways that counter the negative light in which they are so often presented.

During my first years as an NGO educator I worked a lot on media images. I was trying to help pupils and teachers see behind stereo-typical images of the Third World so they could start to see realities behind the pictures. I helped organise a series of sixth form Media Days at the Africa Centre in London, in collaboration with practising journalists. My second example is set in the main hall of the Africa Centre in the early 1980s. Sixth form students from many schools came together with the support of Oxfam to spend the day learning about how Africa is portrayed in the media.

An imaginary trip was made to Batonga in Africa, where we had to report on a sugar cane crisis in a town that was poverty stricken like many of the third world countries. When we got enough information to satisfy ourselves we returned home to England to inform our fellow Britons of the crisis...

We emphasised the fact that stocks and shares would not be drastically affected; the British were not to worry. However, in the article we did not mention that people were dying as a result of hunger, wages were low and the government was uncontrolled. We failed to report on this as it was not in the interest of our readers...

These articles from the very reliable British newspapers were then read out in turn after completion. Having listened to the same report being distorted and vandalised by different newspapers I felt rather confused, as a disaster so severe could be made to seem so unimportant by the media; naturally readers would believe what was reported.

Figure 2: From a sixth former's evaluation of a 'Media Day', reproduced from Oxfam (1984) Deadlines: Media Bias about the Third World – A simulation for secondary schools.

Each Media Day was built around a simulated disaster scenario. Working in groups, the students covered the fictional disaster as reporters for British newspapers like the *Sun*, the *Daily Telegraph* and the *Morning Star*. This proved an exciting and powerful way of getting home the message that the same story can be given very different slants (Figure 2).

In her history of Oxfam, Maggie Black examines the use of the 'starving baby' images used by NGOs to evoke empathy and charitable giving. She dates this back to the Congo crises of the early 1960s, reinforced later by the Biafran crisis of the late 1960s:

> Gradually, image by image, Oxfam was helping to develop a new way of looking at the world, an ideologically charged view of other countries and cultures, a more considered version of the predicament symbolised by the starving child. It is a great tribute to Oxfam that, in today's Britain, almost no-one's idea of the world beyond Europe and North America is untouched by the perception of humanity in need. (Black, 1992: 104)

Many development NGOs followed this trend. They produced hugely negative images of children intended for classroom use, either indirectly through fundraising activity or directly in their early resources produced for schools. During the 1990s there was a reaction against such overly negative portrayal of children's lives. This was due partly to the global acceptance of the *Convention* and the growing understanding and acceptance that children's privacy and dignity should be respected.

But recently NGOs have again started presenting visual media images that appear to feature negative representations of children. This is possibly because fundraising capacity is shrinking in an era of compassion fatigue, so increasing competition among NGOs for public support. However, within the school sections of these organisations, set up to promote learning about world development, it has been agreed that work in UK schools be based on educational over promotional aims. There have been many collaborative ventures over the years, with resources jointly produced, for example the 1992 poster pack produced by four leading development NGOs for learning about the impact of European discovery of the Americas, and the recent *Get Global!* skills-based resource to help secondary age students enquire about the world.

The right of children to learn respect

Children's actions as young citizens can be shaped by their ability to identify with the daily lives of other children in the world. Their rights to action are part of their entitlement to learn values for a better world and their role in helping to achieve this, both in their own communities and globally. This is the spirit of the *Convention* and is made specific in Article 29 for...

> the preparation of the child for responsible life in a free society, in the spirit of understanding, peace, tolerance, equality of sexes, and friendship among all peoples, ethnic, national and religious groups and persons of indigenous origin. (29.1d)

Article 29c provides for education about pupils' varied cultural backgrounds, including 'the development of respect ... for civilisations different from his or her own'. This is important for teachers who are seeking justification for global learning, especially if the idea of 'civilisations' is taken in the widest possible sense to include all learning about other peoples and communities and not just those deemed historically significant, such as the ancient Egyptians or Romans. Learning about daily life in an African township or Indian village should be presented from the point of view of the local people. Pupils should be learning about the culture of a different civilisation from its own perspective rather than about places which they may see as culturally or economically inferior.

I use the term 'respect' to cover the broad area of values education that includes tolerance and respect for the cultures and lifestyles of people other than ones, own. The third scene I have chosen to illustrate takes place in a middle school classroom in Newcastle, North East England during the mid 1980s. Pupils are involved in a simulated debate between settlers from Java and the indigenous residents of Irian Jaya (Figure 3). They have moved to this 'new island' on a government scheme that offers land. This was at a time when there was international criticism of the Indonesian government because the rights and traditional environments of the Papuan people of Irian Jaya appeared to be under threat from this transmigration scheme.

This is one of a number of drama-based projects I was engaged in while working as an Oxfam education adviser in north east England. I was beginning to see the importance of getting children to use imaginative identification with the lives of other people. I worked with teachers to devise and trial simulation activities and these were written

---

The Tree People
We are not being helped because the settlers need money, food, clothes, shoes, rice, land and a house. We wanted the government to stop cutting down our trees and killing our animals but the settlers need land and a house.

The settlers
We have decided to go to the new island because in the city they are very poor and it is far too hot and crowded. And we would not get as much land. They also live in little huts in the city but if we go to the New Island we will get good land and a fine new house.

Figure 3: From TILT NINE *on Teaching about Trees (Oxfam, 1985).*

up and offered to other teachers in a termly subscription magazine called *TILT*. I also worked with Theatre in Education colleagues to develop an interactive performance drama on the history of a Caribbean island: Rich Port, Poor Port.

Children's experiences can contribute to the creating of role-plays. This makes them seem more realistic because they are closer to the lives of the subjects of the activity. Children can learn imaginatively about global issues affecting children and, as active citizens, plan to do something to effect change.

This section on *learning rights* has been mainly informed by secondary level teaching and NGO projects that ran during the 1970s and 1980s. It offers a foundation for principles of global learning in relation to children's rights. Good practice is about:

- inspiring children to express and share their daily realities. This is particularly effective through learning exchanges between schools in different countries

- promoting children's expressions about their own experience, or to challenge or broaden the often limited or distorted images of children's lives too often presented to pupils in UK schools. This requires pupils to learn about media generally and involves them in making appropriate classroom resources

- devising imaginative ways for pupils to learn about children's lives in different places and circumstances, to complement the enabling of direct expression (see first point) or for use where it is not feasible for those being studied to convey their views and perspectives on their lives by direct expression. Use of dramatic methods like role-play can lead pupils to informed and imaginative action as young citizens

All three of these points are further explored in the classroom experience section in 2.3. What the section above does not cover is the right to education itself, which I see more as a provision right. So access to schooling is considered in the welfare rights section which follows. It describes examples of projects carried out in primary schools.

2.2: Welfare rights

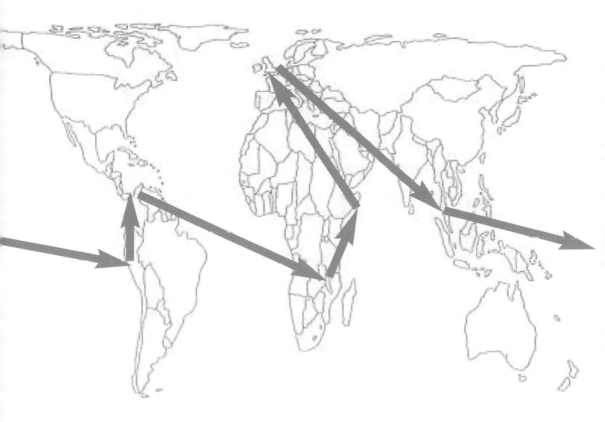

Figure 4: Map of the book's welfare rights studies: from Malaysia to Peru to Panama to Malawi to Somalia to the UK.

The projects described here illustrate ways of learning about children's rights to a decent childhood. Relating the five outcomes in *Every Child Matters* to matching articles in the *Convention* gives them a global focus. I recorded the views of children and these views inform what follows and indicate how teachers can develop their practice in conveying welfare rights to their pupils.

Each section describes a project which has encouraged children to express their views. Their pictures are used to suggest global learning approaches to each of the five outcomes, which I have labelled: security, survival, success, safety and status. The projects are presented in chronological order of their development, but can be used in any order as they are all equally useful for pupils to understand children's rights issues fully.

The right of children to economic security

One of the outcomes of *Every Child Matters* is achieving economic wellbeing. This matches Article 27 of the *Convention* which provides for 'the right of every child to a standard of living adequate for the child's physical, mental, spiritual, moral and social development'. Other relevant Articles include 4 and 5, for the important roles of the family and the state in the life of every child. One of the *Millennium Development Goals* is to reduce hunger and improve family incomes. Although achieving economic well-being is less emphasised in the *Human Rights Act* it does make clear that schools should develop pupils' experience and understanding of poverty issues in the UK and the world.

My fourth illustrative scene is set in a secondary classroom in Kedah State, north west Malaysia during the late 1980s. The pupils are sitting in rows with boys on the left side and girls on the right. Their possessions are in boxes and bags at their feet. The subject of the day's English lesson was their parents' jobs and whether they themselves

Life for the rubber tapper is not easy. I'm sure because my father is a rubber tapper. Before he goes to the rubber farm early in the morning, he only drinks a cup of coffee. He doesn't eat breakfast. It's about 6.30 a.m - he arrives in his farm and starts tapping the rubber trees. He only goes to tap when the weather is good but if it's raining he will not come out.

At 12.30 p.m he returns home carrying two barrels of rubber liquid on his bicycle. He never takes a nap first but goes straight to the hut where the liquid should be coagulated. The coagulated rubbers are machined into pieces. My father gets only two pieces a day.

He sells them once a month. One kilogramme can bring $ 1.25. In a month my father only gets about $ 200. My family consists of 7 people and it is not easy to manage on only $ 200 per month

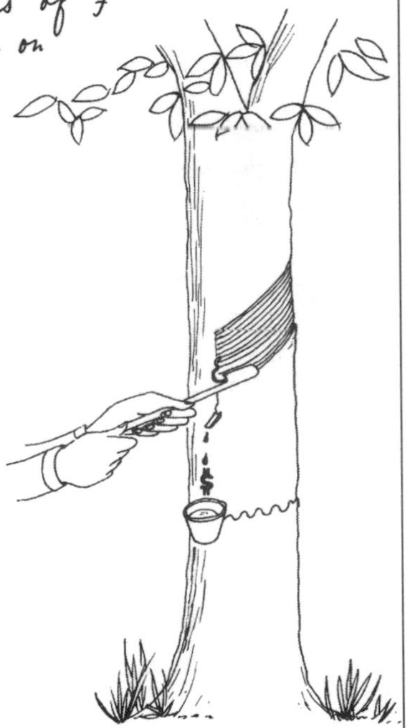

Figure 5: Malaysia – life for the rubber tapper

DIALOUGE BETWEEN A KAMPUNG GIRL A CITY GIRL.

minah : Hello, is that Iz. in Kuala Jumpur?

Iz : Yes, is that minah speaking, from the kampung?

minah : How are you and your life now? Do you enjoy living in Kuala Jumpur?

Iz : Oh, I'm very well now. Of course I enjoy it very much. I have found a good job for me now and I can save some money for my future. How about you, have you found any job by now?

minah : Oh...... not yet, I'm still looking for it until now. There are not to many jobs here, it's hard to find one.

Iz : If you want, come on and join me. I will help you get a job. Do you have an examination cutificate?

minah : Oh yes, I have SPM curtifizate, but is grade two.

Iz : That's all right, you could come. I'll help you to find a job. If you come and join me, yo will meet a midlen range of people with differert kinds of habit.

minah : I want to go to Kuala Jumpur but I find it hard to leave my parents and my relatives because they are close friends and family. Here I can continue traditional entertainment life ....

Iz : In Kuala Jumpur you can keep good health because they are soo many doctors and more medical facilities.

minah : O.K. I'll join you in Kuala Jumpur. I will be there at 7.00 a.m at the bus station. next Sunday. Bye for now.

Iz : Bye. I'll be waiting for you.

Figure 6: Malaysia – dialogue between a kampong girl and a city girl.

would prefer to stay in the rural area when they leave school or move to a city to look for work.

The first piece is about agricultural production in Kedah (Figure 5). A pupil presents a personal view of her family's income, showing some of the realities of work and pay for the local rubber tapper, who supports a family of seven. Dollars flow from the rubber tree into the cup but the text shows that the small-scale farmer gets little of it. Her picture helps develop pupils' understanding of the relation between primary producers and export processes, and shows some of the effects of the international trade economy on family life in a developing country.

The second piece is an imaginary dialogue between a girl who has moved to the city for work and a girl who has chosen to stay in the kampong (home village) (Figure 6). This class task produced a lot of discussion and contrasting opinions among those who aspired to move to a city to seek a better life than their parents had. In this example, the rural girl rapidly changes her mind under her friend's persuasion and decides to go to Kuala Lumpur.

These pupil drawings were part of a Social Topic Exchange Materials (STEM) initiative between a secondary school in Malaysia where I was teaching in the mid-1980s and a school in North Yorkshire where a friend was teaching. The Malaysian pupils express their ideas in English, so making exchanges of ideas and learning easier for British pupils – although, ideally, language should be no barrier to cross-frontier learning. English is widely taught in Malaysia, which was once a British colony.

When I later created resources for Save the Children's new Education Unit, the pupils' words and pictures were incorporated into a secondary Geography pack: *Frontiers: Change and Development in Malaysia and Thailand*. The Malaysian contributions are the product of their classroom English lessons, which included a learning exchange on the topic of homes with secondary pupils in Yorkshire.

Save the Children's field office in Bangkok asked a number of rural schools to produce comparable pictures. The Thai pupils' drawings were exchanged with selected images from rural Malaysia and Yorkshire. The pupils' work was developed in a chain process that originated in South East Asia, linked to Europe and then returned to another area of South East Asia. The primary aim was to exchange pictures and accounts by pupils on a defined topic. Then these would be brought together as a resource for use in the UK, where they would contribute to a debate within secondary Geography about the value of learning about the world directly from young people in their own countries rather than through adult interpretations. The handbook in the *Frontiers* pack provides supporting maps and statistical information about migration and production in Malaysia and Thailand.

Studying household economies helps pupils and teachers to think about children's economic well-being today. Comparing the ideas from two classmates presents different ways of looking at children's wealth issues in distant places. The rubber tree reveals the economic hardship which had not been immediately apparent, concealed as it is behind the facade of the family home. The dialogue adds understanding of rural poverty and why life in the cities may seem more attractive for young people.

Learning about poverty issues is sensitive. One constructive approach is to develop learning about poverty in a UK context and then compare this with poverty in other parts of the world. The ways of seeing richer and poorer countries tends to differ. Schools may be teaching about 'developing' or 'under developed' countries in general without having the resources to study family incomes and the ways children contribute to them. Teachers should be looking for children's perspectives on issues of wealth and economic security.

The right of children to enjoy and achieve

Another outcome of *Every Child Matters* is enjoying and achieving. This corresponds to many rights in the *Convention,* including the right for family care

> States Parties shall use their best efforts to ensure recognition of the principle that both parents have common responsibilities for the upbringing and development of the child. Parents or, as the case may be, legal guardians, have the primary responsibility for the upbringing and development of the child. The best interests of the child will be their basic concern. (18.1)

Governments have responsibilities to provide assistance to parents and guardians through 'the development of institutions, facilities and services for the care of children' (18.2), whether at community or national level. Other relevant Articles include 28 for access to education and 31 for leisure and recreation.

Article 28 of the *Convention* states that children have rights to basic education. If these rights are indeed in place, consideration is required of the right to quality education as identified in Article 29. But not even a classroom can be guaranteed in some parts of the developing world. This can be contrasted with the economically richer world where there is enough money to improve the quality of education for every pupil.

None of the *Millennium Development Goals* specifically refer to children's success and achievement but this can be assumed as the aim of all of them. Recent developments in educational thinking provide ways of teaching directly about happiness. One of the *Millennium Development Goals* concerns access for all children to education at primary level; another is about getting more girls into schools. Article 28 of the *Convention* recognises 'the right of the child to education... on the basis of equal opportunity'. Article 29 provides for the quality of education which should include 'respect for human rights and fundamental freedoms'.

Figure 7: Peru – street play

The outcome 'to enjoy and achieve' focuses more than the *Human Rights Act* does on children's progress and development. Most of the world's children have some experience of formal schooling but there are many who do not because of their family's economic circumstances. As well as helping to bring about universal access to education through campaigning, teachers can celebrate the children who are in school around the world. But it is also good to celebrate achievements that are not gained through education. Inviting children to share their ideas about what they feel good about in their lives brings other experiences into classroom learning.

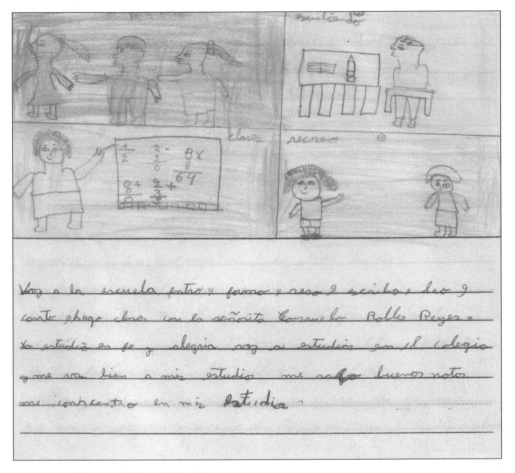

Figure 8: Peru – school scenes

My fifth scene is set in a primary classroom in an inner city area of Lima, Peru's spreading capital on the coast, in the early 1990s. I was shown around the area and met one family in their nearby home in a street which was still being built and which had brick water tanks outside each house. Because there was so much violence, I could not visit the school but the Brazilian photographer I was working with managed to do so. The local project workers arranged for exchange sheets from Bristol to reach the Lima pupils and for them to make their own project booklets on 'My life in the city'.

The first drawing by a primary age pupil in Peru's capital city shows his home area (Figure 7). The dry desert climate allows homes to have flat roofs, where clothes can be dried. Children are skipping and playing with spinning tops on the street between the houses and the traffic. The sun shines down.

The second drawing from Lima shows activities at school including outdoor learning and play as well as classroom writing and maths (Figure 8). The pupil who wrote about her drawings revealed her ambition to go on to secondary school. She was getting good marks and was conscientious about her studies. Many of the children I worked with in Lima had ambitions to be doctors or teachers. With a strong global media emphasis on the children who are not in schools because of poverty, civil conflicts or environmental disasters, it is good to learn from the views of children who are enjoying their lives at school.

The drawings on pages 28 and 29 are from NGO fieldwork with children in and around Lima. They were for the purpose of making a photo-pack for primary Geography, *Lima Lives* (Save the Children 1993). Although the output was one-way, the process entailed two-way communication. Primary pupils in Bristol made pictures of their homes and I took them to Lima to show pupils and their parents. These pictures acted like a passport, showing the kind of resource Save the Children intended to produce. This introduction was followed by an intensive two weeks of fieldwork in three working class settlements in Lima, in an attempt to present a little of the diversity of family histories, current lifestyles and actions for the future. Shorthand notes in translation were made about what the children said about their pictures. Thus the final publication was made up of factual inputs about city lives.

The drawings show a diversity of lifestyles in a crowded working class district of Lima. The El Agustino district has been settled by incoming families desperate for homes. They have taken over a steep hill close to the city centre and the central market which is a source of jobs. Their first houses may be no more than small temporary structures built from woven straw or cardboard but they stake a claim to land from which more permanent brick and plaster homes are developed. The residents then press the local council for water, sewage and electricity services or work co-operatively to provide them for themselves.

The El Agustino children shown in these pictures were happy to share images of their lives in the city with children in the UK. Save the Children initially hoped to produce a two-way resource based on stories from both Peru and England but funding would have had to come from the UK and this was not deemed to be a viable use of the NGO's money. However, the principle of enabling resources about children's daily lives in the UK and Europe to be developed for use in schools in other countries is worth highlighting. With collaborative support and financial backing, genuinely global resources could be produced that would give all children truer and more relevant knowledge than most traditional school resources about their peers elsewhere. There is more on this in section 2.3.

The right of children to safety

Children's rights can be improved by community, state and international action campaigns. Of particular concern is enabling children to learn about issues of access to education and about protection from the exploitative labour which harms children's progress to adulthood. 'Learning and labour' rights are considered in many of the articles of the UN *Convention*. Article 28 recognises that primary education at least should be compulsory and free to all (28.1). In addition:

> States Parties shall promote and encourage international co-operation in matters relating to education, in particular with a view to contributing to the elimination of ignorance and illiteracy throughout the world and facilitating access to scientific and technical knowledge and modern

teaching methods. In this regard, particular account shall be taken of the needs of developing countries. (28.3)

Children who are not in schools are exposed to harmful working conditions in order to add to family incomes. Article 32 of the UN *Convention* gives general protection against exploitation of children. Subsequent articles offer protection from drug abuse, sexual exploitation, trafficking and torture:

> States Parties recognise the right of the child to be protected from economic exploitation and from performing any work that is likely to be hazardous or to interfere with the child's education, or to be harmful to the child's health or physical, mental, spiritual, moral or social development. (32.1)

Being safe is another of the outcomes of *Every Child Matters*. This matches Article 19.1 of the *Convention*

> States Parties shall take all appropriate legislative, administrative, social and educational measures to protect the child from all forms of physical or mental violence, injury or abuse, neglect or negligent treatment, maltreatment or exploitation, including sexual abuse, while in the care of parent(s), legal guardian(s) or any other person who has the care of the child.

Another relevant Article is 39 for rehabilitative care.

None of the *Millennium Development Goals* are explicitly about child safety although in a way they all are. Environmental sustainability implies that environments should be kept safe for children to grow up in. A child's right to 'stay safe' at home and in the community is asserted in the *Human Rights Act*. All children share concerns and feelings for their own safety and that of others. Children may be equally in danger in rich countries and poor. Schools in the UK can celebrate examples of children who grow up safe and protected.

Figure 9: Panama – 'activities we do at home at different times of the week'.

Figure 10: Panama – 'the best people at providing for our needs'.

My sixth scene is set in a little two-class primary school in the Scottish highlands in the mid 1990s. The pupils are finishing their picture sheets showing aspects of their lives. They are to be exchanged with a class of the same age in rural Panama, Central America.

One of the images of daily life in Panama shows a child's daily activities in her community (Figure 9). The other is a child's view of who cares for her best (Figure 10). The first picture gives a strong visual representation of a child feeling safe in her community, helping at home, visiting the farm or walking to school. The second drawing shows a united family, a policeman helping children across the main road through the village and teachers all as caring adults. These pictures of carers for children at home and in the community help pupils and teachers to think about children's safety and who ensures it.

The focus of learning about the developing world is extended to aspects of caring for children and the children's own roles in their family and community. Such learning takes into account a broad spread of rights that include identity and cultural heritage. The essential right underpinning so much is the right to a family.

The *Caring and Sharing* project was designed to share children's ideas and experiences of childhood between schools in Scotland and Panama. There was an historical reason for this choice of countries: Scotland, then an independent nation, had briefly colonised the Atlantic coast of what became the state of Panama, through the Darien Scheme of the late 1660s. Contemporary maps of the coastline of Panama still show Scottish Point (*Punta Escoces*), illustrating how the past influences the present. There can be some validity in linking parts of the world that have already had links of a different kind.

For the project, Scottish and Panamanian children compared their views about who they think cares for them best. In Scotland the role of parents, baby sitters and Welfare State professionals was central. In Panama the dominant carers were the family, teachers, and the police on community service helping children across the road to school.

Two urban and two rural primary schools in each country were selected, and the work was directed at the top classes of eleven and twelve year olds. Worksheets were sent out to all four schools at the same time. They dealt with Caring for Children, Caring for the Environment and Sharing Resources. Each identified the area of enquiry at the top in English or Spanish, leaving the rest blank for the pupils' responses. Accompanying guidance for teachers suggested that responses should preferably be through visual illustration rather than writing, to overcome language barriers. Packages of the pupils' work then crossed the Atlantic by courier to the partner schools. Children in both countries were thrilled to receive direct responses to their own inputs, and the teachers in Panama evaluated the learning highly, as having given their pupils 'a window on the world'.

Other Save the Children projects have focused on children being compelled to work. This often prevents them from developing their full potential for learning and so may limit their future prospects. Child labour which restricts full development is a campaigning issue readily understandable by children who are in full-time education (see Resources for more information).

The right of children to health

Another outcome of *Every Child Matters* is being healthy. This matches Article 24 of the *Convention* which provides for 'the right of the child to the enjoyment of the highest attainable standard of health'. This Article points to the importance of health care and access to clean water and nutritious food. Other relevant Articles include Article 6 for children's rights to survival and development.

Three of the *Millennium Development Goals* are related to improving children's health. For all children to 'be healthy' is less of an issue than in the *Human Rights Act*. Media images and school textbooks often dwell on health issues in poorer countries. Although the disparities between rich countries and poor should not be denied, teachers should think about how they might provide a wider and more challenging picture of what is happening in the world and how children themselves perceive matters.

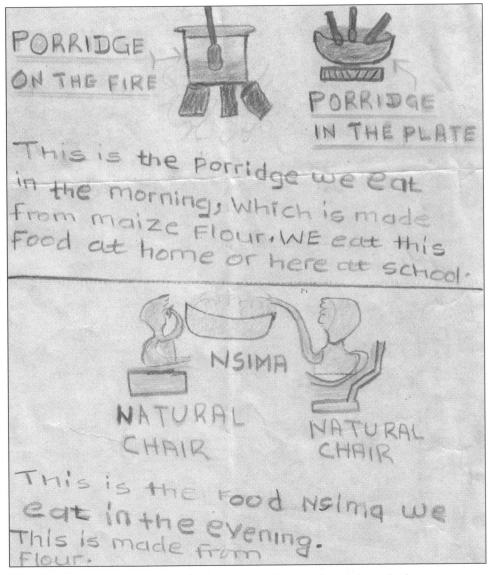

Figure 11: Malawi – 'food: what I eat in the morning and evening'.

Figure 12: Malawi – 'health problems and how I got better'.

My seventh example is set in a primary school in Malawi in the late 1990s. I was on a fieldwork visit to an integrated health project supported by Save the Children, in a town near the Zambian frontier which had one secondary and several primary schools. I brought picture sheets and items from schools in Scotland to show the children aspects of their health, food, play, family and school life. The Malawian pupils were excited by these, regarding them as gifts which they wished to reciprocate. They were amazed at the wrappings of the box of cornflakes and contrasted it to how they grow and winnow their own maize around the school grounds. They also enjoyed their first experience of lego. They gave me handmade spinning tops, footballs and clay figures to take back to the Scottish schools.

The first picture shows maize porridge: the staple food of rural Malawi (Figure 11). The second drawing shows a child coming down with malaria and taking aspirin as a cure (Figure 12). These illustrate aspects of health relating to diet and medicine. Environmental and economic circumstances mean that a typical diet can satisfy a child's hunger without being very nutritious. A mother is shown providing health care for her child but lacking access to appropriate medicine – although aspirin may help alleviate the fever. However, the effective treatment of malaria entails prevention, for example sleeping under a net.

The right of children to participate

The last of the *Every Child Matters* outcomes is 'making a positive contribution'. This matches Article 29 of the *Convention* which provides for education to prepare the child 'for responsible life in a free society'. One of the newest areas of recognition of the rights of children in the *Convention* is for participation, expression and association. Other relevant Articles include Articles 2 for equality and 3 on seeking the best interests of the child. The whole *Convention* can be seen as giving children enhanced status in society.

Figure 13: Bristol – 'actions for the school'.

These pictures portraying how children contribute to their societies may encourage pupils in the UK to think about children's active participation in their society. One of the *Millennium Development Goals* is to build a global partnership for development. Young citizens should be brought into this partnership through learning to take appropriate action at local, national and global levels.

The notion of making a positive contribution is less evident in the UK *Human Rights Act*, even though this fits with current thinking about children being citizens in their own right. When learning about children in other countries, this concept may not be obvious, as ideas may be influenced by adult conceptions of development and progress. So it is important for teachers to look for examples of the various roles children play in family and local economies and as national and global citizens, and highlight them in the classroom.

Also relevant to the idea of children learning across frontiers are the illustrations of children's issues as seen by young refugees and asylum seekers. My eighth scene is set in a classroom in a secondary school in east Bristol during the early 2000s. The pupils were recently arrived refugees, mainly Somalis. It was difficult for these children to find school places in the city in the middle of the school year, but the Black Achievement Team at the school accepted children from newly arrived refugee and asylum seeking families.

Their task was to design drawings for the *Our School, Our World* class booklet. I worked with the pupils in a 'new arrivals' class pending their admission to mainstream classes, giving them a specially designed course in English language and Citizenship. Although the size of the group fluctuated there was a core of about fifteen, mostly girls and mainly from Kurdish and Somali backgrounds. Their ages ranged from 11 to 16.

The Somali girl's drawing here suggests actions that students could take at school to improve the toilets and also to raise awareness of

Figure 14: Somalia – 'Problems I have catching up with my learning'.
'Dhibaatooyinka aan wax la baran la'ahay'

racism (Figure 13). Her picture gives a sense of incoming children feeling safe and successful in their new school communities.

Our School, Our World encouraged the pupils' language skills and their understandings about Citizenship. The pupils created a publication that could be shared with others in the school and community and eventually be featured in a professional magazine for teaching Citizenship – which gave the pupils a powerful incentive. The final publication opened outwards from the pictures and ideas of the group, to the school, the city and the world. The language activities were designed so the pupils could put them onto picture sheets. This enabled every student in the group to work at their own level of awareness and linguistic capacity in English.

The class booklet was produced by young people who have direct experience of diversity and contrast in the world. The same techniques can be used to record the perceived similarities and differences between the known neighbourhood and the places the pupils are learning about. Picture sheets like these can then be shared between pupils in different schools and in different countries.

Comparing homes and family life styles in the examples discussed above show settled communities. This is true even in the case of the images from Lima of migrants who come to the city in search of better lives. Many children experience an unsettled childhood, especially those who are forced to leave their homes because of civil conflict. The resources listed at the end of the book feature images created by refugee children that relate to their welfare, safety and success and their contribution to their new host communities.

Figure 14 shows a desert area of Somalia where a group of children were asked by a Save the Children fieldworker to illustrate the difficulties they encountered in attending school regularly. I requested these drawings from Somalia while I was working at Save the Children's head office in London, so I could add the insights of children themselves to a role-play I was devising about education and participation for Early Years settings in England.

The drawing is of a boy standing on a rough platform scaring birds away from the family crops. He does so out of economic necessity but it prevents him from going to school. This can be taken as an example of participation, in which a child is contributing to family needs. It is also an example of poverty and of child labour. This reminds us how interconnected the elements are of learning about rights issues.

2.3: Classroom experience

This section offers teachers guidance on how to implement global learning in their classrooms. It suggests ways to benefit from cross-frontier exchanges, evaluate media presentations including classroom resources and develop imaginative activities which can lead to action for change.

Exchanging ideas

Encouraging pupils' rights to expression is directly related to promoting their sense of participation in school life and in the world beyond the school. Exchanges can be an effective way of developing learning across frontiers. The children share their ideas about common themes in their daily lives. Exchanges complement resources where there is scope for learning on both sides.

Structured learning exchanges are different from pen pal exchanges of letters or photographs. A sequence of activity based expressions can be developed. For example, in a Futures project for Year Seven English in an urban comprehensive school, the pupils wrote stories about the future and combined them with non-fiction descriptions of what would make a better future. The *Our School, Our World* project described above also illustrates how global learning can be structured into lessons. This project moved from capturing words and pictures for the class, the school and the community to personal accounts of the countries the refugee children had left.

The Malawi link described above demonstrated that exchange dialogues can be developed which follow the interests of the pupils. After the introductory exchange, pupils in one of the Scottish schools wanted to share ideas on the topic of water. So a second exchange of picture sheets was made. The right of children to expression was being realised, since it was they rather than the teachers who were guiding the direction of the exchange project.

Through exchanges of this kind children learn from and with other children across frontiers of nation state, language and culture. But such rewarding exchanges need careful planning and organising. Experience of establishing successful learning exchanges between schools in different countries indicates that good practice depends on certain factors

- exchanges must be based on equality. The participants have to see it as an equal exchange, in which they can learn about differences and similarities by exploring a common theme or experience together

- language should not be seen as an obstacle to exchanges across frontiers. Questions which encourage mainly visual responses are appropriate for younger pupils and should be translated into the first languages in advance

- the children should share their views and the realities of their lives as this makes them feel valued

- the resources selected should show realities of community lives, and particularly the roles of the children involved

- open frame picture sheets with a question or topic heading at the top are ideal, and should be provided along with relevant information about the place concerned. This will provide a frame for pupils' responses. The rest of each sheet is blank, so each child or group of children can express their own realities through words or drawings on it. Drawings will be most useful where the exchange is between countries in which different languages are spoken.

The schools should complete their task so that the two lots of worksheets can be exchanged at the same time. When they receive picture sheets from their exchange school the children already know the topics of enquiry and can readily respond to the visual images they receive from children growing up in a different physical, social and cultural environment. This facilitates comparison, so fostering their understanding of issues of similarity and difference, be they in the games they play, family life or their experiences in school.

Teachers on both sides may need to sustain the motivation of their pupils by building up their anticipation of receiving more exchange material. Many exchanges have been set up in a flush of enthusiasm which soon fades on one side or both. This is not necessarily a total failure as some useful comparative learning will have taken place. However a realistic time scale for the project should be decided by the schools even before they begin.

The validity of the school linking being advocated by government departments and the *Times Educational Supplement* is currently under debate. One question is this: when does a learning or reciprocal exchange link turn into economic dependency? However, the examples of learning exchanges described in this book show how collaborative learning for global understanding can be initiated and sustained between school communities in different parts of the world that have very different levels of economic resource. In these projects, the pupils learned to see beyond definitions of 'development' based solely on narrow economic criteria.

These learning approaches are not exclusive to the NGO sector. I hope readers of this book feel inspired to create their own meaningful exchanges between young people and to learn from them. The key to success is that the purposes of the initiative should be agreed from the outset and that everyone involved should see the results.

These recommendations for improving global learning through exchanges all start from one vital principle: they are based on the genuine participation of the children – both those learning and those learned about. For children in the UK to become global citizens, they need to learn about the social, cultural, environmental, political, economic, spiritual and moral factors that drive the communities with whom they are learning. And they will need to learn how to relate their own lives to these aspects of the lives they are learning about in active and meaningful ways that transcend barriers of fundraising and empathy. Only then can children come to see a single world in which the lives of everyone impinge however indirectly, on the lives of everyone else so that action is possible for a common good.

Evaluating information

If pupils are to understand the similarities and differences between their lives and those of other children, sensitivity is needed. Photographs, films or textbooks used in schools often stress the differences, the exotic, the negative. Such images can be challenged by group tasks or class discussion. Begin, rather, by emphasising the positive and the similar. For younger children particularly it is good to start with a concept of common childhood, showing that all children play and most go to school. Pupils will then be better prepared to appreciate difference and begin to learn how histories, environments and traditions affect how children experience the world in different places. Examine the resources together and follow with group and whole class discussions about the images and the point of view of those who are presenting them.

This is certainly the way to approach topics on health and wealth issues in rich countries and poor. Such studies must be underpinned by the pupils understanding that all children have the same rights to grow up healthy and in economic security. Once this is established, pupils can explore the reasons why this is not true for all children and what might be done to enable them to access their rights as children.

That all children have rights to information highlights the importance of learning through contact with the real world rather than the one constructed by the writers of textbooks and classroom materials. The frontiers of children's learning will be extended by helping them to analyse the misrepresentations in their curriculum and materials and develop their critical thinking skills. It is important that they learn to put images of the world in context and explore why and by whom they were made. It is also important to encourage the participation of pupils in the provision of information. By learning to enquire and to express their ideas they are learning to explore the wider world (see final chapters for practical activities and resources).

Globalisation has created sophisticated means of communication which, if we ensure that children can access them, have the potential to increase understanding. It gives children the chance to make their own media to communicate in their own ways with other young people.

However, the mass media have huge impact on young people's attitudes towards the world they are growing up in. This influences their perception of others whose lives may be visible only through television or cinema screens. Studies of mass media images reveal the generally negative trends in reporting incidents in children's lives. The emphasis is on the sensational: shocking physical or emotional abuse of individual children or mass suffering because of war or disaster. Educators need to help young people deconstruct such messages and learn to look behind them. They need to ask questions about why and how the images were made and how much say the children portrayed had in the image-making process.

Everyone who is involved with children needs to treat images in this way. It can't wait for the teachers of Media Studies in secondary schools. Simply offering a range of visual contexts of urban and rural settlements in an African country may help stimulate thinking about the accuracy of the images. Pupils can take pictures of favourite places in their neighbourhood and add personal captions, then compare their images with pictures from other places, ideally through exchanging similar photo galleries with young people in other countries who have been given access to cameras.

The views of childhood in schools range from *concealed* childhoods, through *constructed* childhoods to *confided* childhoods.

Where children are rarely or never the subject of learning the childhoods are *concealed* or invisible. This is more likely to be the case at secondary school, when pupils move from the child-centred learning approaches of primary school. Courses in world history or citizenship include children in primary projects about, say, daily life in Benin or the Indus Valley but young people are seldom visible in the resources for twentieth century politics. Secondary lessons on the Second World War do indeed feature children evacuated from cities to country areas for their safety but this is merely the exception that proves the rule. As citizens, children have a right to be featured in lessons about all aspects of citizenship.

Flat, stereotypical or traditional presentations of children living in particular times or places, more like cardboard characters than living beings, are what can be termed *constructed* childhoods. 'Children of many lands' used to be a popular approach in primary Geography, with books showing children in colourful traditional costumes. Some rode camels; others picked tulips. National identities have their own truths or distortions in how they are represented. As well as the stereotyping, the children are portrayed as passive, posed and as taking no part in the active lives of their communities. This *National Geographic* or photographic view of difference fosters ideas of distance and strangeness between the children of the world.

The preferable approach is to present *confided* childhoods. The subjects of learning have had some say in how they are presented. Pupils are given images in which the children portrayed are shown as they want to be shown. This is not as difficult or complicated as it sounds. What it requires is for those who produce learning materials *about* children, be they commercial publishers or international development agencies, to ensure that they work *with* children in selecting and producing the images. Then the children learning from the resource will have a more richly fulfilling and honest experience than if some view of childhood has been filtered through remote adult hands. Producing resources on principles of confided childhoods will greatly improve how we learn from and with children about their own childhoods.

The resources for schools that development NGOs produce are best when they have been created through two-way learning processes across frontiers. But it may be impossible to show the lives of children in difficult social, economic and environmental circumstances in this way. And there are other restrictions on NGO educational activities in the UK: they are non government organisations, answerable to themselves, their constitutions and boards of management. Beyond these controls, most are registered as charities so come within UK charity law, and this places restrictions on activities which might be seen as politicised or indoctrinating.

Organisations like Oxfam and Christian Aid raise money and awareness in the UK to help alleviate the effects of poverty, conflicts and natural disasters in poorer parts of the world. The development agenda has meant that they have extended their programmes to support long-term development, although this has to be balanced against the needs for immediate relief. These organisations increasingly follow rights-based principles in developing their field programmes.

The UK-based development NGOs have established education departments that aim to raise awareness of their work for UK audiences. These are often called Development Education units. Although these may receive their funding by supporting the work of the NGO, the educational programmes are usually much wider. NGO development education workers collaborate across NGOs to help support learning in schools which they can base on their direct experience of programme work in developing countries. It can be difficult for teachers to tell whether the messages in an NGO resource have a fundraising or an educational purpose. However, resources of both types can be useful once their purpose is understood.

When doing fieldwork with children it is essential to communicate appropriately and to see things from the children's perspectives. A local researcher, community worker or adult is more likely to achieve this, as they are known and trusted by the children. The fieldworker also needs to be able to communicate directly with the children in their own language. Otherwise the information collected will be stilted and will not truly represent how they see their lives.

In the worst scenarios the information the fieldworker has provided is later altered to fit publishing requirements, and the final publication presents the expected negative image of children growing up in economically difficult circumstances. Thus to learn from children across frontiers demands not only their trust but also the producer's fidelity to what they say and express in their writing or drawing. Children brought into such fieldwork research processes should be clear about the purpose of the activity and how the information they give is going to be used. Ideally they should get to see the published outcomes of their expressions and be given a similar resource about children from the country where their own life stories will be used in the classroom.

When I was conducting fieldwork I found it useful to offer something of myself and my home background at the start. Even a simple colour postcard showing somewhere near where I live, with a personalised message of introduction or thanks written on the back, was well received. The final product and the learning that results will be made more meaningful if the subjects have been involved in selecting and captioning the images, and deciding how they would like their own realities to be presented to the learning community in another country.

The cover of this book indicates how resources can be collaboratively produced for use in schools in linked countries or all countries as a kind of shared book. Plan International has helped develop resources for use in a number of African countries as well as in the UK. Outside the NGO sector with its direct international contacts, LEAs have developed reciprocal learning links for social and civic learning, for example a learning link has been set up between Pembrokeshire in Wales and Zanzibar in Tanzania.

Teachers need to know the following about NGO resources:

- learning about children's rights and realities will be enhanced by using NGO learning resources. NGOs aim to promote good practice for developing materials and have produced an impressive range of resources on global childhoods for teachers and pupils.

- resource creation and dissemination can be improved through positive collaboration between teaching professionals and NGOs that are working directly with children and families in many – particularly economically poorer – parts of the world.

- giving a Globe Mark for authenticity to resources depicting childhood would help to improve teaching courses and learning resources.

A Globe Mark would be a kind of kite mark of educational standards for learning appropriately about the world. It is still only an idea but it might be developed by people who are reading this book. I would like to see some kind of validation developed by educators so that children can be assured of the usefulness and suitability of what they are being offered for learning about the world.

A new resource or project would only achieve a Globe Mark if it provided an authentic view of the experience it purports to represent. It would also be a guarantee that the people represented have had a say in the representation process.

It should be possible for commercial publishers and NGOs producing resources for global learning to meet and draw up an agreed code of practice for Globe Mark validation. If enough prestigious publishers could put their names to a standard mark of this kind, users would be better informed about the value of the resources they are downloading, buying and using.

It would certainly be good to see new or revised versions of learning resources for global childhoods receive a Globe Mark. Teachers will then no longer have to take the NGO on trust just because of its philanthropic reputation. They could tell at once that the resource has been approved by the children it is about. Perhaps we will move towards giving children and young people a voice in their learning which includes their being involved in the production of learning materials.

Imagining children's lives

Imaginative identification enriches fact-based learning about issues of change and community politics. Classroom activities that use role-play and drama are a powerful strategy for learning. Role-plays can help pupils to enter the daily realities of the lives of the children they are trying to help. They can also help to explore the potential and limitations of campaigning actions.

Role-play can be very effective in generating campaigns to improve the lives of children. The scenario should be authentic and open to being entered imaginatively. The children's own accounts of their ideas and experiences give the material authenticity. This was true of the role-plays on Burkina Faso and Somalia which I developed for Save the Children (see Chapter 5). The imaginative identification is helped if pupils understand about the similarities with their own lives. They will more readily put themselves in the situation of the people they are learning about and so better understand the differences in experience which restrict these children's lives.

Pupils can role-play a community meeting along the lines of what they know about local committee meetings, for instance. Imaginative identification is a path to commitment and campaigning activity and is likely to be much more effective than inviting responses to, say, a harrowing film of children in need. The role-play approach brings pupils closer to seeing the real children under consideration, who should be sharing the same rights as the pupils doing the role-play have themselves.

Drama-based learning methods like role-play and simulation are known to stimulate children's sense of involvement with the lives of other children, particularly those growing up in difficult or dangerous circumstances. The authenticity of dramatic scenarios which intro-duce child welfare issues in distant places is therefore vital. But learn-ing of this kind should not be weighed down by too many facts, as this could prevent children from identifying with the lives of others. The ultimate achievement of dramatic learning is its generation of cam-paigns on behalf of the children being learned about.

If teachers wish to foster campaign activities with their pupils, having them identify with the people concerned is the way to start. Resources and exchanges such as those described foster such identification. But too many resources about poverty and development fail to make the children featured vocal or visible, leaving the UK pupils feeling they are being asked to identify with adult communities. Learning exchanges may not be viable where the people most involved are not in school or have no access to communication resources such as computers and the Internet. Children in conflict situations might not want to communicate their personal views and experiences, even though knowing that children in other parts of the world are interested in them can be powerfully supportive.

School-based campaigning can evoke controversy. Pupils and their parents may perceive what the teachers initiate as being politically motivated and regard it as indoctrination rather than education. But the Citizenship agenda has raised awareness of legitimate areas of campaigning activity. Learning for social action is valued alongside learning for employment and academic achievement.

Children engage more readily in local campaigns than international or global ones. It is easier for them to survey local issues and express their ideas about them. There are many examples of pupil involvement with local councils, for example to make known their ideas about improving play facilities for children. Some councils have set up youth committees to facilitate such interactions.

Issues at national level become larger in scale and harder to influence. Writing to local MPs, inviting them into the school or arranging a visit to parliament are all valuable skills for political literacy. A class may study a national issue reported in the press and discuss their views on it. There must be opportunities for pupils to share their views more widely in the local community or the national press so their ideas do not go unnoticed.

However, pupils can be helped to feel empowered to make a difference globally. They can join supporter groups and receive information about campaigns like saving wildlife species that are threatened with extinction. They can express their opinions in writing and pictures which they communicate online. They can hold fundraising events for charities.

NGOs can support pupils and teachers with information and ideas for suitable activities. Older students might be able to work as volunteers in local or national NGO offices. They can contribute their skills either by directly supporting campaigning organisations or by organising their own campaigns.

Make Poverty History is a recent example of school-based campaigning. The campaign invited pupils to present their views at the G8 Summit in Scotland. A coalition of NGOs working under the banners of the Global Campaign for Education and Make Poverty History led the campaign. Pupils made and painted cut-out characters of their 'buddies' to show their concern for an imagined friend who could not attend school. The buddies were created from a downloadable template or designed by pupils themselves, then collected and taken to Scotland where they were displayed during the summit of world leaders. This campaign exemplifies how pupils can contribute their ideas to a common concern which is of global importance.

World AIDS Day, held on the December 1 each year, has an on-going global campaign in schools. A changing consortium of NGOs leads the campaign, using posters, badges and a creative website of classroom campaigning ideas. But the most successful global campaigning in schools has been for Red Nose Day. Inspired by Comic Relief, its combination of learning and action ideas has engaged children in helping to create a better world for the least well-off of the world's citizens. So if schools wish to develop global political awareness and capacity for action in their pupils they will find numerous sources of support.

There was once Empire Day, then Commonwealth and United Nations Days. Now Children's Day is celebrated each 20 November, to mark the date of the UN *Convention on the Rights of the Child*. Schools can obtain action calendars for assemblies or classroom activities. Special awareness days, like the global campaigns, motivate pupils to express their concerns about the state of the world and explore what actions they could take to improve matters. The number of worthwhile campaigns can make it difficult for teachers to cope with the pupils' choice of campaign. Pupils may feel moved to act on behalf of animals, the environment or economic injustices as well as issues which directly affect the opportunities and rights of children.

Multiple literacies

Active young global citizens require economic literacy. But they also need to develop political, social, environmental, emotional literacy as well as conventional literacy, particularly where the communities seeking to learn from and support each other do not speak the same languages. Guidelines are needed to help teachers achieve a common approach to this complex area of learning.

Active learning for global commitment should involve learning to take part in action at many levels. It is valid to learn global, act local, re-learn global. Pupils who carry out a campaign to clean up the local environment can exchange what they have learned with pupils carrying out similar environmental activity in another part of the world. This enables all the pupils to see the world as a global community of which they are part. There can be many learning benefits from global exchanges. The pupils in the economically poorer world see that there are unsolved problems in a part of the world they have been led to see as richer and more successful than their own. Pupils in the richer world can see the power of action resting in the hands of young people in the supposedly poorer and more passive world beyond the familiar. If the pupils on each side of the exchange recognise that they have problems in common, they can learn ways of supporting each other to find mutually beneficial solutions.

Figure 15: Checklist for teachers to evaluate resources on global childhoods

Process

1. Who has produced this and why? Is the purpose made explicit?

2. When was this produced? How recent is it and will it be updated?

3. What role have children had in the production? What is acknowledged about the subject children or about children involved in trialling?

Content

4. What aspects of childhood are presented? Does the emphasis seem excessively positive, excessively negative or value-neutral?

5. What areas of the world are covered? How localised is this resource in accurate portrayals of family and community life?

6. How much visual or verbal evidence is there? Is there a real sense of these children's lives?

Method

7. What range of learning activities is provided? Is there a variety of learning approaches to 'distant' childhoods, including exploring media images and stereotypes?

8. How interactive are the learning activities? Does the resource offer creative ideas for classroom use or rely too much on a knowledge response or worksheet format?

Context

9. Is there scope to link with other relevant resources? Does the resource provide teachers with wider ideas, such as using links and school exchanges to learn more about children's lives?

10. What do you think about this resource? Is there an invitation to comment on and help improve the resource, for example by enclosing a return questionnaire?

Summary – interactive learning for children's rights

This chapter links the words of children and their pictures to their *learning* and *welfare* rights. These illustrate a variety of ways for increasing learning *about* children *from* children and show the diversity of art and presentation styles which children from different places and cultural backgrounds use when describing something of their lives and feelings. Much can be learned from their work

- The so-called poor world is rich in its potential for children to express themselves, and capacities to learn from one another. The possibilities can be explored through structured learning exchanges.

- Children can absorb complex values and understandings which challenge negative views of distant lives conveyed by the media and many textbook images. NGO resources are a source of corrective positive information about children's lives.

- Imaginative drama-based methods of learning are a way of developing understanding of the lives of other children and can lead to informed action like campaigning and support for charities.

- The comparisons made by young refugees and asylum seekers between the lives they had to leave behind and the lives they are making in the UK can be a source for learning about the world.

3
Crossing frontiers

Childhood as experienced by children around the world can and should be a valid source of learning in schools This chapter considers children's rights as a learning area in a holistic way, building on the specified outcomes of rights already described.

The movement for rights education in the UK is analysed and a forward-looking vision for classroom learning set out which gives importance to children's rights and to children learning about these rights in global contexts. Childhood is thus made a properly acknowledged source for school learning and this affirms children's rights to learn in its methodology and content. Such learning embraces the welfare rights of all the world's children.

Introducing understanding of children's rights can be merged with the practice of making children a subject in their own right of school learning. Curriculum reform on its own is not enough: also required is awareness of the need for improvement in the whole life of a school. Global childhoods cannot be taught about only within the constraints of fixed subjects. The entire school environment needs to respect the immediate rights of pupils to awareness and their own expression.

3.1: The movement for rights education

My ideas derive from my experience as a teacher working for NGOs and encouraging young people to express and share their ideas. The innovative approaches we used are part of a growing movement for education about, for and through rights which originates in the ideals of the United Nations for peace, tolerance and education 'regardless of frontiers'. It is supported by the UN *Convention* of 1989 and fits with peace education, development education, environmental education, multicultural education, antiracist education and global education.

The terms used in the fields overlap and can be confusing. The table below offers clarification.

EDUCATION – conceived and inspired by external organisations, e.g. UNESCO, NGOs	*International* education *Multicultural* education *Environmental* education	*Peace* education/ education for *peace* *Development* education/education for *development* *Citizenship* education/education for *citizenship*	*Values* education/ education in-for-through *values* *Human rights* education/education in-for-through *rights*
STUDIES – directed by and for teachers and curriculum needs	*Global* education	*Peace* studies *Development* studies *Citizenship* studies *World* studies	

Classifying these educational movements in this way emphasises that the purpose of human rights education is to enhance understanding of a plural set of values, as distinguished from movements aimed at achieving a single abstract entity like peace or development for all. Education about, for and through children's rights is a special subset of human rights education.

Following the Second World War, the United Nations agreed the *Universal Declaration of Human Rights* and set up UNESCO to promote international exchanges in education, and UNICEF to help care for children in greatest need.

UNESCO enabled the sharing of good educational practice across frontiers. An agreed set of *Recommendations on Education for International Understanding* (EIU) was drawn up in 1974. In the UK, the DES sought to influence educators, putting out a schools' circular in 1976 and setting up a Standing Conference on EIU in 1978. EIU is based on UN principles of peace and tolerance and aims to teach the next generation to understand countries and cultures outside the UK. 'International' is key concept, as much of the learning was about global politics and relations at country level. So EIU probably made most impact on upper secondary students, through courses in current affairs or external sixth form conferences.

From the start, UNICEF has worked to benefit children in need in the poorest countries. It has worked with governments to promote health care and education programmes, from which development education programmes have grown. UNICEF UK provides teachers with resources and training programmes for learning about children growing up in poverty.

Other approaches to learning globally and learning about children were also developed in the UK. In the late 20th century NGOs like Oxfam and Christian Aid helped to develop resources and resource centres for Development Education, which originated from a concern about poorer or less developed countries. Save the Children has a similar concern particularly with children. Amnesty International was created explicitly to focus on human rights. What the teaching world could see then and now is a diverse range of ideologies or educations from which teachers could choose approaches to world mindedness that they could develop with their pupils. From this wide-ranging field the term Global Education emerged as an umbrella for bringing all these educations together. Today the DCSF encourages a global dimension to school learning.

The shifts in the development of human rights education in the UK is illustrated below.

	Global/International	Peace/Development/ Citizenship	Values/Rights
1940s-1950s	UN/UNESCO	UNDP	UN UDHR (1948)
1960s-1970s	UNESCO *Education for International Understanding* (1974)	New Right criticism of *Peace* and *World Studies* UN Development Decades and growth of *Development Education* by NGOs, DECs and DEA	
1980s-1990s	Oxfam *Curriculum for Global Citizenship* (1997)	*Citizenship* as a theme in the England NC and Crick Report (1998)	*Values* in England NC. *Education in Human Rights Network*
2000s-	DfES/DfID support for *global dimension* in schools	QCA revision of KS3 *Citizenship*	DCA support for *human rights* in Citizenship at KS3

The strongest impetus for Human Rights Education followed the Second World War and the UN Charter's belief in avoiding peace and promoting respect for rights. The *Universal Declaration of Human Rights* (UDHR) appeared in 1948 and the terminologies and practices of education in human rights education were set down. These still inform the British and international movements. UNESCO promoted Education for International Understanding, emphasising the value of learning about human rights. During the 1960s and 1970s the independent Schools Council supported projects for integrated humanities and world studies, so developing learning approaches and materials for rights education.

In the following two decades an informal Education in Human Rights Network of NGO staff and teacher trainers met to produce guidelines and share ideas through a regular newsletter and annual conferences. Centres for the study of human rights were established in teacher training institutions, including the universities of Leeds, Leicester, London and Roehampton. Amnesty International, Oxfam, Save the Children and UNICEF, among others, published teachers' and class-room resources. Today many institutions are offering modules for Education Studies students on human rights education and related fields of development, environmental and global education.

The subject of children's rights still requires higher educational status but movement is in the right direction. The Qualifications and Curriculum Authority (QCA) offers a Key Stage Two unit for human and children's rights and the CITIZED website (www.citized.info) sets out specific guidance for children's rights learning in the early years. So there is progress. In 1998 George Flouris compared national educational curricula and found that there was far less on human rights in the UK than in France or Greece, and that in the UK there were 'no references to children's rights found in any of the subjects' (Flouris, 1998, 103). This is slowly being remedied. Education in the UK today allows for a new, lively and valuable movement for children's rights.

Human rights and wrongs are as old as human history; as old as the time people began making arrangements for how to live together in societies. Concepts of individual rights against governments grew during the revolutions in England (seventeenth century), America and France (eighteenth century) into the flourishing international human rights culture at the start of the twenty-first century. A key landmark was the creation of the United Nations after a world war ended in 1945 and the *Universal Declaration of Human Rights* (UDHR) in 1948. However the UDHR has been criticised as a formulation of western values, since the founder members of the UN who created it were primarily the victorious allied powers and the countries still under European colonisation had no voice in it (Freeman, 2002: 34-42; Pagden, 2003).

Nonetheless, the fundamental values enshrined in the UDHR – justice, peace, tolerance and respect – seem to have held up through more than fifty years of international tension. And the later United Nations agreements have more approval from the global community as the UN came to represent, albeit imperfectly, almost every world citizen. The UDHR does offer a minimum 'common standard' of values in an increasingly secular age, as expressed in its Preamble. The 1989 *Convention on the Rights of the Child* complemented the UDHR by clarifying rights for all children.

So human rights can shape a fundamental value system for creating viable educational policies. Implementing such policies in schools requires developing methods for young people to be learning about their rights and testing their social responsibilities. As universal values, human rights underlie courses in social and citizenship education, which should place greater emphasis on the specific area of children's rights.

3.2: Models for rights education

This section considers the case for making childhood and children's rights more centrally important in schools. It explores the potential in current subject areas for achieving a wide-ranging and forward-looking view of child rights education which emphasises the importance of children learning globally.

The increased interest in children's rights, especially participation rights, has created a climate for involving children more visibly and vocally in their social education, whether through personal and social education courses, the humanities or whole school initiatives. Since the UN *Convention* in 1989 a child-focused approach to subject learning has been growing in strength.

The *Convention* acknowledges children's education rights and also their participation rights, even if these are kept apart in the official text. The education articles (especially Article 29) provide teachers with a top-down recipe for teaching about peace, tolerance and justice issues today. This is compensated by the articles providing children with rights to expression (Article 12), to share information with others through any media of their choice (Article 13) and to have access to beneficial media information (Article 17). Teachers can focus on the subject matter of children and childhood as a rich source of exciting, motivating and child-friendly learning that can help to make issues come to life and have relevance in classrooms across age ranges and frontier divides.

Human rights education stresses that children should learn about all their rights. Before the *Convention*, children's rights were often regarded as something adults provided for children and a matter of protecting them. What is new about children's participation and expression rights is that children are now seen as active members of their communities and not just the passive recipients of adult support. There is scope to improve learning about specific childhood experiences worldwide and about the rights of all children. If rights of expression are not developed, pupils may receive an education in rights that is tokenistic, passive and adult controlled. But when expression rights are operating, children become active learners and members of their school communities. An emphasis on global childhoods broadens the picture, so that children come to understand their creative roles in their own societies.

The study of rights in childhood explores two main questions: 'what is life really like for children?' and 'how can pupils find out more?' The first question relates to perceived images of childhood and the ability to deconstruct them, for example when learning about a developing locality and viewing children in an African village setting toiling with buckets of water. The question challenges the image by prompting pupils to ask: how much does it show of the African child's real life? Who constructed the image? For what purpose? And what role did the children themselves have in deciding its final format?

The second main question follows: if pupils decide that there is more to be learned about these children and their communities than is shown by the resources, they should be encouraged to carry out further research. They might, for instance, interrogate the image makers in depth, perhaps inviting publishers or NGO education staff into the class. Or the range and depth of direct contact with the lives of the children being learned about is extended by scanning internet sources or seeking direct contact with the children in their own communities.

The most important thing is to not be bound by perceived frontiers of any kind in today's globalising world. In the past, as represented, say, in Thomas Hardy's novels of Wessex life, communication relied on hand-written notes – which were sometimes wrongly delivered. In today's world of globally connected communities it is possible to initiate exchanges via the internet, setting up e-mail dialogue, discussion groups or video conferencing. E-learning about children's lives should not be the only learning method, but experience of setting up cross-frontier learning initiatives on the internet has proved that they can be valuable experiences for everyone who takes part. When a 'global rights to expression' dimension is built into learning, it increases the scope for rights-based learning in schools. We live in a time when the possibilities for children's rights through global learning, regardless of frontiers, are constantly expanding.

The school can drive the learning about rights by means of its child protection policies and pastoral or personal education programmes or, alternatively, by its whole school and subject-led provisions for rights awareness. Ideally, the two approaches should work together. The former approach works outwards from the needs of individual children, the latter from the wider awareness inspired by the needs of children in difficult, rights-denying circumstances.

Some courses and resources have been constructed around what we can learn about children's daily lives in different countries, while others start from universal principles as enshrined in the *Convention*. The first approach is evident in, for example, the many secondary Geography lessons that focus on 'developing countries' and feature children – if they show them at all – as passive sufferers of poverty and exploitation who must be minders of younger siblings and carriers of firewood and water buckets. The latter approach connects with Personal, Social, Health and Citizenship Education lessons, in which pupils learn about the *Convention* and what their rights are. Many learning resources produced by development aid organisations seek to bridge the two approaches by relating issues of childhood poverty to the rights being denied to children. Such resources emphasise how children can help themselves and be helped by their families and communities, and by external aid, to gain these rights.

Such portrayals are clearly inadequate: much is missing about global childhoods. Focusing on the economically poor areas of the world tends to skew the subject matter of childhood too forcefully towards the negative. Some contextualisation of childhoods can be achieved when the learning is introduced through a photo-pack of, say, village life in India. But this may still provide pupils with only a narrow and inadequate view of childhoods in India today. Scaffolding children's learning by starting with portrayals of people's daily lives and moving them towards a grasp of abstract principles is complex. It is especially complicated for younger pupils, to whom it is not easy to explain why conceptually, a right is not the same as a need.

Writing on behalf of the Council of Europe, Hugh Starkey stressed the importance of trying to achieve more integrated models for human rights education in schools, especially secondary schools:

> The early years of education have a tradition of nurturing and caring. Post-primary education has often been a much harsher environment. Educators have increasingly come to realise the advantages of a caring and community-based approach to secondary education... Of course, a helpful school climate is not sufficient in itself to promote human rights education. There is a need... for 'a sequenced and meaningful' programme of study. Such a programme does not have to be based purely on knowledge. (Starkey 1991: 60)

For the youngest children, rights to survival, development, family care and health are fundamental. Logically these should be areas of rights that children learn about from the earliest years of formal schooling. A rights-based curriculum would look at how young children flourish and learn social values in a variety of settings. The Early Learning Goal for 'understanding the world' usually concentrates on child's immediate experience.

Bold colour maps and images broaden children's spatial understanding of the wider world. NGOs have produced innovative resources for this age level and details of some of them are given in the final chapter.

UNICEF's guide to *First Steps to Rights* offers teachers a broad range of child-centred learning ideas for introducing understanding of rights concepts with young pupils through, for example, using objects hidden in feely bags that relate to rights.

The Ragdoll Foundation/Save the Children produced a set of children's films from six countries called *What Makes Me Happy*. The films bring visual, aural and sense reality to the way children grow up, the ways in which they help in their own communities and how endlessly creative and inventive they are in using the simplest recycled resources.

During the middle years of schooling children can more readily identify global issues and their own potential role. At this age the rights to identity, information, expression and association become more meaningful in their lives. Two resources are particularly suitable for teachers to use at this stage:

Save the Children's *Young Lives, Global Goals* video resource pack supports an appropriately child-focused curriculum. In the video, children themselves speak directly to camera, describing some of the harsh realities of their lives as they grow up in conditions of poverty. There are eight interviews with children from four countries, allowing concepts of poverty and economic literacy to be understood through comparing the daily lives and prospects for a boy growing up in rural Ethiopia with, for instance, a girl growing up in the capital city, Addis Ababa.

Equally suitable is the primary teaching guide *Our World, Our Rights*, published by Amnesty International. It offers many useful activities based on a wide range of rights for teachers to use in class.

At upper secondary age the general provisions of the *Universal Declaration of Human Rights* become manageable. For adolescents it is appropriate to shift the emphasis to rights of protection from harmful labour, sexual abuse and exposure to drugs. NGO resources illustrate the effects of unfair trade on household economies in ways that are appropriate for secondary classrooms. This remit embraces personal, social and global views and provides at best an impressive array of wisdom from children in many parts of the world.

Global childhoods and universal rights are inter-connected and learning about them in schools is best done when they are addressed together. The chart overleaf suggests an appropriate integrated programme for pupils to learn about global childhoods and universal rights.

	Global childhoods	Universal rights
Early schooling (e.g. 3-7)	Positive comparisons e.g. laughing	Provision rights e.g. health, happiness
Middle schooling (e.g. 7-14)	Similarities and differences e.g. learning	Participation rights: e.g. expression, association
Late schooling (e.g. 14-19)	Negative comparisons e.g. labouring	Protection rights e.g. security, sexuality

This is inevitably simplified but the strands can be brought together through topic areas such as Celebrations, Futures or Child Labour. Because learning about rights must be developmental and progressive, so that children learn about the issues at their appropriate age, a checklist should be kept of their progress all through their schooling, to ensure breadth, balance, geographical spread and the possibilities for affirmative action.

A child-RICH curriculum

The learning strand of Rights in Childhood (RICH) can be incorporated in all schools and across frontiers. Focusing on RICH equips all pupils to become active, globally aware and concerned citizens who are learning to ensure their own rights and those of other children.

RICH is not a school curriculum subject that is taught to pupils by teachers. Learning will only be meaningful when educators and children actively co-operate. Child citizens who wish to present their own image will benefit from working in collaboration with skilled and experienced adult educators. Teachers should explore the possibilities for learning together and enabling children's expression about their childhoods.

When learning about global childhoods and children's rights in a sustained programme supported by dedicated resources such as those

Figure 16: A 'rich' curriculum

The following questions will be a stimulus for teachers and an aid to lesson planning.

*1. **Rights**: are courses based on rights principles?*
Is rights learning made explicit through studying rights documents? Or is it implicit in a set of principles underlying the course or lesson?

*2. **International**: is there a global dimension?*
Here the term international is an extension of the 'in' of Rights in Childhood. It comprises international learning in the exact sense of learning about interactions between countries and the cosmopolitan sense of accepting diversities of experience and viewpoints among people. Does it have specific global content or does it have a general dimension that looks outside the classroom and beyond visible frontiers of experience to inform learning?

*3. **Children**: Do children feature largely?*
How much are children a source of learning? Do pupils see pictures or hear voices of real children in courses and lessons? As well as a rights and a global dimension, is there an additional child dimension to school courses? Do schools teach about and through the experience of children?

*4. **Childhood**: Is childhood itself an area of study?*
The concept of childhood is a valid area of study in its own right – is childhood rather than adulthood a key area of school learning? Are the experiences of what it means to be a child in today's world central? Or is there an over-emphasis on the lives of individual and isolated children? Is meaning given to children's rights as a universal aspect of being a child?

described in this book, pupils encounter insights into the daily realities of childhood scenarios from around the world and they find them intriguing. At primary school they acquire a basic understanding of fairness and the rights that apply to all children. Scenes of playing and family life show them the positive aspects of children's lives in a variety of countries.

Once pupils have a basic understanding of the world's diverse interests and life styles they can connect more easily with, say, a disaster that suddenly strikes in some distant place on the world map. The event can be the subject of an assembly and in the classroom learning that follows the pupils can do internet research to learn more about the background and what happened. They learn about the event from a sustained global perspective. They find out what daily life was like for the local children before the disaster, and how matters could be improved. This approach gives scope for pupils to learn about the basic principles of international aid and development, and about ways of helping people to help themselves. Finally, they might consider what they might actively do about the situation, for example by raising funds in the school or local community.

With a firm foundation built at primary schools, pupils should continue learning about the world at secondary school. They are receptive to acquiring deeper understanding of why poverty is difficult to eradicate, why more boys than girls go to school in many countries and how environmental factors contribute to hunger and famines. Pupils who experience curriculum models of this kind will leave school as informed global citizens equipped to learn further about the world in collaboration with other young people and to take action for improvements they deem necessary and achievable.

Although *Every Child Matters* has identified five impact areas to make childhood better and ensure that all children in the United Kingdom get their rights, it does not go far enough in identifying childhood, and specifically global childhoods, as a source of learning. It is concerned with 'economic well-being' but does not link this to global learning or offer a global perspective.

The areas of government that are concerned with children and their education need to act in unison. While the DfES, now the DCSF, is advocating learning for citizenship, the DfID a more global approach with positive school linking and the Ministry of Justice more awareness of human rights in schools, there is no co-ordinated programme. A coherent set of guidelines is needed for children to learn about, from and with children.

Teachers need specific training if they are to teach children about children's issues on global lines and as informed by humans rights principles in the ways outlined in this book. Workshops for teachers on children's rights and responsibilities should be directly linked to child protection issues. Teachers and trainee teachers need to have a solid grasp of the global dimensions of childhood so they can compare the lives of children in other schools and communities with familiar rights contexts.

A book like this, focusing on learning about children's rights and realities with a global dimension, will, I hope, help to build up a valid learning area – but it is not a new school subject. If all new teachers were to follow courses in global childhood studies, the next generation of teachers will be far better equipped than the present one to teach children about children and to listen to children.

Summary – childhood as a source of learning

How children learn about the world beyond their immediate environment has engaged educators for many years. How can children in a community know and learn about children in other communities, particularly those distanced by space, time or culture? How do we help them overcome cultural distancing – the differences which have been created between countries because of economic or democratic differences. This book is about how children in the so-called developed countries can learn more truthfully and effectively from and about children in the so-called developing countries. This is a two-way process. Another book is waiting to be written about how children in the developing countries can learn from children in the developed countries.

Each time they plan or evaluate courses, teachers should ask these questions:

- Is there a global dimension to the course – does it entail learning beyond the locality and nation state?

- Does the global dimension include learning about children – are children's daily lives made visible, showing them with their families and communities?

- When children are presented, is it in light of their rights – whether these are affirmed or denied – rather than as if they are passive, silent, dependent on adults?

Bringing together aspects of human rights, children's views and global perspectives in newly perceived and practised ways suggests a significant shift in teaching and learning. What matters most is that teachers learn to listen to what children themselves express. We need to examine how the voices of children from other places reach our classrooms and how to ensure that communication is improved through encouraging children to speak out for themselves. But this is seldom easy.

Children facing difficult economic or environmental circumstances are unlikely to think that talking to a strange adult pointing a camera and microphone is a priority. But once they understand that they are being given an opportunity to speak and be listened to by the world community who teach about their lives, they may see the potential it offers for making changes to their circumstances.

When pupils and teachers in UK schools start to think along more global-local lines and set about trying to communicate with some of the children who live in the poorer parts of the world, they may understand their circumstances and develop the capacity to claim their rights more effectively. The *Millennium Development Goals* make it urgent for educators in the rich world to refocus their ideas through the lenses of childhood. When children are introduced to the concept of rights from an early age, as described in this book, courses in children's rights can be designed to fit across curriculum subjects and profoundly influence the schools' values and policies.

4

Practical guidance

This book takes a holistic approach to children's rights as a learning area, building on the specified outcomes in *Every Child Matters* for children's health, wealth, safety, celebration and contribution to society. It illustrates the ways in which childhood as experienced around the world today can be a valid source of learning in schools and how the most appropriate basis for such learning is the UN *Convention on the Rights of the Child*.

New approaches

For children themselves to be the subject of school learning the whole life of the school needs to change. The school environment has to respect the rights of pupils and affirm the positive messages being offered by the teachers. And the debate about how children's rights relate to their responsibilities has implications for how pupils conduct themselves in school.

In a survey by Birmingham University of ideas about citizenship for 7 to 11 year olds reported in the *Times Educational Supplement*, a Year 3 boy declared that 'children are citizens who do not get their rights met' (*TES*, 2/2/2007, p15). And a report by UNICEF in 2007 asserted that children in the UK are cared for less well than children anywhere else in the rich world. These surveys indicate that children need to learn at school that they are valued citizens with rights of their own.

The concerns discussed here cross the frontiers between the fields of human rights education, citizenship education and global education. Where the three meet, a new field is created: child rights education which is global in scope and which leads to positive action by young citizens. The NGO resources, which provide images of children in different parts of the world source the exploration of the new field. The book closes with accounts of activities and child-to-child projects for sharing views about the world and claiming rights to expression and to be heard, and gives details of the relevant publications.

The resources described feature the words and images from children in various countries. They are a rich stimulus for comparing childhoods in today's world. They can also act as longer-term sources for reflection on what children's participation could mean both for integrating the right of expression into schools and for extending this right to a truly global dimension.

> Through recognising children as citizens and engaging with student voices, educators, policy-makers and researchers can increase their understanding of learning and teaching processes and of what constitutes a successful learning community. Moreover, by drawing on the CRC as a framework they can ensure that the principles of inclusion and non-discrimination are built into their agendas. (Osler and Starkey, 2005: 39)

There is general international agreement that global citizenship education should be based on learning values for democracy, inclusion and human rights. But it seldom focuses specifically on the rights of children. This means that pupils will only be offered information and ideas which are based on adult conceptions and interpretations of democracy, inclusion and rights. And these are inappropriate for pupils who live in a global society that has signed up to the *Convention*. The task for educators is to incorporate children's own views of their lives so that their learning about global childhood rights and experiences is based on children's own understandings of reality.

Rights education teaches about universally accepted values. Participating in the world as global citizens entails sharing ideas about the world so that we come to understand other people, their ways of life and their values.

Pupils need to learn to see beyond the simplistic portrayal in the media and school materials of children's lives. This chapter outlines some activities to use in the classroom. They range from short discussion tasks to large-scale simulations and illustrate how resources which focus on children's lives in developing countries can be used constructively in the classroom. The examples that follow are drawn from various sources and can be adapted by teachers and pupils to suit their own learning.

Activities and approaches
Developing visual literacy
1. Integrating visual images

Photographs are powerful learning sources. They merit careful examination and discussion. Textbook images or class films are often afforded little more than a glance. Children will learn little from pictures they look at in this way. Stategies are needed for slowing things down so that they have to engage with the image.

The pupils need to work actively with the pictures they are given, rather than just looking at and discussing them. This can be done in several ways.

■ The power of the captions could be explored

■ The pupils to reflect on the pictures could write on the pictures.

■ Or they could cut them up, then crop and caption them.

■ Or the pupils could extend the focus of a picture by drawing what they think might be outside its frame.

We gave pupils photos which depicted children's lives in a range of contexts. They discovered that by attaching different sets of emotive words to them, the same pictures can be presented in either positive or negative light. This stimulated discussion about which images they think are accurate and representative.

When introducing the study of a particular locality, we need to start with a range of contrasting images of the place. Classes who make an imaginary journey to a chosen location might begin by presenting a travel agent's version of the country, featuring images of city hotels or beach resorts. They can then contrast this with a more realistic study of an African or Indian village.

2. Every Child Matters Everywhere

NGO development education units and the Geographical Association have produced locality packs for key stage Two Geography. The example illustrated here uses photographs of three children growing up in Lima, the capital city of Peru (Save the Children's photo-pack *Lima Lives* (out of print)).

The activity starts with a consideration of children's lives in the UK. The discussion is based on a simplified summary of *Every Child Matters* which relates the five outcomes to rights terminology as found in the *Convention*. The pupils can discuss the issues in groups or the discussion can take the form of role-play as an imagined family.

In the second stage, the pupils embark on an imaginative journey to investigate children's lives in another place. The discussion topic remains about rights, but in the new context. The discussion sheet is adapted to the different environment. The class should look at maps and photographs beforehand so they have a better idea of the reality of the place and the children who live there. Alternatively, photographs of different families can be given to the groups, as in the *Lima Lives* resource.

Finally, the pupils compare their thoughts about the two different countries, either in groups or as a whole class. In a role-play where the teacher is in role as an international child rights expert, the class can express their views in the form of a drama. In comparisons between the UK and Peru, for example, pupils quickly understand that the children in Peru are in need of material support for the decent housing and clean water that are their right. Infusing conventional learning about contrasting localities with issues of children's rights provides a common value base from which to compare the two countries. Without such a base there is a danger that rich world and poor world localities are over-contrasted and the differences between them amplified.

Developing emotional literacy

Fluent verbal and visual expression contributes to children's development of emotional literacy. In language and literacy lessons, pupils can be encouraged to express personal and global values. Knowing that their communications – be it a drawing, a piece of prose or a poem – will be read by other people besides the teacher is likely to motivate pupils to do their best. They will be far more engaged when they see that their letter is not going to be merely marked and returned but will be sent to a chosen destination and may well evoke a reply.

English offers scope for telling stories, learning from other cultures and expressing ideas, so it is ideal for increasing the range and quality of learning from children's experiences. Popular stories for children by such authors as J K Rowling, Jacqueline Wilson and Philip Pullman can be used to build up pupils' curiosity about the worlds of children's imagination and expression. Writing by children themselves that has reached publication, like the diaries of Anne Frank and Zlata, are also popular in schools. What is required is access to more such writings and for teachers of English to intensify the focus on children's own literary and artistic products.

Developing political literacy

Pupils use their imagination when they play games such as Christian Aid's *Trading Game*. It provides a microcosm of global economic inter-actions in which richer and poorer countries meet in the marketplace, so encouraging children to plan how they can act to help poorer countries.

3. High Seize

Other activities simulate global action campaigns to help pupils explore ways to set up and run their own campaigns. High Seize was developed during the 1990s as part of a European awareness campaign for young people about drugs and development. The simulation was run within the framework of regional youth parliaments convened to explore the global trade in drugs and aimed to influence European policy. It was designed to enhance the understanding of the youth delegates who later met with European parliamentarians in Strasbourg.

The setting for High Seize is an international conference on a ship in the Atlantic – hence the pun. Delegates from cocaine producing areas meet with traffickers, users and politicians in Europe. The scenario is intentionally implausible – a matter that is explored after the simulation is complete. At the simulated conference each party puts across its own perspective on the drugs issue and in inter-group discussions an attempt is made to reach some consensus.

This is a model for global campaigning which could be developed to focus on changing children's worlds, not only in relation to drugs policies but also more comprehensively. Pupils and teachers could use High Seize to devise campaign-based simulation models where children's parliaments in the rich world interact with those in the poor world in child-to-child political action. The simulation offers endless creative possibilities for pupils to explore.

Developing thinking about rights

This section describes classroom activities intended to help pupils explore their own rights values. They use group discussion activities which can stimulate thinking about aspects of children's rights. Simple to set up, the activities are models for promoting children's expression rights in the classroom and encouraging pupils to voice their opinions and share ideas.

4. Wants and needs cards

The UNICEF picture cards are designed to enable pupils to think about differences between wants, needs and rights. They are available in the *Time for Rights* pack (2003) or the basic idea can be adapted and the cards locally designed.

Some cards illustrate things which many people would rate as wants: an i-pod, a bicycle or a seaside holiday. Other cards illustrate basic needs like food, water, shelter and health care. A third set of cards illustrates rights concepts like justice, education, protection and participation. Because these are more abstract, they are harder to convey in a simple illustration. This is all part of the learning objectives and can be discussed after the activity is complete.

Pupils work in groups with the three sets of cards all mixed up. Their task is to sort them into three piles, agreeing which they think are wants, needs or rights. As they do so they should talk about what these words mean to them as individuals and as a group. When the task is complete, each group shares its decisions with the rest of the class and discusses the cards they found especially hard to place.

With the three key words written on the board, the class can determine what each means. Pupils generally decide that 'wants' describes things we would like to have but don't really need; that 'needs' are things that we have to have for life and development, but that 'rights' are more than basic survival and are also harder to define. If pupils have their needs and rights they will have a better life than if they have to live without them.

The cards can be used to help pupils learn that rights are given by society and that the rights of other people should be recognised. Responsibilities are necessary. So although the sorting activity is suitable for young children, the introduction of the concept of rights as universal values may be more readily understood by the older primary pupils. Also relevant is the wider learning context: the activity could be presented as an introduction to a topic on children's rights or it could be used for comparative learning about other children's lives.

5. Circles of rights

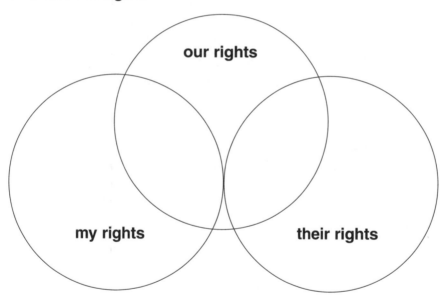

Draw overlapping rings and label them *my rights, their rights* and *our rights*. Discuss the implications of this model for building a coherent framework for children's rights education in schools. The left circle relates to how pupils learn about their own rights and related responsibilities, generally in PSHE or Citizenship. The right circle is about the denial or achievement of rights for children who are distant from them, as considered in humanities areas of learning, assemblies and fund-raising initiatives for international charities. The middle circle implies that pupils see their own rights and those of other children as related – although this may not be happening in a coherent way in their schools. The children's learning about their rights will only be fully achieved when all these connections are made.

Learning about 'my rights' – i.e. what official documents provide for my protection and development as a child – and about 'their rights' – i.e. how some children in the world do not have all their rights and why – should not be done separately. It is important that educators see and present 'our rights' and 'their rights' as connected. This is the only way that pupils can gain understanding about which groups of children are most at risk of lacking certain of their rights. Effectively connecting learning about the rights of children in the rich world and the poor develops pupils' skills of empathy and desire for action.

6. The Island Game

Amnesty International's Island Game is an activity for learning rights in the context of Citizenship. It provides a simulation model for pupils to think about universally agreed rights. Students space themselves around the classroom in groups of four to six. The scenario is that they have landed, in their groups, on a cluster of uninhabited islands after their plane crashed. In order to survive as a new society they will have to agree some principles for organising themselves and living together. Each group is given a large sheet of paper on which to draw up their charter of rights.

This simulation idea can be developed in many ways. When it is used to focus on ideas, each group presents its charter and these are discussed. But the Island Game can be extended by convening an inter-island meeting with the teacher in role as the UN Secretary General who has flown in. Still in simulation mode, each island can become aware of a neighbouring island and move to share ideas together. These larger groups can agree a general Magna Carta which incorporates the ideas in their own island charters. Whichever story-line is followed, the essential elements of this activity are to share ideas for basic rights principles for a good society, first in small groups and then as a whole class.

This should always be followed by an out-of-role discussion about what the pupils have learned from taking part in the activity. This may invoke explorations of what rights are, as well as the specific issue of whether the groups looked at democratic models for running their societies. Teacher facilitators may well find that they learn from running this activity with different groups in different learning contexts.

Another variation gives pupils relevant information at the outset about each person in the group, to prompt thinking about equality rights. For example, they might be told that each of them represents ten men and women, adults and children, able and disabled and so on. It all depends on what area of rights learning the activity is being used for: it can be a conceptual introduction or a detailed examination of certain rights.

5

Resources

Selected NGO resources relating to rights
Amnesty International: www.amnesty.org.uk

- *Human Rights in the Curriculum* (subject series: French, History, Mathematics, Spanish)

- *Learning about Human Rights through Citizenship* (secondary)

- *Our World, Our Rights* (primary: new edition forthcoming)

- *TeachRights teacher network*

Christian Aid: www.christian-aid.org.uk – Learn Zone

- *The trading game*

Council for Education in World Citizenship: www.cewc.org

- *Youth parliament on drugs and development* (final report)

Development Education Association: www.dea.org.uk

- *Human Rights: Guidance for Key Stages 2 and 3*

Oxfam: www.oxfam.org.uk/coolplanet

- *A curriculum for global citizenship*

- *Developing rights* (secondary)

- *Global Citizenship: The handbook for primary teaching*

- *Oxfam catalogue for schools* (annual)

Peace Child International: www.peacechild.org

- *Stand Up, Speak Out: a book about children's rights* (secondary)

Plan International: www.plan-uk.org – Plan-ed

- *Take your rights* (card game based on the *Convention*)

The Refugee Council: www.refugeecouncil.org.uk

- *Global Communities: Learning about Refugee Issues* (primary and secondary teaching resource)

UN: www.un.org

- *Teaching Human Rights: Practical activities for primary and secondary schools*

Unicef: www.unicef.org.uk – TeacherZone

- *Rights Respecting Schools* award scheme

- *Talking Rights, Taking Responsibility* (secondary)

- *Time for Rights* (primary and middle) with Save the Children

Save the Children resources relating to children's rights

Save the Children: www.savethechildren.org.uk/education

- *Citizens by right: Citizenship education in primary schools* (with Trentham Books)

- *Children's Rights: A Teacher's Guide* (ideas for teachers)

- *Eye to Eye* (photographs from refugee camps: www.savethechildren.org.uk/eyetoeye)

- *I've got them! You've got them!! We've all got them!!!* (booklets on children's rights and responsibilities)

- *One Day We Had To Run* (paintings from refugee children)

- *Partners in Rights* (art activities – see page 93)

- *Rights, Camera, Action* (for Media Studies) www.savethechildren.org.uk/mediastudies)

- *SCALES* (active learning examples   downloadable at www.savethechildren.org.uk/scales

- *What Makes Me Happy* (films inspired by children, with The Ragdoll Foundation – see page 92)

- *Young Lives, Global Goals* (child poverty and the Millennium Development Goals – see page 96)

The section below gives more detailed information about a selection of resources on children's rights produced by Save the Children. This is meant as a case study of how and why a certain NGO produces classroom resources for teachers.

For the early years
What Makes Me Happy – six films inspired by children in different countries

Available as a DVD, this set of films is the product of a creative partnership between Save the Children, which provided global reach, and the Ragdoll Foundation, which brought their expertise at entertaining and educating young children, as evident from their Teletubbies and Rosie and Jim television programmes. Save the Children set up workshops with teenage children in six countries to explore their memories of what had made them happy in their early childhood. With Ragdoll, scripts were created and young actors chosen to make the memories into films. The outcome is a collection of positive life slices in which children in places and circumstances that are usually portrayed negatively in the UK – such as Ethiopia and the Occupied Palestinian Territories (OPT) – paint, play and laugh together. In the film set in the OPT, Mahmoud is seen balancing his obligations to serve his local community through running errands against his longing to have time on his own to pursue his own ideas.

Teachers who have used these films have their favourites. One is the Sri Lankan story, filmed on location after the 2005 tsunami had devastated the coast. The film is about a girl, Hashi, who finds a damaged kite and – with the ingenuity and help of many other people – succeeds in repairing and flying it. This sense of fun in children's creative play is also evident in the film from Anhui Province in China, where Save the Children has a number of health and education programmes. Here, a boy, Junjie, uses scrap materials scavenged from the streets and people of the city to design his own toy.

These films use children's ideas to broaden global learning in the early years through relating to the similarities in children's experience. Children enjoy them because they see childhoods which are not too unlike their own. This suggests some parameters for effective global learning about childhoods. Both similarities and differences should be presented. Acceptance of similarities is the first step to appreciating differences. The dimension of happiness is vital – a major step forward for an NGO that exists to help children in the most difficult and damaging circumstances. But the difficult aspects of children's lives, particularly in the most distant and underdeveloped countries where Save the Children runs programmes, should not be disregarded. It seems vital to portray the good and the bad experiences in children's lives and not just the more common images of a terrible childhood.

Barriers to Learning role-play – access to schooling in Somalia

Somalia has been seriously affected by droughts and civil conflicts. Many families struggle to find basic food and water for survival. Although they regard education as very important it often has lower priority than migrating around the semi-desert land to feed families and livestock. Mobile teachers have traditionally provided some education for these nomadic families. Although schools provide greater resources as well as socialisation with other children and teachers, many families will not make the effort to send their children to school if it is hard to reach or evinces discrimination or if the toilets are inadequate. This is especially the case for the girls. Children in rural Somalia also responded to the specific questions on worksheets described in section 2.2).

The Somali children's drawings were used in primary schools in England to help trial a role-play activity for Early Years called Barriers to Learning. The children's pictures enriched the photographs of children's lives in Somalia. They helped the English pupils to identify with the children in Somalia. In a hot-seating activity the English pupils were invited to feel as if they were Somali children asking their parents – role-played by the teachers – to explain why they could not go to school.

This was followed by a role-play activity in which pupils in groups performed sketches to illustrate the obstacles to education faced by the Somali children, such as drought, hunger and poverty. The groups role-played families trying to work out how to overcome the obstacles. This active learning approach led the English pupils to identify strongly with the Somali children's lives and made them look for ways to help them get more schooling. They simulated action learning and planning campaigns. Fundraising activities and writing letters evoked eagerness to find out more.

This resource is available on-line from Save the Children as a downloadable role-play activity to help pupils enter the lives of these children imaginatively (www.savethechildren.org.uk/scales).

For the middle years
Partners in Rights – an arts-based pack on rights in the UK and Latin America

Funded by the National Lottery, the Partners in Rights project enabled a team of creative artists from Scotland to run arts workshops with children in Brazil, Cuba and Peru. Giant puppets were exchanged, and the participants made collages of what they saw as important in their lives. The outcome is a learning resource and website in three languages: English, Portuguese and Spanish. This ensures that everyone who was involved can see the results of their efforts and learning.

The artists led creative activities with children in the three Latin American countries. In Recife, Brazil, the project workers worked with groups of children in an Afro-Brazilian cultural centre, rather than in schools or family settings. They used a variety of arts techniques and gathered data from interviews in group sessions using interpreters. One child's response would set off others and soon a group would be conversing animatedly.

It is difficult to capture the children's spontaneity, and the nuances and complexity of the discussions when children talk things over together and with an adult from outside. And it is difficult to convert this rich experience into a printed resource. But it will inevitably be quite different to the typical formula of 'a day in the life of ...'. Instead of presenting one child the materials aim to provide a group or community portrait.

The best stimulus for sharing was to tell traditional tales. We chose a tale from Europe: *The Pied Piper of Hamelin*. Groups of children were encouraged to choose a tale from their continent and retell it by directing an adult artist to illustrate it. The point of this is to try and establish common areas of experience so that the outside adult researcher is drawn in and is no longer a stranger. This lively beginning generated spontaneous group conversations because the children understood what kind of insights into their lives were being sought and what information would be considered appropriate for the project.

Mining Minors – child labour in West Africa

This is a role-play, based on a project to combat child labour in West Africa. Children working in the gold mines in the north of Burkina Faso shared their experiences and voiced their concerns. Supported for many years by Save the Children, the project is now run by a local NGO.

Children do jobs in the local gold mine that are damaging to their health. Boys work underground in dangerous conditions to try and earn some money for their families in a part of the world where frequent drought conditions during the year make agricultural production virtually impossible. The boys bring rocks out of the mine and the girls work with their parents to sift through them in search of grains of gold. The children are working in family units, playing a role in their community. But they do so at the expense of their education and prospects in life. That children are out of school and in the workforce at a young age is recognised in richer countries as contravening the rights of children and instead education is compulsory.

The role-play based on this project allows the children to express opinions at a community meeting which would traditionally be dominated by adult male voices. Mining Minors was devised and trialled in UK primary schools. The role-play is set in a meeting that has been called to investigate children's working conditions and decide what can be done to stop or improve them. The participants represent different interest groups: elders, mine owners, parents, NGO workers and the children themselves. The elders' decision for the community prevails.

This resource is also available as a downloadable role-play activity at www.savethechildren.org.uk/scales

For older pupils and students
Young Lives, Global Goals – child poverty in four countries

The Young Lives Global Goals video pack shows the lives of certain children in Ethiopia, India, Peru and Vietnam and is designed for secondary Geography and Citizenship. It is based on a project for measuring and reducing poverty in families with very young children which was supported by the Department for International Development. The older siblings of the study children – who were all born in 2000 – feature on the video. This is about far more than holding up a camera to a child who is living in difficult economic and environmental circumstances. Teachers who use the videos appreciate the insights it offers into childhood worlds. It provides a realistic insider perspective for exploring with pupils the very topics that are often negatively treated topics in schools in the UK.

Brighter Futures – experiences of young refugees

Brighter Futures is designed to develop awareness of racism in host communities in three urban areas of England. Young asylum seekers and refugees meet regularly to share experiences, support each other and develop their communication skills. Brighter Futures groups have presented at national conferences. They maintain a website so they can spread awareness of the lives of young asylum seekers and refugees in the UK and some of the problems they encounter with immigration authorities and social services and the difficulty of gaining access to higher education. The visual montage is related to experiences of racist bullying that occurs in school and community settings and which also invade the privacy of mobile phones and personal computers. Such awareness raising demonstrates the positive contribution young refugees make through use of such media as the Brighter Futures website (www.brighterfutures.com).

At the time of writing, a role-play activity on *Rights against racism* is in progress. The Brighter Futures group of young asylum seekers and refugees in the north east of England is developing dramas based on the racist bullying they themselves have experienced. The idea is to use the specific examples of bullying in the classroom, around school, at leisure centres and through emails at home, and to re-enact them in various ways, for instance as a television reality show, where the simulated audience votes for appropriate strategies to tackle the bullying.

From beyond the UK

Save the Children's extensive educational programmes around the world have generated other valuable resources, such as the Listening to the Waters project in Cuba. Pupils made a study of flood patterns in their area, mapping out areas likely to be at risk. Then they set up an awareness raising programme for their parents, to show them how important it is to move to higher ground before the waters rise too high. There is a sense that the children are taking on community responsibility and educating their elders, recognising that their own rights to care and protection can be strengthened through action for the care and protection of everyone in the community (see scukcuba@enet.cu) with a booklet. Also available is a DVD: We are Prepared: Listening to the Waters).

Bibliography

Alderson P (2000) *Young Children's Rights: Exploring Beliefs, Principles and Practice.* London: Jessica Kingsley

Black M (1992) *A cause for our times: Oxfam, the first 50 years.* Oxford: Oxfam

Brown M and Harrison D (1998) 'Children's voices from different times and places', in Clough N and Holden C (eds) (1998) *Children as Citizens: Education for Participation.* London: Jessica Kingsley

Cunningham H (2006) *The Invention of Childhood.* London: BBC Books and BBC Audio Books

Eliot T S (1944) *Four Quartets.* London: Faber and Faber

Flouris G (1998) Human rights curricula in the formation of a European identity: the cases of Greece, England and France, *European Journal for Intercultural Studies*, 9 (1)

Freeman M (2002) *Human Rights: An interdisciplinary approach.* Cambridge: Polity Press

Freeman M (ed) (2004) *Children's Rights Vols 1 and 2.* Aldershot, Hants: Ashgate

Harrison D (2003) 'What are you going to teach asylum seekers about citizenship, Mr Blunkett?' *Teaching Citizenship* 5

Hicks D (2003) Thirty years of global education: a reminder of key principles and precedents, *Educational Review,* 55(3)

Lister I (1991) 'The challenge of human rights for education', in Starkey (ed) (1991) *The Challenge of Human Rights Education.* London: Casell

Osler A and Starkey H (eds) (2005) *Changing Citizenship: Democracy and Inclusion in Education.* Maidenhead: Open University Press

Pagden A (2003) Human rights, natural rights, and Europe's imperial legacy, *Political Theory,* 31(2)

Starkey H (ed) (1991) *The Challenge of Human Rights Education.* London: Casell

Times Educational Supplement. Democracy? I vote for Shilpa: Forget politics: citizenship for many pupils means fish and chips and 'Big Brother', February 2, 2007, page 15

UN (1989) *The United Nations Convention on the Rights of the Child.* New York: UN (referred to throughout this text as 'the Convention')

Index

Amnesty International 3, 63, 65, 71, 88-89, 91
asylum seekers *see* refugees

Brazil 96-97
Bristol 40-43
Burkina Faso 54, 97-98

Cameroon 14-15
campaigns 54-57
child labour 31-32, 36, 44, 71-72, 97-98
Children's Day 57
Christian Aid 50, 63, 84, 91
citizenship 7, 15, 20, 41-43, 47, 62-65, 69, 72, 79, 87-88, 98
Comic Relief 56
Community Service Volunteers 5
Council for Education in World Citizenship 84-85, 91
Council of Europe 70
Cuba 96, 99
curriculum models 72-75

Declaration of Geneva 2, 5
development education 51, 62-63, 91
disasters 50
drugs 71, 84-85

drama and role-play 19-20, 53-54, 59, 83; *see also* simulations

Education for International Understanding 63-64
Education in Human Rights Network 65
English 14, 41-43, 84
European Convention on Human Rights 9
evaluations of resources 47-53, 58, 68, 81-82
Every Child Matters 3, 8 9, 22-44, 74-75, 79, 83
exchanges 44-47

geography 25-26, 30, 83, 98
Geographical Association 83
Global Campaign for Education 56
globalisation 48
Globe Mark 53

Indonesia 18-19
interactive activities
    Circles of rights 87-88
    Wants and needs cards 86-87
International Year of the Child 3

Lima *see* Peru
literacy 57, 82-85

Malawi 37-39, 45
Malaysia 22-26
Make Poverty History 56
media *see* right to information
migration 19, 24-25
Millennium Development Goals 9-10, 22, 27, 32, 36, 41, 77

non government organisations 17-18, 50-53, 56-57, 59, 64, 80, 91-99; *see also under separate* NGOs

Oxfam 16-17, 19, 50, 63-65, 92

Panama 6, 33-35
Peace Child international 92
peace education 62-64, 92
Peru 28-31, 83, 98
Plan International 3, 52, 92
poverty 26, 44, 59
PSHE 69, 87
Red Nose Day 56
Refugee Council 92

refugees 40, 59, 92, 98-99
responsibilities 6-7, 11
rights
    economic security 22-26
    enjoy and achieve 27-31
    equality 4, 89
    expression 13-15, 51-52, 61
    health 36-39
    information 15-18, 47-53, 82
    learn respect 18-20
    participation 39-44, 66
    safety 31-35

Save the Children
    fieldwork 39, 42-44
    foundation 2
    resources 15, 25-26, 30-31, 35-36, 65, 70-71, 83, 93-99
Schools Council 65

simulations
    Deadlines 16
    Every child matters everywhere 83
    High Seize 84-85
    Island Game 88-89
    New island 18-19
Somalia 40-44, 54, 95-96

teacher training 75
Thailand 26

UK Human Rights Act 9, 22, 28, 32, 36, 41
UN 57, 62-64, 88, 92
UNESCO 63-64
UNICEF 3, 15, 63-65, 70, 79, 86-87, 92
Universal Declaration of Human Rights 4, 63-64, 66, 71

values education 62-64

World AIDS Day 56